W9-BKR-141

NARRATION AS KNOWLEDGE

Tales of the Teaching Life

NARRATION AS KNOWLEDGE
Tales of the Teaching Life

edited by
JOSEPH F. TRIMMER

Boynton/Cook Publishers
HEINEMANN
Portsmouth, NH

Boynton/Cook Publishers
A subsidiary of Reed Elsevier Inc.
361 Hanover Street
Portsmouth, NH 03801–3912

Offices and agents throughout the world

The editor and publisher wish to thank those who have generously given permission to reprint borrowed material:

Excerpt from *The Iliad* by Homer, translated by Robert Fagles. Translation copyright © 1990 by Robert Fagles. Introduction and Notes copyright © 1990 by Bernard Knox. Used by permission of Viking Penguin, a division of Penguin Books USA Inc.

Excerpt from *The Iliad of Homer*, translated by Richmond Lattimore. Translation copyright © 1951. Reprinted by permission of the publisher, The University of Chicago Press.

"Telling Stories About Stories" by Joseph F. Trimmer originally appeared in TETYC, October 1990. Copyright 1990 by the National Council of Teachers of English. Reprinted with permission.

Excerpts from *Fresh Ink, Essays from Boston College's First-Year Writing Seminar*, edited by Eileen Donovan-Kranz and Lad Tobin. Copyright © 1996 by McGraw-Hill. Reprinted by permission of the publisher.

Excerpts reprinted by permission of Sharon Jean Hamilton: *My Name's Not Susie: A Life Transformed by Literacy* (Boynton/Cook-Heinemann, A subsidiary of Reed Elsevier, Inc., Portsmouth, NH, 1995).

"Satire, Sartre, Cookies, and the Classroom" by Joel J. Gold. Copyright © 1997 by Joel J. Gold. Previous versions of this essay have been published in *The Chronicle of Higher Education* and in *The Wayward Professor*, published by the University Press of Kansas, 1989.

Library of Congress Cataloging-in-Publication Data

Narration as knowledge : tales of the teaching life / edited by Joseph
   F. Trimmer.
     p. cm.
   ISBN 0–86709–436–2
   1. College teaching—United States. 2. College teachers—United
States. 3. Reading (Higher education)—United States. 4. English
language—Rhetoric—Study and teaching (Higher)—United States.
I. Trimmer, Joseph F.
LB233.N287   1997
378.1'25'0973—dc21   97-41508
                                  CIP

Editor: Peter R. Stillman
Production: Vicki Kasabian
Cover illustration and design: Jenny Jensen Greenleaf
Manufacturing: Louise Richardson

Printed in the United States of America on acid-free paper

01 00 99 98 97 DA 1 2 3 4 5

Contents

PART 3   STORIES ABOUT CULTURE

Acknowledgments

Narration as Knowledge has many beginnings, but I want to thank Jeanne Gerlach for what I see as its symbolic beginning—an invitation to read one of my teaching stories at a conference she and her students organized at West Virginia University. I also want to thank Peter Stillman for encouraging me to publish a collection of such stories by other teachers. Of course, I would like to thank the teachers who allowed me to publish their stories in this collection. Their narratives have expanded and deepened my knowledge of the teaching life. And finally, I want to thank Jennifer Light for helping me prepare this manuscript, and Vicki Kasabian for guiding it through the various stages of its production.

Introduction

JOSEPH F. TRIMMER

The last time it happened I was sitting on the edge of a crowd of English teachers in a hotel ballroom listening to the keynote speaker outline the intricacies of something called *narratology*. He began with a brief apology. Narratology, it turned out, was a complex subject shaped by subtle assumptions and slippery assertions about the relationship of narration and knowledge. I opened my journal, clicked my pen, and prepared to follow his lead. But I was too late. He was already out of the blocks—hurdling abstractions, stretching syntax, and rounding the corner in full stride into theory-speak. I tried to keep pace. But the words came in such dense clusters, I had to drop out.

I looked at the two words I had written in my journal: *narration* and *knowledge*. I knew they went together, but the speaker was connecting them in some deep code I could not crack. Discouraged, I closed my journal, clicked my pen, and scanned the room. My colleagues seemed attentive. Nobody was fidgeting. Nobody was leaving. The man next to me and the woman a few seats beyond him were taking notes. Maybe it was just me. It wouldn't be the first time I refused to respond to the litany of nouns and names.

I checked my watch. Twenty minutes to go. The speaker was still circling the possible meanings of narration and knowledge. Desperate for diversion, I began my own little game. I marked each time the speaker used an active verb, and then I watched the sweep of the second hand until he used another.

I was keeping myself amused—clocking the speaker at about twenty-second intervals—when suddenly, out of the recondite buzz, I heard one simple sentence: "Stories intensify life." STORIES! STORIES! Had this guy been talking about STORIES? No wonder I was lost. His theoretical speculations had distorted his subject beyond recognition. My little game clinched it. Stories could not *intensify* life unless they *enacted* it. No verbs, no action. No action, no life. I opened my journal, clicked my pen, and wrote my response to narratology: "Theories . . . theories . . . and theories ABOUT stories, but NO stories."

Trusting Stories

All English teachers can tell a version of my narratology story. We became English teachers because we loved stories. We loved reading them, writing them, and talking about them. We loved the way they intensified our lives and helped us understand other lives. But as we worked our way into our professional lives, we slowly, almost imperceptibly, changed our attitude toward stories. We lived in a world that did not trust them. Stories were not true. Stories were not reliable. If we wanted to keep stories in our lives, we had to convert them into something else. Something more serious. More scientific.

Begrudgingly, we signed on. We studied stories and storymaking and taught our students to do the same. We smiled knowingly as they discovered the magic of reading. But we had to get down to business—teaching them the terms of analysis; the theories of interpretation; the strategies for converting stories into psychological profiles, historical documents, and aesthetic inventions. We told them that such work would deepen their appreciation of literature and help them understand how stories had shaped their culture.

We told them the same sort of thing about their writing. At the beginning of the term, we asked them to write a personal narrative—a story about some event that had transformed their lives. But we did not read their stories as stories. We diagnosed them, marking the errors that excluded them from academic discourse. We told them that they could not use stories to report learning. That purpose was reserved for the privileged rhetorical forms—analysis and argument. We moved on, teaching them to write *about* stories, encouraging them to dissect plots and theorize themes. Such work, we said, would sharpen their analytical thinking, prepare them to challenge the claims of literary critics.

Teaching Stories

If we have had difficulty trusting stories in our teaching, we have had even more difficulty trusting stories about our teaching. We love stories about teaching. We love to set the scene, quote the students, and reveal the trick we used to resolve the plot. We repeat these stories in the coffee room, embellish them in convention bars, and collect those that hit the mark or bring down the house. But while we treasure such stories for their wit, we do not trust them to convey knowledge. They are merely entertainment, comic relief in the high drama of academic discourse.

Most of our professional training has debunked teaching stories. They are not reliable. They are not verifiable. They are not statistically generalizable. We can use them as anecdotes, as introductions (like my narratology story), but this is simply a hook—a rhetorical device (like the speaker's apology) to attract our readers' attention. To write about teaching, we have to follow the procedures sanctioned by one of the two schools of educational research.

According to the empirical school, our first task is to remove ourselves from the classroom. Teaching in our own research projects distorts our findings. So we use criteria such as age, gender, and test scores to select other classes that are statistically homogenous. We call one the control group and the other the test group. Then we design a research project that adds one experimental variable to the mix. The test teacher introduces this variable to the test group, and then we measure the performance of both groups on a standardized test to see if the project has made any difference.

Reports on such research look remarkably similar. There is a discussion of the methods used to ensure the similarity and anonymity of the two classes; a discussion of the project, the measurement device, and the findings; and then pages and pages of charts and graphs. The researcher, or narrator, argues that this data reports knowledge. Readers who try to decipher empirical studies complain that the narrator cannot tell a story.

According to the ethnographic school, our first task is to join a class. We cannot teach the class, but we can observe it. We can interview the teacher each day about his or her goals for the class and reflections on how it is going. We can also interview the students about their work; study their assignments; and read their notes, papers, and tests. But mainly we watch, observing and recording the interaction of the class in every possible situation. We attempt to compile "thick descriptions" of this activity. Then we reflect on how these descriptions change the way we interpret what we see.

Reports on ethnographic research also look remarkably similar. There are lengthy reflections on the researcher's initial bias about the teacher, the curriculum, and the students. There are transcripts of the researcher's interviews, copies of the teacher's lesson plans, and drafts of the students' written work. And there is constant reflection about how the researcher's growing knowledge of the personal and academic lives of the teacher and students is changing the study—refocusing its observations and revising its interpretations. This researcher, or narrator, does not argue that this work proves anything. The object of ethnographic study is to report what the researcher has learned. But the researcher does argue that the multiple variables of that education are embedded in the many documents in the text. Readers who try to plough through ethnographic studies complain that the narrator cannot find a story in these stories.

These Stories

The stories in this collection were written to explore different ways to report information on teaching and learning. They do not follow the sanctioned procedures of educational research. They are not written in the privileged forms of academic discourse. Instead, they play with all of the devices of storytelling (scene, dialogue, point of view) to render moments that suggest an educational encounter.

The narrators, experts on literature and literacy, try to avoid presenting themselves as heroes. These narrators know that the classroom is an exciting but uncertain place. No one, not even the teacher in charge, understands all the subtle assumptions and slippery assertions enacted in the daily exchange of information. And so these narrators try to spin "true" stories about the partiality of their knowledge and the vulnerability of their power.

They also try to avoid presenting their students as "them"—agreeable abstractions that act in unison, as in "they read this," "they wrote that," and "they learned this." These narrators know that students have distinct attitudes toward learning, that student voices and silences scatter the enterprise on the syllabus into side alleys and dead ends. By clocking these detours, teachers know they are always behind. But they know they are making *good time* and they will have a tale to tell.

These tales, while engaging and insightful, are not exotic. They represent a range of recognizable teaching experiences, ordinary classes made extraordinary by the knowledge and skill of the narrator. They braid the *reading* and *writing* that is present in any English classroom with the *culture* that shapes teachers' and students' lives.

For convenience, I have sorted these stories into three sections: *Stories About Reading*, *Stories About Writing*, and *Stories About Culture*. But given their complex view of teaching and learning, any of these stories could be re-sorted into another section. What binds them together is the title of this book. Each writer sees *Narration*, the process of storytelling, *as* a way of making *Knowledge*.

Stories About Reading

The stories in this section portray the delights and difficulties of teaching reading. Michael Martone celebrates the classroom (his mother's and his own) as a place "where stories happen." By telling us how he reads his favorite stories, particularly *The Odyssey*, he shows us how "we live in and are mapped by the stories we tell." Joy Passanante dramatizes her students' reaction to another old story, *The Iliad*. By reading different translations, they discover how different words can shape and reshape the same story. Kim Stafford wonders what reading Chaucer's tales can do for one of his students and what it has done for himself, a strayed medievalist. His pilgrimage to a penitentiary provokes tales about healing and provides thoughtful answers to his initial question—both for his student and himself.

Patricia Shelley Fox introduces us to the difficulties of reading problematic texts. Her younger students read Louise Mallard's "epiphany" in Kate Chopin's "The Story of an Hour" as betrayal, while her older students read it as liberation. Placed in the larger context of women's narratives, these readings create the possibility for "finding the selves we set aside." Victor Villanueva Jr. describes a similar difficulty as his students debate the status of American Indians in Leslie Marmon Silko's *Ceremony*. But his major obstacle is trying to deal with the arguments of the class's articulate bigot. Joseph F. Trimmer recounts the challenges he faces teaching different students how to read the same story. Their responses to Alice Walker's "Everyday Use" leaves him puzzled about the consequences of contradictory readings.

Stories About Writing

The stories in this section trace the troubles and transformations of teaching writing. Chris M. Anson records his uncertainty assessing a powerful but technically flawed personal narrative. His story and his student's story, provide provocative "beginnings" but no satisfactory ending. Lad Tobin's selection of student writing for a collection of essays prompts him to wonder how students could write incessantly about "death, disease, and dysfunction." But as he writes about his own life as a student, he begins to wonder "how they could *not* write" about such things. Toby Fulwiler documents the activities of his advanced writing class on "personal voice," blending his students' voices with his own. He realizes that his celebration of "the best writing class I've ever taught" requires a second story, one that reveals the complications and compromises buried in his initial narrative.

Sharon J. Hamilton presents a story of "a life transformed by literacy." She describes her attempt to solicit student criticism of her writing and shows how that criticism transforms not only her text but also the life of one of its most "promising" critics. Neal Bowers explores the power of writing from another perspective. When challenged to reveal "the secrets" of poetry, he confesses that he does not know many. But he acknowledges that his challenger, though she may not realize it, already knows those that matter. Lynn Z. Bloom summarizes the master plots of teaching stories but then confesses her own complicity in the story of "the worst course I ever taught." She recalls how her own version of storytelling shatters the course into fragments when it collides with the sanctioned versions of educational discourse.

Stories About Culture

The stories in this section suggest how the inevitable interplay of personal and professional issues complicates teaching in our culture. Ruth Vinz renders her struggle to control a disruptive student, her own vulnerability, and the desire for power in us all. At the end, she confesses that her story, like her disruptive student, "could not be tamed." Lillian Bridwell-Bowles also tells us one of those stories that leads to others. Each one resembles a film clip, an episode in the story of how she was shaped by a racist culture. Although she tries to reform others, she discovers that she is often blinded by her own history.

Joel J. Gold and Cecelia Tichi give us contrasting stories about the classroom and culture. Gold reports that the students in his Honors Proseminar in Satire learn their lessons so well that they form a comic community—performing a series of intricate tricks on their befuddled teacher. Tichi describes how the students in her American Literature Survey form an intellectual community to debate the distinctions between Emerson's self-reliance and Tocqueville's individualism. Unfortunately, the distinction seems to be erased by the slogans of the larger culture, and the "Teflon lesson" does not stick.

John Clifford and Sondra Perl explore the complicated relationship between the culture teachers and students bring to class and the culture taught in class. Clifford is perplexed about how he can create a democratic classroom when the serious cultural differences among his students prevent them from talking to one another. Perl is tormented by the prospect of teaching the enemy, the children of the people who would have killed her family had "we been born there instead of here." By exchanging stories, she and her students try to come to terms with the suppressed stories of their shared history—the atrocities of the Holocaust.

Wendy Bishop concludes this section (and the book) by taking on those events, students, and subjects that "a happily practicing teacher has to block out." In particular, she tries to understand what's at stake for teachers and students in their entangled personal and professional relationships. She suggests that our teaching stories become "more important as we age, weary, or wear . . . and have even more need of spiritual help." Rather than abstract our teaching into empirical research or bury it in ethnographic studies, we need to face "the real moments" we encounter each day. And we need to trust our stories of these moments. To narrate is to know. We need to tell our teaching stories if we are to understand our teaching lives.

1

Stories We Tell Ourselves

MICHAEL MARTONE

I grew up in a high school English class. I mean this literally. My mother taught freshman English at Central High in Fort Wayne, and one of my earliest memories is of sitting at a big wooden desk by the door and listening to my mother tell stories about the stories she taught.

My mother is fond of repeating that she had me in August and by the beginning of the next semester in January she was back in the classroom. Her mother babysat me from then on, and as soon as I toddled I rode with my grandma downtown to pick up my mother at school. As a preschooler I got to go in and fetch my mother, and I wandered the huge locker-lined halls. I would burst into my mother's room where she would be erasing the board or lining up the desks. To me, everything seemed huge, perhaps doubly so since Central was an old beaux arts box with high ceilings and ornate fixtures. Mom taught on the third floor in a corner room that looked out across Barr Street at the massive St. Paul's Lutheran church and school. Its bells were geared to Westminster chimes, and as I watched my mother teach she seemed to pace her presentation to pause in time with the ringing of the bells. The pigeons startled from the window sills, a cloud of them wafting around the spire. My mother and her students waited through the bonging and then picked up where they had left off, drilling gerunds or talking about Silas Marner.

Many days my mother would simply take me to school with her. My father would drop us off in the dark. Through the day, I would sit at my desk and draw or look at the pictures in the Golden Book encyclopedia I was now collecting from the supermarket. I half-listened to the buzz of the classroom. Very soon I realized that my mother was saying the same things to each new

1

class, but each time she presented the material as if it were completely new. In the late summers before classes resumed she would read to me as she prepared her lesson plans. *Romeo and Juliet, Great Expectations,* "The Necklace." To this day one of our inside jokes is a line from *Our Town.* "Mother," I will say, echoing our little drama from the time I was five, "am I pretty, Mama, am I really pretty?"

After I started going to my own school, Mother would sometimes let me cut and come with her to Central. On days when there were pep sessions, I sat with her homeroom and cheered in the stands. As I learned to print, I helped her grade, blocking in the letters in her grade book. The perforated half-pages always amazed me. Most amazing, I was the lucky boy who ultimately received all the projects that my mother's students made. I got the sugar-cubed walls of Troy. I got the tin-foiled cardboard breastplate of Achilles. I got the toothpick longboats of Odysseus. All of these crafted popsicle sticks and toilet paper rolls came to me by default as her students failed to pick them up at the end of the term. My bedroom was crammed with collages and pastels, maps and charts, models of temples, the great globe itself twirling on a string from the ceiling.

I am forty years old, and I have spent most of my life, year in and year out, in a classroom. First I was a student, and now I am a teacher. What have I learned?

Well, beginning with my time in my mother's literature class, I learned that the classroom was the place to read and appreciate a particular kind of art called literature. I always liked the stories my mother taught. I took to this kind of art. But I also sensed that my mother through her alchemy as a teacher was able to "bring to life" narratives such as *Wuthering Heights, David Copperfield, Huckleberry Finn,* and *Jane Eyre* to students who were economically, historically, and culturally far removed from the particulars of those books. Those who teach literature as part of their own classrooms continue this struggle to transmit to students the codes that will allow them to participate in—to translate actually—these things called novels or poems or short stories and perhaps to go on to compose their own. This is being done in a very difficult time. Not only are these traditional forms of narration competing with other narrative delivery devices—movies, television, comic books, twelve-step programs—but they also are being faced with the anxiety of late century existential questions as well.

We now know that much of the twentieth century has been about *aboutness,* that is, calling into question all forms of certainty and authority. Hierarchies, canons, and curricula are all in play, all being questioned. At the college where I teach it is quite easy to now complete a degree in English without having read a novel, short story, or poem. We joke that our students can deconstruct the Graduate Record Exam but cannot pass it. No clucking of tongues or shaking of heads over this matter. I simply rehearse it here to remind myself that these are the obvious professional interests of the English classroom. It has and will always present a subject matter formally, be it Bob Dylan, Charles Dickens, or Jacques Derrida.

But I want to talk about the English classroom as a place itself, a site where stories happen and where they are created, not just as a place where they are presented, appreciated, and consumed. I realized while sitting in my mother's classroom that the classroom itself would make a great story. And so I repeated it here. The Westminster chimes, the crash of pigeon wings, the students stumbling through their memorized sonnets, my mother clapping chalk dust from her hands, a little boy sitting in the corner drawing cyclops after cyclops with his crayons.

I like the part in *The Odyssey* where Odysseus and his men make their escape from Polyphemus, the Cyclops. Odysseus almost blows it once again. He has told the giant earlier that his name is "Noman." This cleverly confuses the neighbors when the wounded giant called them for help. "No man has done this to me, etc." But now Odysseus calls out, "Polyphemus, when you are asked who blinded you tell them it was Odysseus, son of Laertes, of Ithaca, etc., etc." Big rock, close call.

I marvel at the confidence of the hero's boast more than the wiliness of the alias, and I always imagine that years later Cyclops in his cups would be telling a friend that Odysseus son of Laertes of Ithaca did this, and his companion would respond, "So who's he?" This scenario doesn't occur to our boy from Ithaca. He wants to get the facts straight. He wants his name in the story.

I teach a course in contemporary rural and agricultural literature, and I was doing so at Iowa State University where most of the fifty students attending it had grown up on farms or in small towns. This is nothing special. It was just the demographics of the college.

A student asked one day why we were studying these books about hog farmers and dairymen in places such as Iowa and Indiana. Existential questions again. I asked her what she thought we *should* be studying. "Well, something important. Something like Greek mythology."

I said, "Okay, let's study Greek mythology. Odysseus has been away from home for twenty years. He has just hit town. He has to overthrow the suitors. Needs to lay low while he plots. Where does he go to hide out?" A long pause. "To his oldest friend, the swineherd."

The kids from the pig farms laugh. "Odysseus's dog, by the way, almost blows his cover," I continue. "We find the animal lounging where? That's right, on the dung heap".

These Iowans know the smell of manure, of course. They have been scraping the shit from the gutters of their own barns as diligently, if not as heroically, as any Hercules.

Every patch of ground has its stories. The world is old and people, the ani- mals who tell stories, have been everywhere upon it now. The documents we use to transfer a patch of ground as property suggest this; we call them *titles* and *deeds*. Some places seem more storied than others. You are riding a bus in Greece, on the island of Eubea. You rush by a rocky plain the size of a foot- ball field, one of the few open places you've seen. You think to yourself that this must have been the site of a battle, and, sure enough, upon consulting your *Blue Guide* you discover there were eight skirmishes in the Hellenistic period. In Greece it is nearly impossible to build anything new for all the ar- chaeology that needs to be done first. There are all these layers to live with. And the modern Greeks, believe me, get pretty tired about watching where they step. But all places contain such layers. All that is needed is a *Blue Guide* to narrate the place.

I was once helping a farmer during planting season. This was in Turin, Iowa, a place named Turin because the hills there reminded a one-word sto- ryteller of the Italian hills. And those hills, loess hills, are composed of wind- blown glacial till. As a geological feature, loess hills exist in only two places in the world: China and western Iowa. A special place but one rather unsung, and I was sitting on a red tractor there vibra-shanking the soil while the farmer was feverishly planting corn a few rows behind me. Incredibly, Vivaldi was playing on the cab radio, *The Four Seasons*, and I got so distracted by the violinic braying of donkeys in the Tuscan Hills of Italy scored in the music that I stalled the tractor. The farmer's son, discing in the next field over, saw my plight. I couldn't get the tractor out of gear to start it up again. He came rushing to my aid by finding a raft and poling across a ditch flooded with spring runoff. This was years ago but this summer when I visited that place again, Eric, the son, said, as I knew he would, "Remember that time when you stalled the tractor, and Dad was bearing down on you, and I found the raft and pole." And I do remember.

All of this happened on a field called Cottonwood, another one-word story remembering the trees that had been there once and are still there in the name of the place. I exist and my exploits exist as long as Eric tells the story. And now, you, like the recipient of a virus, know of another patch of ground because I have told you of the loess hills of Iowa, of Turin, a field called Cottonwood, a young man named Eric who, at this moment, is probably harvesting the corn in that field, listening to the cab radio and remembering the time he went to help an awkward city slicker named Michael. You are infected now by that mosaic chip of information, that bit of DNA that begins to replicate in you the details of a story, and you'll go home and find that you have this story to tell your family, your students, other hosts for the infection, this story about storytelling.

It was I, Odysseus, son of Laertes, of Ithaca. When you tell the story of what happened here, Polyphemus, say it was I, Odysseus, of Ithaca, son of Laertes who blinded you. Look, I can see Eric floating on his raft calling to me.

The stories of the heroic age of ancient Greece, the ones we have studied, that have survived in our literature, that have crept into our modern pathology as narcissism and oedipal, those stories were told originally by a bunch of farmers and fishermen, wine merchants, and barflies perched on the rubble of rocky peninsulas and islands in the backwater of the then known world. But they took themselves and their stories very seriously.

Mythology by Edith Hamilton was another book my mother prepped each year. I remember the wonderful line drawings inside. On the cover was the picture of the bronze Perseus holding his bent sword in one hand and Medusa's head in the other. It was the Mentor paperback edition trimmed in bronze piping. Here the stories of the classical mythologies were glossed, and my mother read to me about the flying horses, the monsters, and the gods. But even then, I realize now, I was most taken with the people who seemed . . . well, so like people. I am Odysseus, son of Laertes, of Ithaca. And his wife Penelope who undid her patient weaving and who attempts to trick her trickster husband with the riddle of their bed. And later in my own freshman English class we used Hamilton's book. Her picture on the back, a cloudy black-and-white head shot that smacks of the thirties studio pose, her hair done up in a cloud of gray, her skin glossy. She looked just like Miss Colchin, my teacher, who was fond of telling us that when she was a little girl she sat on James Whitcomb Riley's lap. That is, Edith Hamilton looked like the schoolmarm she was, retired headmistress of Bryn Mawr School and now the great popularizer of the ancient classics.

Think about it. How do I know, how does anyone know, the ancient Greek classics? As far as I knew, the lady wrote them herself, made them up on her own. Then I noticed that her brief biography also mentioned her childhood in a place called Fort Wayne, the very place where I was spending my own childhood and the place where I sat studying the stories of a bunch of long dead braggarts and blowhards. But wait, there is more. Walking home from Franklin Jr. High School I would cut through Hamilton Park, cross Alice Street and Archer, and then cross Edith Avenue. Not only did I grow up in the same city as Edith Hamilton, I actually grew up on land that had once been owned by her family. It was long thought that my school had been named in honor of Benjamin Franklin. Its yearbook was called the *Kite and Key* and its newspaper, where I broke this story as an investigative reporter, was called the *Post*, as in the *Saturday Evening Post*. I discovered that my school had been named after its Franklin Street address, and that Franklin had not been Ben but Frank Hamilton. The surrounding street names all bore the names of the other brothers and sisters.

In 1957, Edith Hamilton, at ninety, was made an honorary citizen of Athens. The ceremony took place in Athens before a performance of the Prometheus, using her translation in the Herodes Atticus, the huge amphitheater nestled beneath the Acropolis. The Parthenon and the Temple of Zeus had been lit at night before, but in Hamilton's honor the Athenians lit the Stoa for the first time in history. Hamilton spoke to the hillside full of people, and then her version of Aeschylus was staged. As a bookish ninth grader raised on all this heroic stuff, this was pretty cool to me.

And the paradox was not lost on me. It was not just cool that someone from my hometown had gotten a bit of fame, had talked to the king of Greece and gotten a free trip to Athens. We all have booster feelings when we realize that some soap star or golf pro hails from our town. As the recent play and movie reminds us, we are all but six degrees of separation away from each other, and so perhaps any of us are only a hop, skip, and jump away from someone with a modicum of fame or notoriety. No, as I thought about Edith Hamilton, the gushing adulation I felt was of another order. It had to do with authoring and creating. You see, Hamilton herself in her writing had inscribed in me the very notions about fame and famous deeds that now swelled my breast. For me she was a kind of meta-celebrity, for in order to understand celebrity itself I had to digest the great stories of heroes that she, Edith, had composed. It was as if Hamilton were the wizard from Kansas. Do not pay any attention to the man behind the curtain. A girl from Fort Wayne, Indiana, had in a very real sense kept the civilization of Ancient Greece alive, not by doing the chores of Hercules or by defeating the Trojans in battle but by writing about those heroes and deeds. She was epic in a so self-effacing way. She was essential, invisible, the medium of transmission. And to me this is a great story.

Hamilton Park, where I played, had once been a trash dump, a hole dug deep in the ground and filled with rubbish. Now it is a grassed-over crater, the refuse heaps when it closed not quite reaching the lips of the embankments that surround it. When I played there as a child I loved the days after it would rain because on those days the junk that had been buried beneath the ball diamonds and picnic tables would work its way to the surface. I found old blue medicine bottles and pearl buttons, tin cans and bed springs. Sometimes whole tires would appear overnight in the middle of the football field, or as you slid into second your spikes would slice open a burrow of coiled hose. There were hummocks of eroding books too, the weathered pages like geological strata. And once the door of an icebox emerged near the scoreboard. You could open it, and it was like opening a tomb, a hatchway underground or back in time. The grassy banks around the park, I used to imagine, must be like the hillsides of Greece—Epidaurus, Dodoni, and even the cliff of the Acropolis where the Herodes Atticus was carved out. I thought of my playground as a theater, as a stage, and as a kind of automatic archaeology with the history of this place, the old used mechanisms of its working, its gears and balance wheels, its urns and amphora bubbling up at my feet.

Mythology of course was a religion for ancient peoples, and though we are reminded of that by the dutiful teachers and in prefaces to collections of stories, it is hard for us to imagine these tales as such. They come to us in literature classes as beautiful vessels, shells of cicada, and we admire them for their aesthetic power, perhaps for some of their ethical lessons, but mainly, I think, it is odd to us that people found in this set of stories an immense system of belief. Of course, our religious nature has been tutored by another set of stories. Though certainly stirring and equally compelling, the episodes of the Bible don't strike us the same way. One big reason has to do with point of view. The gods in ancient mythology did not write the text of the religion. Its writers, though perhaps inspired by gods through the muses, treat the deities as characters and actors. The Bible, especially the Christian testament, strikes us as more rhetorical, its stories are illustrative of the revealed word of God. To the Greeks, I think, the telling of the story itself was the religious act. Their church after all was a theater. There they listened to the retelling of a vast structure of connections. Their stories were all happening simultaneously. Theseus knew Oedipus, palled around with Heracles. They were related. They intermarried. The gods were everywhere, too. And this all had taken place only a few generations ago. The Bible reads more sequentially. After all, its great purpose is linear, to record and predict the one big story of God's drama with His creation. The stories were over in mythology. There is no revelation and no apocalypse. In the world of the Bible, we live in the middle of a great unfinished narrative and we are waiting for and participating in its ending. The Greeks lived within a labyrinth of stories, of finished tales whose intricate structure promises infinite variation.

I went to graduate school at Johns Hopkins University in the late 1970s. Hopkins is known for its medical institutions, but it maintains a small liberal arts and sciences campus and is the site of the first graduate schools of the humanities and sciences. I went there to study writing. I had never been outside of Indiana before, while most of my colleagues were Easterners fresh out of Ivy League schools. As I have said, I learned my lessons well, and my first efforts at writing stories were derivations of the stories I had read in other classrooms. It was after class in the Grad Club, where we debriefed over beers and fried food, that I related the more or less true stories of Indiana. My listeners were well traveled but knew far more about Europe, England, even India than they knew about Indiana. Indiana to them was as remote as the planet Mingo, and it was then partially in response to their response, partially as an expression of homesickness, and mainly as an application of my understanding of mythology that I began writing stories about Indiana.

When I wasn't writing stories I would wander the campus and make myself a nuisance in the biology labs. At that time, the revolution in genetic engineering was just getting started. The technique of snipping genes with certain enzymes and pasting them onto the chromosomes of another had just been patented, and the graduate students in the biosciences practiced doing that, snipping and pasting DNA, as if they were practicing scales. I had a friend named Eric, another Eric, who worked in the labs and one day pulled out a tray of slides to show me. See, he said, these are *E. Coli Ericson*. He told me he had attached a gene from a frog onto the bug that lives in all our guts. The smears I was looking at were a new form of life, and he named them after himself. I am Odysseus, son of Laertes, of Ithaca.

Today scientists at Hopkins are putting together the human genome map. The project began in the desire to identify the deleterious genetic material, the genes that actually cause inherited diseases, and has expanded to the incredible feat of identifying the function of all one hundred thousand genes packed on the twenty-three pairs of human chromosomes. An early discovery is that there are very few genes that directly cause things; however, the map reveals that there are thousands of genes that create a disposition, a likelihood of certain consequences. In my goofier moments I fantasize about the possibility of the storytelling gene. They have discovered the location they believe indicates an aptitude for musical ability. I fantasize that there is a gene that makes us all storytellers and hunger to hear stories.

Mythologies, whether ancient or Hoosier, seem to me to be like the human genome. Both use a limited set of building blocks, alphabets or proteins, in near infinite combinations to transmit complex collections of information, codes, and instructions. The way we have come to think of our biological inheritance is a metaphor based on storytelling. Isn't it curious that when groping for a model to explain how we reproduce we have settled on explaining it in those terms? It seems right to us to figure this apparatus of inheritance in terms of sequence, of language, of narrative, of story. And embedded in each level is the wizard behind the screen, the story gene, this disposition, this hunger for stories, almost as if our very essence is tied to the creation of story. We tell stories because we are human and we are human because we tell stories.

Mythologies to me seem to be always local and scaled to a human size. Even the monsters, the giants, and the gods behave in ways we recognize. "I like you Noman," says the cyclops Polyphemus to Odysseus. "I will eat you last!"

The advent of mass media—the book, newspaper, radio, television, etc.—distorts that human scale. It is easy to feel that we know the O.J. Simpson story better than we know our own stories. Locally, do you know the mil rate of your township tax assessment? Are borders, always arbitrary, of one's neighborhood, city, state, country even viable anymore?

The stories we tell ourselves create the very space that we as a group, any group, inhabit. Place is made by story. Recall the end of the *Odyssey* when Odysseus is instructed by the gods to hoist an oar on his shoulder and walk inland until no one recognizes the tool, until someone asks why he is carrying the winnow out of season. The true regions of the world we live in are mapped by the stories we tell.

Mythologies are connected stories that ultimately form a cultural map of a place. I have pushed my own stories to include the space that has been known as Indiana, but those stories have tended to seep into the surrounding region. The Midwest is a good example of the kind of placeless place but where stories are beginning to construct it. Where is it? My students in Iowa would not include Indiana in the Midwest. As a Hoosier, I think of Kansas and Nebraska as part of the Plains, at least, if not the West itself. To be a midwesterner is to begin with the justification of using that name, and what it means is still abuilding through an interweaving of local stories. In my own case, I discovered while reading about Edith Hamilton that as she lived her final years in Washington, D.C., she took to visiting the incarcerated Ezra Pound in St. Elizabeth's Hospital there. I was writing a story about Pound, who had his first teaching job at Wabash College in Indiana, and I included Edith Hamilton as an unnamed character in my story. The current governor of the state of Indiana was in my dorm at Indiana, and my most recent project, stories narrated by Dan Quayle, began when I rediscovered a letter he wrote to me when he was my representative in Congress praising my first book of poems set in Fort Wayne.

Mythologies, finally, are always also about storytelling. Mythologies are self-conscious of their cultural mission of mapping a place as well as mapping themselves. Recall that Odysseus himself is asked to recount his own travels to the court he is washed into after leaving Calypso. He is moved to tell his story after he has listened to a singer sing the story of the fall of Troy. Mythologies are self-conscious because they acknowledge the human problem and advantage of memory itself. Recall that the mother of the muses was memory. And yet individually we are trapped in perceiving time sequentially. Mythology—and I keep thinking of a biological/mechanical metaphor—seeks to attach a cultural memory into our experiential wiring. Stories are viral. A good example of this is the collection of folk legends, both urban and rural, that get repeated as the truth. There are many factual inaccuracies in my Indiana stories. I am self-consciously altering the details or making up ones I do not know. In so doing, the storyteller faces the existential dilemma of fact and fiction. The things we do are done. We are always left with the residue of events, evidence. And all that residue can be by definition manipulated and shaped for many purposes, one of which is the myth building I have been speaking of.

Myths are local, connected, and self-conscious. Tell them I am Odysseus, Laertes' son, of Ithaca. In the stories we tell ourselves, we tell ourselves.

I noticed as I sat in my mother's classroom that from time to time she would refer to me as an example of something under discussion in the text at hand. I was Piplike or the way I played games in the neighborhood mimicked the structure of the quest they were discussing. I had a strange feeling sitting there in my big desk as all the eyes in the class turned to the little boy in the corner. I was being read. I was a text. And at this moment, in my own text, my memory searches for a reference. I think of Elizabeth Bishop's poem "In the Waiting Room" in which she says of a similar moment, "I was an I/ I was an Elizabeth" (Bishop 1983, 159). I also think of the wonderful experiments in child development in which researchers daub a smudge of ashes on the foreheads of observed children. The children of several ages are playing in a room of mirrors, and it is only ones of a certain age that notice their reflections and stop before the mirror. They understand that they are in the mirror and that the ash is on their forehead, and they now know to wipe it off.

I, whoever I am, am a text created in my mother's classroom. I am a lucky boy since the transmission of my biological and my cultural heritage took place under such circumstances, in such close proximity. I am Michael, my mother's son, of Fort Wayne, Indiana.

Only recently my mother visited my classroom. We were discussing Robert Waller's *The Bridges of Madison County*, which my mother had read. She did not sit in the corner but jumped into the discussion, and I was a child again with the ash on my forehead, a mark where my mother touched me. And in the mirror of the moment I contemplated rubbing it off, considering how in doing so I would now have the ash on my fingers, how I could transform my sons or my students. As my mother talked I saw her metamorphose into this character, a mythological being, the one you see before you now whose ashes are in the air of my words, the words you have just inhaled.

Works Cited

Bishop, Elizabeth. 1983. "In the Waiting Room." *The Complete Poems of Elizabeth Bishop*. New York: Farrar, Straus, and Giroux.

Wilder, Thornton. 1938. *Our Town*. New York: Pocket Books.

2

Up River, Down River, and Across the Aegean

JOY PASSANANTE

On the surface of it, and for the forty other characters who make it what it is, this story begins one crystalline afternoon at the end of August on the cusp of the new millennium, the commencement of another academic year. The setting is the Northwestern United States, the Idaho Panhandle, Room 209 in the building occupied by the College of Forestry, Wildlife and Range Resources of the University of Idaho.

For some in the classroom, this is the first day of college; for most, this is a just another first day in a seamless succession of semesters. For me, a teacher for nearly half my life, today marks my first encounter with the university's version of Literature of Western Civilization (a misnomer, to be sure, but that is another story). I am amused that the registrar has housed us in the forestry building. After saluting the mounted caribou and moose heads in the hallway, I walk into my classroom, my backpack digging into my shoulder, weighed down by the hefty Norton anthology. I stack my notes on the podium and scan the shelves of glass-eyed owls and labeled pine cones in varying-sized canning jars, around which I know I'll have to navigate when I start pacing.

Truth to tell, however, this story begins much earlier and two thousand miles away—in 1956, in the heart of the country, a St. Louis suburb, a time and place most of my students can barely imagine. It was my ninth birthday, a day memory gives me again and again in the sight of the waxy magnolias and the scent of apple trees behind the play house and the jungle gym in my backyard—and in one particular gift. Along with a Madame Alexander doll in a silver tutu, my parents gave me a copy of *The Iliad*, a children's prose version with full-page pictures of warriors wearing stylized

12

masks and armor and hefting red and orange shields. My first reaction was disappointment. At age nine, in the 1950s, how many girls wanted a book about war? But I picked it up late one steamy evening, and when I next looked at the clock it was 2:00 A.M. and my heart was still racing. The next few nights, I used a flashlight under the sheets so as not to alarm my parents. And when I read how Achilles dragged Hector around the citadel, my tears astonished me.

This drama was still unfolding much later, when as an undergraduate I studied Greek epic poetry and drama from a man who mesmerized two hundred of us by reading Hector's funeral in ancient Greek. I read *The Iliad* twice, every word (Richmond Lattimore's 1951 translation), and wrote an overlong paper on it. And after graduation, I made a sort of pilgrimage to Greece, where one light-soaked afternoon, I plunged into the Aegean Sea and splashed up libations to Poseidon.

Nearly three decades later I find myself immersed in the Herculean task of choosing texts for a semester that sweeps across twenty-seven centuries in sixteen weeks.

"Teach *The Odyssey*," my colleagues advise. "They won't like *The Iliad*." Most of these advice-givers, I surmise, have been seduced by the resourceful Achaean hero. But I cling fast to nostalgia; have faith in the humanity of Hector and Andromache, Priam and Patroclus, and in the raw potency and allure of Achilles' rage.

But in addition, I recognize another level—a hidden agenda, a subtext. For me, literature—reading it, writing it, understanding it, remembering it—has always been about passion, but inextricably bound to language. I studied it not for the theoretical challenges it presented but for the feel of the words in my mouth.

Propitiously, while I'm fussing over texts and syllabi, I happen to read a review of the 1990 translation of *The Iliad* by Robert Fagles, and I discover that Fagles' work has been chosen for the sixth edition of the Norton world literature anthology. As I read it, I become increasingly conscious of the differences in its resonance from that of my old undergraduate Lattimore. I read once again in Book VI how when Hector returns home to his father's palace he, "splattered with blood and filth," strides through the city gates

> clutching a thrusting-lance eleven forearms long;
> the bronze tip of the weapon shone before him,
> ringed with a golden hoop to grip the shaft.
> And there in the bedroom Hector came on Paris. (206)

I note the force of the language, the tight-fisted punch of the Anglo-Saxon. And then, scanning the next three lines, I do a double take, let out a whoop, and go scurrying to my dog-eared Lattimore. And then it all falls into place, and I am ready for the onslaught.

This first day, as always, I poll the class, asking people where they are from. One says he's from Lenore. I ask him where that is, and he says, "Below the Dworshak Dam." Another says she lives "upriver from Riggins." I like the way they draw on a vernacular rooted in pragmatism and place. When I ask them why they're taking the course, thirty-eight of the forty say "Because it's a requirement." Several fold their arms and scoot back in their chairs. In the back corner, a young man eyes me as if daring me to say something significant. His nectarine-tinted hair falls straight from a burgundy velvet beret. He's distinctly not from around here. . . an alternative high school?

We don't get to *The Iliad* for a couple of weeks. And the gods are with me: by the time we puzzle through the roles of Chryseis and Briseis, scope out just why Apollo is shooting those poisoned arrows, and zoom in on the argument between Achilles and Agamemnon, we have become comfortable with each other. I have grown to love the students I have taught for twenty years at the University of Idaho. They are mostly from Idaho. Although a sizable number bear the citified stamp of our swelling state capital, most are from the wheat-growing, sugarbeet-producing, cattle-raising, mountain-rugged rural parts of the state. For them, trekking north to the university in Moscow (population 18,455) is like moving to a metropolis. When they go out to dinner with their visiting parents, they are likely to order chicken fried steak; their heads hold complex data about guns and elk and negotiating truck-scarred unmarked logging roads in the moonlight. They're canny and helpful, and when I'm piecing together the details of a fictional scene about hunting or wheat fields or rock climbing or cabins by a lake, I have a list of resources to call.

And we're close to this level of comfort by the time we get to Book VI, which Fagles has named "Hector Returns to Troy," but which I am mentally calling "Meanwhile, Back Inside the Scaean Gates." This section of *The Iliad* is realistic and sensitive, concerned with Hector's relationships with his family—his parents and siblings and his wife and baby son. Having sustained a marriage of twenty-odd years and reared a family of my own, I have fostered a particular fondness for this book, but now, in class, instead of lingering over its tender images, I find myself rushing through the first pages of it so I can—as I have imaged it to myself—ascend the battlements of poetic understanding and "drive the bronze clean through."

And so, when finally we get to lines 96–97, the lines I've been awaiting for weeks now, I ask Tom to read the passage aloud. Tom's hair is as black as the T-shirt that bisects his biceps, and has a sheen to it. His veins strain against the skin like a painting of Michelangelo. His mellow bass resonates from the back of the class. I can tell he is used to hearing it. He's a sophomore and unafraid to say things.

> And there in the bedroom Hector came on Paris
> polishing, fondling, his splendid battle-gear,
> his shield and breastplate, turning over and over
> his long curved bow. (206)

Some eyebrows arch at the word *fondling*, but mostly there is no reaction. A young woman with caked eye makeup and an anachronistic perm stares at the lab sink. I am silent for a second, masking my disappointment, then dig in. "Is there a particular word that seems a little odd in the context of describing a warrior and his armor?"

Tara looks up from the tassel of the thick auburn braid from which she has been picking split ends. She's been quiet until now, absorbing. But when she's ready, she sparkles. She has a raw edge; a week or so from now, her expression for Achilles in his grief will be the same as her description, later in the semester, of Hamlet's angst: "whacked out." Tall but a bit too awkward to play on the varsity basketball team, she plans to be an elementary school PE teacher. "I'm not so sure a warrior would actually *fondle* his armor," she says. There are some titters. The woman with the curlicue hair stops examining the sink.

"Oh, I don't know," another deep voice from the back row offers. "What else would he have to fondle?"

After a stunned nanosecond, the class explodes; some crane their necks to view the source of this wisecrack. It's Shane, his long wheat-blond hair tied with a rubber band at the back. Fagles' term "long-haired Achaeans" floats to consciousness, but I keep focused on business, seize this opportunity. I haul out the Lattimore from my backpack under the podium, whip out an overhead transparency, dim the lights; I'm playing it brazen and broad. "Take a look at this different translation." The overhead projector limns the lines from Lattimore:

> He found the man in his chamber busy with his splendid
>   armor,
> the corselet and the shield, and turning in his hands the curved
>   bow . . . (Lattimore 1951, 161)

I repeat the phrase, "busy with his splendid armor."

"Hey," says Tara. "This one doesn't use that word at all!"

I read the Lattimore once more. "What's the difference with between 'busy with' and 'fondling'?" I ask.

"'Fondling' sounds like he's making love to it," Tara says.

And then Tom pipes up, attention full now, "Or making love to himself."

"Hm," I say again, pause a bit. They laugh, and I know I have them. Shane unfolds his arms, happy with his part in this.

I jump on this attention. "OK. Now, is this erotic—or auto-erotic—implication appropriate for this scene? What's going on? Who's in the bedroom with Paris?"

"Helen," Tara says. "The slut."

Heads turn toward her. Sink long forgotten, the young woman with glamorous eyes now snaps shut her compact.

"Slut?" Heidi's voice rings out. "Slut?!" Heidi evidently doesn't remember that Fagles has Helen call herself a "bitch" and a "slut," but I'm happy someone besides me is leaping to Helen's defense.

"It says it right here in black and white." Tara jabs the Norton at line 141 and reads—"and all for me, slut that I am!" Several voices rise at once, and it surprises me how many of the women, led by Tara, are suddenly, vehemently anti-Helen. At the height of the cacophony, I glance at The Perm, who shakes her head, as if, with me, grateful for Heidi's outrage. I hold her gaze for an instant, searching for her name. Something unusual, I think, like Estelle, or Audrey. An abstraction perhaps? Faith?

I wave my hands, whistle for attention, and they quiet down. "OK, OK. Let's talk about the black-and-white thing. Lattimore—this one on the screen—calls Helen simply 'dishonoured.' If I do not mistake myself, Lattimore's version is also, er, in black and white." I let that sink in.

And then, The Perm makes eye contact, a sidelong glance, as if we share a complicity, and it suddenly comes to me, her name: Harmony. The irony helps me regroup.

"So which is the *real* version?" Troy asks. Troy, who is putting himself through school by cutting wood, is a business major. Already an entrepreneur, with his chain saw and lemon yellow truck, he hauls and splits to order. I don't know it yet, but I will become a customer when the semester's over. He lives alone and longs for more time to ramble and hunt in Idaho's generous forests. He wears sunglasses inside this windowless classroom.

"Yeah, why does Fagles change it? Are you trying to say that both these guys are just way subjective?" Tara throws out.

It's a painful oversimplification, yes, but so is everything else in a class that has to cover so much ground, and her canniness pleases me. "Like this slut thing," she continues. "So Fagles thinks she's a slut, and Lattimore doesn't."

"No," Heidi says. "Fagles thinks *Helen* thinks she's a slut. Lots of women feel insecure about themselves in that way. Y' know what I mean?"

Before we can explore the centuries-old problems of women's self-image, Tom says carefully, for him, "So when Fagles says 'bedroom' and Lattimore says 'chamber,' old Fagles is pointing out the sexual nature of this whole mess . . . and that leads back to Helen." He slaps both hands flat on his desktop, clearly pleased with himself. Tom plans to transfer at the end of the semester to enter nursing school, and I find myself already missing his presence.

As seductive as the situation's sexual politics might be to discuss, I am relieved to backtrack a bit, to set the scene more purposefully, to focus on language. "So what's the difference in the kinds of words these poets choose? What's the difference between 'bedroom' and 'chamber'?"

"One is fancier," a fellow in a starched white Navy uniform offers in a voice I can hardly hear. I smile as I recall how Lattimore's style is described, in a recent *College English* essay by Lawrence Venuti (as well as by the translator himself forty-five years ago), as "plain."

"*Chamber* is an old-fashioned word. We would never talk like that." This is Tara, reasserting her status as the self-proclaimed spokesperson for the culture of the class.

Then Troy the Logger joins in. "A chamber can be any room. But a bedroom is the place you sleep . . . or whatever."

"Yes, and it looks like it's the 'whatever' that's important here. At least for Fagles," I say. Eager to be entertained, they laugh. "And why might that be?" I press on. "Why doesn't Lattimore play up the . . . uh, whatever?"

The bell rings, and I let the question conclude the class, hoping it will resonate and they will take this notion back with them to their computer labs and fraternity rooms and dining halls.

To the next class meeting I bring a handout with three translations: Pope [1732] (1909), Lattimore (1951), and Fagles (1990). The passage is from later in Book VI. I want to hang around a while longer inside the Scaean Gates, tarry here because it presents both the gnashing passion of the warriors and the poignancy of the love between Hector and Andromache.

Because I am overly ambitious and no doubt cloyingly eager to include everything I can about the way language works, I start with line length.

"Squint your eyes and get an impression of the passages. Which one would you read last?"

"The second one," says Troy, indicating the Lattimore, which occupies more than a third of the page. Several nod.

"Why? What are the differences?" I ask. "Don't even read the words; what do you notice about how it looks on the page?" Finally, the young man sporting the beret—the memory flickers across my mind that he is from Seattle—says, "The Lattimore looks longer."

"Why would you want shorter lines?"

Shane offers that we're not used to reading long sentences. Beret-man suggests that sentences everywhere, even in popular magazines, are shorter.

"And why are we conditioned to respond to and expect quick, exciting images?"

"MTV," several yell out. "Sesame Street."

I ask for volunteers to read the first half of the three passages in chronological succession. Beret-man tackles the Pope. His soft-edged voice astonishingly lends itself to the subtleties of the text and the eighteenth century.

> And yet no dire presage so wounds my mind,
> My mother's death, the ruin of my kind,
> Not Priam's hoary hairs defil'd with gore. . . (Pope, 122)

Here Beret-man pauses; scattered giggles bubble up, I assume at *hoary* since I'm positive most don't know the word *defiled*. He forges ahead so earnestly I'm sure he's met Pope before:

> Not all my brother's gasping on the shore;
> As thine, Andromache! thy griefs I dread;
> I see thee trembling, weeping, captive led! (122)

Do I imagine it or is there a quiver in his voice as he reads the last line? I do imagine it. A fellow in a baseball cap nudges his desk partner, another fellow in a matching baseball cap. Harmony snaps open a compact under her desk. I wait.

"It's just so cheesy," Tara says finally, breaking the tension. "I mean, all this *thy* and *thine*. And all those exclamation points. Homer must be afraid we'll miss the point."

"Whoa," Tom jumps in. "*Homer's* afraid? This doesn't seem like the SAME Homer we were reading before."

Tara waves him away with a flick of her large-boned wrist. "Oh, Pope, OK. Pope's afraid that we'll miss the point." She sounds like she's puzzling through it out loud, and then Troy's question becomes hers, takes her by surprise. "Wait a sec! Whose story are we reading, anyway? Which one *is* Homer's?" Everybody looks at me. They're beginning to get an inkling that they're squaring off with translators—each from his own era, focused on his own agenda, toting his own assumptions. "Hold that question," I say. "Let's get all three versions in our heads first."

Because he seems at home in the world of words and there's an edgy sensitivity about him, I give Shane the lyrical Lattimore. He navigates the swells of the syntax smoothly:

> But it is not so much the pain to come of the Trojans
> that troubles me, not even of Priam the king nor Hekabe,
> not the thought of my brothers who in their numbers and
>   valour
> shall drop in the dust under the hands of men who hate them,
> as troubles me the thought of you, when some bronze-armoured
> Achaian leads you off, taking away your day of liberty, in
>   tears. . . (165)

Although Shane does the passage justice—gracefully interpreting the cadence, emphasizing the "not"s to clarify the contrasts, coming down hard on the alliterative consonants, pausing for commas—most of the faces register only politeness. A foot kicks the desk chair of the person in front of it. "Sorry." Several rubberneck at the clock. Nothing to make fun of. Not much to interpret, I suppose.

At this awkward moment, I'd love to return to Tara's question but decide to toss a third version into play first, hoping my point will make itself. "Now for the Fagles. Take it away, Tom. Read it like you mean it."

His voice rises on the first line, and he gesticulates palm up, exaggerating, sweeping the room. The class eats it up. But as he continues, he becomes more serious.

> Even so,
> it is less the pain of the Trojans still to come
> that weighs me down, not even of Hecuba herself
> or King Priam, or the thought that my own brothers
> in all their numbers, all their gallant courage,
> may tumble in the dust, crushed by enemies—
> That is nothing, nothing beside your agony,
> when some brazen Argive hales you off in tears,
> wrenching away your day of light and freedom! (210)

Faces register . . . what? Something new.

"Which version is the most exciting to you?" I hazard.

"Fagles," says Troy flatly, as if I've posed an obvious question.

Tara says, "Yeah, Lattimore is bland."

Beret-man says, "I like the Lattimore, but I think the problem is the verbs . . . Look at this. Lattimore says 'troubles' and 'leads you off' where Fagles says 'weighs me down.' 'Leads you' sounds like they're going into a party, but Fagles isn't messing around. And then there's the word 'wrenching,' which is just plain 'taking away' in Lattimore."

Shane joins in. "And then there's 'under the hands of men who hate them' versus 'crushed by enemies.' Fagles is much more graphic." Yes, I think. Here we go. Beret-man and Shane toss each other the visual equivalent of a high-five.

I almost miss Heidi's saying, "I think part of what makes Fagles good is that he uses words to paint things more boldly. Remember what he says about Helen, for godsakes." She is a bit smug that she's got her licks in about Helen. I cheer silently for her. "And it's not just the words he chooses to use but how he puts them together."

"Good point. Now answer yesterday's question. I believe it was something about whatever . . . why is one of these guys talking about a chamber and the other a bedroom?"

Tara is especially quick today. "Oh, I see. Because of sex, Paris took Helen, and that's why they've been fighting the war. Fagles is just more sexual."

Heidi squirms in her chair and plays with the zipper on her ski sweater. "I think he's just more like us," she says impatiently, and with that comment I know I won't need to belabor my point. Heidi is pretty, with a small gold stud in her nose. She hails from Sun Valley, went to a private school, one of only a handful in the state, is one of the few English majors in the class.

"Us?" I say, trying to sound provocative and not condescending. "What do you mean by us? What are some of the characteristics of us—of our culture?"

"Sex and violence!" I hear this in a single voice.

"I don't think it's just our generation but the whole friggin' world," Troy quells the eruption of laughter. I can picture him with his orange hunting vest hanging loosely over his shoulders, his gun rack in the back of his truck, and I wonder a bit at his defensiveness.

I refocus us on the language.

"Heidi, show us. Read the lines," I demand.

Heidi studies her page for a while, then reads: "That is nothing, nothing beside your agony . . . ."

"And Lattimore says?"

She scans the Lattimore passage a couple times. "Oh, here. 'As troubles me the thought of you. . . .'"

Troy says, incredulity bordering on righteous indignation, "That's the same line? Coulda' fooled me."

I ask Troy to read the climax of the passage in Lattimore—the last two lines—and he does so, stumbling over the thick syntax: "'But may I be dead and the piled earth hide me under before I / hear you crying and know by this that they drag you captive'" (165).

"OK, Tom. Now the Fagles." Not to be outdone by Troy, Tom really gets into Hector's voice, hamming it up. And when he shrieks, "No, No," there's laughter, but it dies as he lets his voice ease into earnestness: "'Let the earth come piling over my dead body / before I hear your cries, I hear you dragged away!'" (211)

"Wow!" Troy says—the first glimmer of passion for the plight of Andromache.

"Why'd you say that?" I ask.

"It's just so sad." But then, as if anticipating my question, he adds, "But it's not so sad in the Lattimore or the other one. I mean, you can really see your wife being drug away . . . ."

"But doesn't Lattimore also use a form of that word? He says, 'know by this that they drag you captive.'"

"It's just not as clear—"

"Or strong. The word *captive*. I mean, how often do you hear that word? It's just so old-fashioned," chimes in Tara.

I pursue the advantage.

"What else is going on here? Let's go back to that difference between Lattimore's 'troubles me' and Fagles' 'weighs me down.'"

"Oh, I get it. 'Weighs me down' is much more physical," says Tara, the future physical ed teacher, at home in her own field.

"And the Lattimore?"

"More abstract," says the midshipman, pleased.

"How about Pope's way of taking care of that phrase?" I continue.

"Uh, 'wounds my mind,'" calls out Tom, like he's just kicked a goal.

"So, is that closer to Lattimore or Fagles?" There is a difference of opinion, but those who see Pope's rendering as emphasizing the physical appear to carry the day in arguing that at least in *that* phrase, Pope anticipates Fagles and the sexualized nineties.

"Hold on, hold on," Troy the Logger objects. "This guy is NOTHING like Fagles! Look at those singsongy lines, duhDA duhDA duhDA duhDA duhDA. And the rhymes, and the weird words like *hoary* and *defil'd* and *thine*."

This is a risk, I know, but I decide to intervene. "Let's back up a minute. Anyone familiar with the rhythm Troy's spotted?" I ask Troy to repeat.

Beret-man offers sheepishly, "Aren't those heroic couplets?"

I exaggerate my nod, smile, say "wow," make sure he and the class know I'm impressed, and decide I can sneak in some stuff about rhymed iambs. Heads turn toward him. "And what's the important word there?"

"Hero," Tara blurts out while arms unfold into the air. I want badly at this point to confess my nostalgia for Pope's exquisite handling of this form, but just before deciding not to press my luck, I take one more step out on the limb. (Fagles would no doubt say *branch.*) "Let's read this out loud together." I lead in the effort, as if I'm conducting a choral speaking class, making them slow down, creating tension against the forward movement of the couplets' rhyme:

> May I lie cold before that dreadful day,
> Press'd with a load of monumental clay!
> Thy Hector, wrapp'd in everlasting sleep,
> Shall neither hear thee sigh, nor see thee weep. (122)

No one laughs this time. And I can tell they like the feel of the words in their mouth.

"OK, let's pretend we don't know anything about the eighteenth century." I say this with barely repressed irony since it's a pretty safe bet that no one knows much about life, not to mention literature, two hundred years ago. "Just from reading these two stanzas, what would you say, just off the top of your head, Pope's culture valued?"

"Cheese," Troy blurts out, then turns around to take in the response.

"OK. But what do mean by that?" I press.

He can't answer, but Shane takes up the slack. "The kind of words he uses. They're so sentimental."

"Or just emotional," says Heidi. I'm glad she's back in the fray.

Shane interrupts, "I'm not putting down Pope or anything, but the Fagles is a lot more gut-wrenching." He pounds his abdomen with a well-controlled fist; I'm not sure he even notices he's doing this.

"You can really *see* it in the Fagles," Tara adds.

"And when you can see it it's called an—" I don't even get to finish.

"Image," Heidi tells us.

"Read the last three lines of the Fagles one more time, Tom," I command. This time he reads it with more . . . well, passion.

> That is nothing, nothing beside your agony.
> when some brazen Argive hales you off in tears,
> wrenching away your day of light and freedom! (210)

And there is silence. Charged, glorious silence.

I let the class feel that power for a few seconds, then say quietly, "So what's the answer to Troy's question? Which text *is* Homer's?"

Shane speaks smoothly, as if he's been practicing this answer in his head. "I think each of these guys represents his own lifestyle, but in some ways they're all good. You know?"

"So, lemme get this straight," Tom says. "We're reading not Homer but someone else with their own ideas of what they want us to hear."

"And what they want us to feel," Beret-man points out, letting that resonate.

And somewhere in all this I am able to see myself as a guest at a sloppily executed but serendipitous double wedding: Culture and Passion; Plot and Poetry.

I am aware that I am saying nothing. But I keep turning over in my mind how now all the pieces of the puzzle are laid out before us. We already know what picture we're forming: how what we read is mediated by the translators' visions. The outlines of these latter-day bards, people who represent their own cultures as much as Shane and Tara and Heidi and Harmony represent theirs, are gradually coming into view. And so I am ready to pop the big question: "Which one of these three is your favorite?"

"That's easy," says Troy, ignoring the hands popping into the air. "This Fagles, he seems like a good guy. Let's ask him to class."

On the last day of the semester, *The Iliad* now ancient history, Harmony stops me as I carry my zipper-strained backpack toward the door, I smile uncertainly. As if we had been in the middle of a discussion of class goals, she blurts out, "I think the most important thing I learned in this class was to pay attention to each word. I never knew you were supposed to do that." She flashes me a smile, her first and only of the semester. I notice that her teeth are wired with braces. She adds "You don't get THAT from Cliff's Notes!"

I linger for a bit, letting that gift glimmer while she disappears down the hall. But when I finally close the door, I feel, oddly, melancholy, wondering what else these students will take with them. Will Troy, when he's building an empire from the acreage he and his father have planted and plowed, think of Achilles and Peleus? Will Tara, when she chooses a girl in her PE class as captain of a team of boys, recall Andromache advising her husband from the battlements? Will Tom, in an emergency room with blood-spattered bodies and the stench of human cells, conjure up Ajax slashing his way across the plains?

And I find myself hoping for them that, like the little girl weeping under the sheets in 1956, they will keep with them the images that have made their blood race and their eyes fill, but also that they will have something more, something interwoven with the images—the words that shape them and stitch them into memory.

Works Cited

Fagles, Robert, trans. 1990. Homer, *The Iliad*. New York: Viking Penguin.

Lattimore, Richmond, trans. 1951. *The Iliad of Homer*. Chicago: University of Chicago Press.

Pope, Alexander, trans. [1732] 1909. *The Iliad of Homer*. London: George Bell & Sons.

Venuti, Lawrence. 1996. "Translation and the Pedagogy of Literature." *College English* 58.(3): 327–44.

3

Pilgrimage at
the Penitentiary

KIM STAFFORD

A double question: What can Chaucer do for a student—one who may never follow literature as an outright calling—and what has Chaucer done for me, a strayed medievalist who now teaches the making of stories rather than the study of their master?

> There was a student in my Chaucer class,
> back in the days when most chose grades or grass,
> but he sought neither. Neither jock nor nerd,
> he seemed to find his pleasure when he heard
> a story or an ancient poem read aloud
> with verve. He worked and read and starved, too proud
> to mention anything but books and art,
> and how these treasures gave his mind and heart
> good solace. But when others talked of life
> beyond our college, of work, of man and wife,
> of bold ambition, he was still. His look
> went far, as if these things outside his book
> were nothing. We wondered how he'd ever find
> his way in this hard world, where cruel and kind
> are sometimes hard to tell apart. He spoke
> but seldom. His style was thrift and mend. He woke
> each day with volumes by his bed, and slept
> to fire his hunger for the books he kept.

How do I remember this about one among the student hordes who wandered through my classes when I was faithful, a scholar searching for a tenured job? How do I remember that one night, late in the term, when we held class at his apartment, the poor student's garret room—a mattress on the floor, a stack of books, and a bowl? I do remember that short list. By then, we had agreed as a group we could no longer meet in the formal seminar room assigned to us. Chaucer had led us abroad, to mingle with the pilgrims of our time. So I remember the night we met at that student's place. The problem is I can't remember his name. Maybe this is the way with teachers of story: I remember my students by the stories they tell, not by their names I briefly learn, names to which I give a grade and then lose. The stories they tell have a way of surfacing years later, far beyond the work we shared together.

I'm a teacher of writing now, no medievalist, and thinking back, I'll call this most quiet student of those days the "Pilgrim." He was tall and a runner, lean. His face had a kind of eagerness most pronounced at the eyes. His hair fell over his face when he sat reading or writing, and when someone spoke, he might glance up without brushing it away. With a keen look, he considered the world through that dark fringe of his own perception. I taught all kinds of things, but what would he and the others learn, finally, from Chaucer himself, the old master of our multitude?

One day in class, I remember saying, "Hard times make good stories, and good stories make rich lives."

"Is that true?" the Pilgrim said.

"What would Chaucer say?"

"It depends which pilgrim is talking, " said the Pilgrim. He would say not more, but the rest of us were off into one of those pinball conversations woven of text and private story, of Chaucerian pilgrim talking back to parent, to brother or sister, to a troubled friend, or to one's own unruly life.

I was the adjunct professor, the visitor hired to teach medieval. Arriving at night from afar, I seldom met my colleagues in the old brick building where I was assigned to meet my class. Like a ghost of the ancient world, I carried texts of Chaucer and Langland, of Gower and old Anonymous, and tried to re-member how my own teachers had pronounced these poems older than thirty grandmothers in a row. Before our class, I haunted the hall where anthropologists had filled glass cases with Indian baskets—Kwakiutl and Klamath, with Paiute and Pima inventions of willow and spruce root and shell bead and the tiny curled feathers of quail, all woven watertight. Something in that careful work brought me back to the interlocking syllables of Chaucer's lines:

> Ther was also a Nonne, a Prioresse,
> That of hir smyling was ful symple and coy;
> Hire gretteste ooth was but by Seinte Loy;
> And she was cleped madame Eglentyne. . . . (11. 118–121)

It was a cold Oregon fall, with oak leaves whirling past the windows on darkest nights. Across the street from campus, the tower of the state capitol building rose in a blaze of light. In seminar room 12B, we held our own against the world, we the Miller, the Prioress, the Parson, and our own increasingly eccentric circle. For among his many entertainments, Chaucer nudged us toward our own quirks, our ragged edges, our checkered pasts, if we were lucky enough to have such. I remember the young Hupa woman who began to share stories of her tribe, first synopses of traditional ones, and then longer portraits of her Native neighbors back home, the odd and the strangely wise. I remember the man who rode his Harley to class and gradually began to bring us stories of marginally legal deeds on distant roads. I remember the editor of the student newspaper, the gossip-monger, increasingly rich with stories that would never find their way to print. I remember the sorority girl who told us wonders of the bizarre family at home, a tribe her house sisters would never know. And I remember the Pilgrim, quiet in his corner, drinking in the poetry.

How does a loner find his way? How does a bookish sort reach out, as the Chaucer pilgrim did, to find help from the whole pantheon of the spirited and dangerous:

> And shortly, whan the sonne was to reste,
> So hadde I spoken with hem everichon,
> That I was of hir felaweshipe anon,
> And made forward erly for to ryse,
> To take our way ther as I yow devyse. . . . (ll. 30–34)

What does it take at the party of our days to circulate the full circumference of the room, and find in each life some pertinence for our own?

Halfway through that term, I was moved to take my group to the Oregon State Penitentiary. The idea came to me before class one night, as I stared through the rain at the capitol building across the street. It was such a short journey from college to capitol—all inside the stifling tunnel of the aristocracy, and life is so short, and I wanted the inconvenience of experience to smuggle us along another road.

It was after the opening round of reading quizzes, after the Middle English pronunciation conferences, and before the term paper. We were just working our way through the "General Prologue," and a friend who worked at the State Department of Education but also taught at the Oregon State Penitentiary nights had invited me to tell her students *inside* about Chaucer. I decided to invite my whole class.

"Next week's class is Halloween," I said. "Meet me at the main gate to the prison, if you dare, and we'll teach in there together."

"Halloween! Do we have to?"

"What would Chaucer say?"

The next week, in the dark of the prison parking lot, from a class of twenty I met the five most faithful.

"Where's everyone?" I asked.

"Ah, there's a dance tonight," said someone in the dark.

"OK for them," I said. "Ready?"

"Let's go for it!" Two women and four men, we clambered into my car, and cruised slowly toward the gate. At the end of the long aisle of swaying poplars leading into the compound, a tiny speaker on a steel post asked who we were.

"State your name, and your purpose," said a guard's voice through the speaker.

"I'm Kim Stafford, these are my students, and we are here to meet Barbara Wolfe."

"Total count?"

"Six."

"Just park to your right and go in, Mr. Stafford."

We left the car under bright lights at a wall crusty with barbed wire and went where a door swung open to receive us. Inside the visitor's room, a woman in white moccasins, a beaded band around her head, waited to teach her Indian Heritage class. A crew-cut man with a Bible waited to read to "The Kingsmen." My friend Barbara arrived, and together we gave up our keys and pocket knives and gum, stepped single file through the metal detector, and started down the pale apricot tunnel. A motor in the wall hummed, and a steel gate slid away. We stepped through, the motor hummed again, and the gate clunked shut behind us.

Inside, all the prisoners were dressed in blue denim. All had faces quieted by doing time. We spiraled up the stairwell of the education wing. On the wall there, a handwritten sign: "The freedom workshop has been canceled." And then we were inside the classroom itself, with tables, scattered books, and chairs—all familiar but for the bars on the windows. My students stood around, close together, and only the Pilgrim sat down with his book and began to read. Barbara sat at the edge of the room to watch. The man who introduced himself as Chico Montezuma, the first prison student to arrive, settled in across the table from me. We talked about the books scattered between us, about his last week's class, and about how many men might show up tonight. I saw that his slender hands were folded over a paperback copy of *The Canterbury Tales*. Then he looked at me.

"Why do you come here?" he said.

"I want to see how people live," I said. "Everywhere."

"You're curious then," he said. "That's what most say. I always ask."

Then the literature class filed in, and the speech class joined us from another room. All together we were forty lives. Barbara killed the lights and I showed slides of bright pages from medieval books, the devotional calendar of plowing and harvest, the image of the Duc de Berry snug before his fire screen, and peasants blowing on their frozen hands outside. We looked at bold illuminations: pilgrim, hermit, martyr, saint, the seething throng of the damned tumbling into the flaming mouth of hell, and the holy souls led free from that fire by angels. There was Chaucer's Miller drunk with his bagpipe, the good Wyfe with her whip, the old Knight poised on his horse branded "M" for Milano. In the dark, I looked around, for Barbara had told me stories. Among us were the three who raped women, the one who killed a child, and armed robbers of all kinds. I didn't know who was whom, only saw in the dim room their eyes lit by these illuminations from the past. And each face was the medallion of a life, my students, my friend, attentive strangers all in blue.

When the slides were done, and the tube lights buzzed again above us, I blinked and looked around.

"Any questions?" I said.

No questions. We stared at each other. My students sat very still. There was a sense of polite waiting for more. So I told about pilgrimage in the Middle Ages. About holiness and malnutrition, about visions and the healing blood of St. Thomas. About life on the road—Chaucer himself robbed twice under the same oak, and the Pardoner vagabond with forged salvation in his wallet.

"Chaucer and some twenty-seven pilgrims," I said, "set out to find a healing place in the spring, when birds sang sleepless and everyone wanted simply to hit the road and be gone." I looked out over forty faces made somehow mute by the fact of our confinement.

"Next time you hit the road," I said, "where will you go to be healed? Where is that place for you? Let's each try writing an answer."

Some faces brightened, kindled by memory, by hope. Then they all bowed over paper, and a few began to write. Soon, everyone was writing. Memory kicked in, contagious. There was a steely tone of intensity in the room. I, too, bowed and wrote. After twenty long breaths, I looked up. No hand was idle, no face was raised. Each looked down into a well of possibility, a door to freedom small as a page, deep for some, glimmering. It took a long time for us all to be done.

"Would anyone like to share what they have written?"

In silence, Chico raised his brown hand. He read that he would seek the quiet of the desert. He described that desert in detail, an exact place with an Indian name, where a spring came secretly from the rock: "*Mas allá del sol.*"

"Right on, man!" a brawny convict shouted from the back.

"*Hermano, sí!*" shouted a man to my right. Then he read his own: He would go to the mountains of south Mexico, he said, where trees are blue by the light of haze, and the people all speak Maya.

"All right!" Shouts all around. "Tell 'em, brother!"

Another read that he would take the Larch Mountain road, near Portland. At the end of the road, he said he would follow a trail he knew. And where the trail ended, he would walk out into the meadow where the only sound was wind and the buzz of insects in the sun. And butterflies, lots of them.

Shouts: "John, that's your place, man! Tell it!"

Another read that he would go to Portland, find his way down the dark aisle in a movie theater filled with strangers. The film wouldn't matter, he said, only the darkness. And people would sit there, not caring who he was or what he had done. "And I know I'll cry," he said softly, "people trusting me."

"Right on! That's it!"

My students were stunned still, listening. I looked into the face of the biker: a grin. In the face of the Hupa woman: a collective portrait of many lives from home. In the editor's face: news, and stories too long and richly strange for news. In the face of the sorority girl: a slow retreat from fear of the odd. And in the Pilgrim's face: that same look he showed when he read aloud—allegiance to the possible.

Finally, a quiet man in prison blues held his paper in both hands and spoke about the house in which he was raised. "It's in the mountains," he said, "and no one lives there anymore. The windows, last time I was there, had all been busted out. But I'll go inside to find the room that was mine. You lie down on the floor there, and outside you hear this stream going by. You close your eyes, you breathe easy, you put your troubles into the sound of the water, and you let that water carry all your troubles away. And then you go to sleep."

I looked around the room. Mouths clenched, faces turned to each other, and out of the corner of my eye in the midst of it all I saw a hand lift one of the books I had brought, and I thought, "Good, someone is moved to take up a book." All around the room the talk went on of these exact journeys we each should one day make.

Lockdown, cell count time. They all stood, turned away, and were gone. As I moved with my students to gather up our things, I found that my book was gone. The B-text of *Piers Plowman* was in a prisoner's hand, traveling down some tunnel toward a cell—that text in Middle English that tells about the tower of heaven, the dungeon in the valley of hell, and between, the fair field full of folk, working and wandering as the world asks:

> In a somer seson what softe was the sonne
> I shoop me into a shroud as I a sheep weere;
> In habite as an heremite, vnholy of werkes,
> Wente wide in this world wondres to here. . . . (ll. 1–4)

We had been there: "wide in this world to hear wonders." I turned with my students, back down the stair, along the hall of bleak pastel, out through the gate. They departed. I got in my car, and drove north through the rain.

The term ended. I turned in my grades. That college no longer needed me, and I went forth. In my life now, I don't teach the *Canterbury Tales*. I don't teach literature at all—part of the strange evolution of a life. All things change in time: I lost my brother, I parted from my wife, my father died. I learned what I learned, and I forgot what I forgot. But somehow, through all that maze of change, a letter followed me. It came from the Pilgrim to my new address. As I said, I can't remember his name. And by now I've lost his letter, but his story, this one episode in his own journey, stays.

It seems that after some years of searching on his own, he was returning to college from far to the east. He was driving an old car with his books, a few clothes, and a primitive computer he had bought used, somewhere in New Jersey. He had to drive pretty much day and night, he said, to make it west in time for registration. The car held up as far as Elko, Nevada, where it conked out dead. And this is how I remember his tale:

> I had twenty dollars left, and I knew I needed friends more than anything else, so I went to a bar and shouted to the room that I would buy for everyone. In a flash, my twenty was gone, and I was center to a motley circle of carousing enthusiasts. We raised our drinks to life, dashed them off, and when the time was right, I asked my new friends for advice about car repair. I'm on the barter system, I said to them, and after that last round, I have precious little to trade.
>
> All my new friends in that bar fell into heavy consultation. Remember this was Elko, den of gamblers, honeymooners, cowboys, miners, and the red neon of the twenty-four-hour sign at the brothel called Mona's. All kinds of pilgrims wander through. But my rowdies somehow came to agreement, and the consensus was that I should try these two Shoshone mechanics out on the edge of town.

Someone had a truck, and together we found a chain to borrow, and then we hitched up my car and chugged through back streets to that Shoshone garage. These two guys there—I think they were brothers—they talked and prodded the engine and looked me over and finally took my computer in trade for fixing the car, and then by driving through the night, I made it to school just in time to register.

Chaucer's pilgrimage of story, his fragmentary *Canterbury Tales*, is as unfinished and as perfect as a life at the end. There is more to do, and suddenly, in a whisper of last breath, all is done. Finally, my career as a Chaucerian becomes a collection of stories, not a professorship or a list of publications. Would my student, without Chaucer, without our pilgrimage to the penitentiary, have sought help in that room of carousing strangers or traded his computer to a pair of Indians in the manner of a pilgrim? I don't know. In the teaching life, we never have that answer.

And what about me? Medieval literature is the country I abandoned, when my own writing led me into other lands. Gladly would I learn, and gladly tell my tales. A pilgrim in the company now, I join the ragged cavalcade, story by story to the end. And how does Chaucer teach me now?

There is a trail that follows Separation Creek into the Three Sisters Wilderness in the Oregon Cascades. The signs along that trail were made in the wood shop at the Oregon State Penitentiary, as part of the vocational training program there. One says, "Separation Creek." That is where I first went on my honeymoon, twenty-five years ago, in another life. One says, "Honey Lakes." That is where I went with my late brother once, and lightning almost killed us both. One says, "Abandoned Trail." That is where I go to be healed:

Up Separation Creek there threads a trail
where snowmelt from the mountains, melted hail
and rain come rushing through the snaggling yew
and cedar thickets. Travelers there are few
along the track they named "Abandoned," trace
for deer path now, opening to meadow's grace
of butterflies and lupine, paintbrush fringed with red
where sunlight's dazzle empties clean my head.
And beyond? I reach to touch the whittled sign,
the lettered plank that trusties carved with whine
of router in their prison shop, as should
my dear old teachers toiling for my good
to send me on, beyond where they could go,
up past the timberline where clean winds blow.

Works Cited

Chaucer, Geoffrey. [1933] 1957. *The Works of Geoffrey Chaucer*, edited by F. N. Robinson. Second ed. Boston: Houghton Mifflin.

Langland, William. 1975. *Will's Vision of Piers Plowman, Do-Well, Do-Better and Do-Best*. Edited by George Kane and E. Talbot Donaldson. London: The Athlone Press.

4

Finding the Selves
We Set Aside

PATRICIA SHELLEY FOX

The room is quiet except for the scrape of pen tips on paper. Twenty-seven freshmen women and I crowd into a room built to hold twenty-four. The extra desks jut every which way from the available corners, and I have had to fetch my own chair from the room across the hall again. The air is stifling, the window swollen shut from last night's rain, the hallway too noisy to open the door to let us breathe. I know the drama of this story, and I don't want the outside noise to break the spell. Mrs. Mallard's mystery.

It's Monday in English 201, Intro to Lit, and in this 8:00 A.M. class, fifty-one-year-old Donna and thirty-five-year-old Jane sit side by side in front row seats to my left among the mostly eighteen-year-olds and the dozen or so joint enrollments—high school seniors taking college English for credit toward graduation. I have given them Kate Chopin's "The Story of An Hour." The story is laid out in a single column on the left-hand side of the paper, and I have asked them to read one paragraph at a time and record their responses—movies of their minds—before they move on. The class reads and writes in virtual silence. But then, in the corner, Donna pauses in her reading. "Ohhhh," she moans, just audibly, then wipes her eyes as she continues to write.

On Tuesday the storm front still hovers. Students stagger in late, wet with their umbrellas. If anything, the room seems tighter, the air even heavier as I look around and then offer my invitation: "Let's begin by sharing our responses to the story we read yesterday."

Carrie makes the opening move. "What goes around comes around," she says with the conviction of a fresh insight. "She got what she deserved."

"Can you say more about that, Carrie?" I ask reluctantly, braced for what I sense will follow.

"Well, at the beginning of the story I thought that Mrs. Mallard would be sad and upset at her husband's death. I felt sorry for her. But then when she goes upstairs, sits in front of that window and starts thinking—well, I was shocked . . ."

"She sounds selfish," Rachel interrupts. "She didn't truly grieve in her soul. She never really loved him. She's happy because she didn't want him around. She seems so shallow."

Becky agrees. "She has a twisted outlook on things. She cares only for herself. She seems so self-centered. I mean, how oppressed was she? Did her husband beat her?"

"Yeah, did he beat her, abuse her?" Jessica wants to know. "And why 'free'? He loved her. Didn't she love him? I was really shocked. Yes, the years will belong to her, but without the one she swore to spend eternity with. *Love* binds you to another. 'Powerful will' doesn't bind you. A marriage shouldn't be like that at all."

"If she was so unhappy she should have done something like get a divorce or go to counseling," Carrie concludes.

"Whew," I think to myself, trying to maintain an appearance of teacherly objectivity, "youngsters on a witch hunt. Were the sixties and seventies a dream? Or is this just how eighteen-year-olds think?"

Meanwhile, to my left, Jane and Donna are silent. I give them the old raised eyebrow, pitching for them to pull us back to center, but neither responds. Jane stares, with a Mona Lisa half-smile, at the floor in front of her desk, while Donna just looks sideways at me tightlipped and shrugs her shoulders as if to say, "I'm not getting into this."

Later that morning in my office, Donna unloads. "I swear," she says, her Brooklyn accent a comfort to me, "I'm never takin' day classes again. These kids just don't get it, do they?"

Donna is my age, a daughter of the 1950s. Happily married for twenty years to Sam, she has three grown children by a rocky first marriage to a bully, an abuser who, she says, did not bring out the best in her either.

"When I think of how I screamed in front of my kids. . . ."

As we sit beside my second-floor office window overlooking the campus, her response to Chopin's story lies between us on the desk.

"I must tell you," I turn to her, "I've been dying to read this—to hear what you wouldn't share in class yesterday."

Donna picks up her paper and holds it out to me.

"I'd like to hear you read it," I say, handing it back to her.

She reads:

Herself. Her Self was emerging. She was letting her*self* come to her. The *power*—the joy of her*self* still alive. It's not a jumping joy or a shouting joy, but a knowing joy—a finding joy. To know that the one she remembered was still with her.

The divorce. Then Sam, who saw in me what I could no longer see in myself. Coming to college. Finding me under it all. Reading, writing, pondering—all the things I left behind in my teens—mine again.

She puts her response down and looks up, her eyes glistening.

"That's where I lost it yesterday," she explains, her eyes now brimming once again with tears. "I was right there with her, sitting at that window. Louise had lived her role as *Mrs.* Mallard so perfectly that no one, not even she, guessed she could be an individual with her own wants and needs. She probably never reflected on her life, just did her duty."

Donna pauses, looks toward the window. "At that moment, when she sat in her armchair and looked out that window, she saw possibilities. I had my first moment like that—my first epiphany—when I was scraping the yellow wax off the kitchen floor. I was twenty-seven, pregnant for the third time, on all fours, and it hit me: This can't be my life. I collapsed right there and cried and cried for my lost self."

"It's easy for women to set their selves aside in marriage," I offer.

"Oh, I was trained to do that," Donna explains. "I was an expert. I grew up in a family of women who modeled for me that no matter what the cost to them—physical pain, emotional suffering—no matter what, their job was to keep the family together. My mother always said I was her smart one, but she would also warn me, 'You're never gonna find a husband if you don't stop reading.' She meant no harm. She just didn't know who I was. And *I* didn't know who I was either."

"Oh, I remember getting messages like that," I recall. "Keep a lid on it. Don't beat the boys in races. Don't let them know you're good in math."

"I was always afraid of my parents, afraid of disappointing them," Donna continues. "When I was eighteen I asked them if I could move around the corner into a little studio apartment—a room of my own. I needed a place to read, to think—an escape to get away from it all and find myself. I thought my father would kill me. He said, 'You leave here in a wedding gown or a coffin.'—Guess which way I left?"

"The same way I left. I went from living with my parents to living with my husband. I have never lived alone," I muse.

"My mother had the same training," she continues. "My son Steven said after she died, 'I never saw Nana without a dishcloth in her hand.' That's sad.

My mother was a bright, educated person. She was a good writer. But it was only when I went through her apartment that I discovered how bright. Saw what she might have become. She wrote the manual for the altar guild. We found all these wonderful things . . . even the love letters. Under chairs and in her underwear drawer my father had written to her *I love you.* He was an Italian hothead, so they had lots of stormy times. But he adored her. All three of us, their children, have been divorced."

"My parents love each other too," I say, my eye fixing on a new magnolia blossom just outside the window, "but it's not the kind of love that would have ever worked for me. Not the kind that my mother would choose again either, if she were choosing today. But they do love each other."

"That's what those knuckleheads don't get," Donna blurts, "that loving someone and needing space are two separate issues. My first husband used to say, 'Why can't you be happy with the way I love you?' and I would say, 'It's not about you. It's about me.' But he never got it. These kids don't either. Neither did I for a long time.

"In 1994 I came here to register for my first classes. Afterward, I walked right there," she points out the window to the fountain at the center of the quadrangle, skirted now with the bright coral blooms of the season's first azaleas. "I cried all the way back to my car. I was forty-eight years old, and I was finally starting something I had set aside when I was nineteen. I kept saying, *This is it. This is me. Finally, Donna.*"

I gaze out the window, listening to Donna's story, and thinking about a similar moment. "You know, the same thing happened to me," I turn to her, "and it happened just that way, on a college campus. I was pregnant with my second child. Despite the vow I made as a college freshman, I married at twenty-one, gave birth to my first child at twenty-two and tumbled into domesticity so easily I hardly noticed. Then came the moves, first for my husband's graduate school, then for his stint in the Navy. One day, when we were having lunch in the wardroom on his ship, the girlfriend of another junior officer asked me, 'Well, what do *you* do besides change diapers?'

"I wanted to protest, to assert that I had once been a person in my own right, but I let it go. Then I went back to grad school, and . . . I'll never forget this moment . . . one crisp, clear, starry summer night I was heading across campus to my Keats seminar. My husband was deployed for six months to the Philippines, my three-year-old son tucked safely at home with a sitter, and I was walking across the campus at San Diego State—great with child—my notebook held tightly to my chest, the cool night breeze sweet on my arms and in my hair, and I suddenly realized, 'Here I am. This is me.' And I knew that I had found myself again."

"How many women are like us," Donna wonders aloud, "you know, women who have found themselves again when they return to school?"

"Louise Mallard never had that choice."

I grew up in the fifties and sixties in the suburbs of Long Island, a baby boomer. Upwardly mobile, my father had served his time in the Navy during WWII, come home to wife and child and was, as he was wont to remind us, "darned lucky" to find a job with the New York Telephone Company climbing down manholes and up telephone poles to put food on our table and a roof over our heads. My father, like Brently Mallard, commuted to work daily—two hours door-to-door each way on the Long Island Railroad—to a job he hated but felt obligated to continue because he was the provider and knew no other way. He would come home at night angry at nothing or no one more particular than a world and a lifestyle that had him by the short hairs. As far back as I can remember, the thing my father wanted most in the world was to retire.

Our small family started out in a one-bedroom apartment in Brooklyn, New York, then, gradually, as my father worked his way up to a white-collar job, stretched our way out to the suburbs of Long Island, first to a two-bedroom 1930s bungalow in Baldwin, then to a three-bedroom, two-bath, post-Levittown, housing-boom split-level in Massapequa in 1952. I remember thinking, as we moved into that new house on my seventh birthday, that our lives were so perfect that things could only get worse.

In the meantime, my mother lived the life of a typical 1950s housewife. Trapped at home—although I don't believe that at the time she saw it that way—she fed us, clothed us, loved us, laughed with us, and saw us off to school. Then she cleaned the dishes, made the beds, washed the clothes, dusted and vacuumed. In spring and fall, she changed the curtains and slip-covers, cleaned the storms and screens, raked the leaves, and mowed the lawn.

My mother was June Cleaver, and our house was the social center for all the housewives on the block. After their household chores were done on weekdays, the neighborhood women would wend their ways—Monday through Friday—across the backyards or down the street to our house where they would occupy the corner nook in the kitchen, smoke countless cigarettes, drink—as my mother still recalls—"four pounds of coffee a week," and talk about God-knows-what until it was time to head home to make dinner and wait for their husbands, whose train pulled into the Massapequa Park station promptly at 6:17 P.M. Sleepwalking their ways through the American Dream. No obvious wants. No expressed urges to change. No apparent need for lives other than the ones they were living. No sense of what the future might hold for themselves or their daughters.

Then, in 1963, I left home for college in Pittsburgh where, during my freshman year, I encountered a book that gave me new ways of seeing and thinking. As I read, I knew Betty Friedan had my mother and the women in our neighborhood in mind, and I was seeing them again for the first time through new eyes:

> On an April morning in 1959, I heard a mother of four, having coffee with four other mothers in a suburban development fifteen miles from New York, say in a tone of quiet desperation, "the problem." And the others knew, without words, that she was not talking about a problem with her husband, or her children, or her home.
>
> Suddenly they realized they all shared the same problem, the problem that has no name. They began, hesitantly, to talk about it. Later, after they had picked up their children at nursery school and taken them home to nap, two of the women cried, in sheer relief, just to know they were not alone.
>
> Gradually I came to realize that the problem that has no name was shared by countless women in America. (Friedan 1983, 20)

As I recount my freshman-year discovery to Donna, she, too, remembers. "A lot of my mother's anger came from that same frustration. I watched her teach the young women of the church. She trained them for the altar guild, and she was such a good teacher."

"Sewing, ceramics, rug hooking," I recall my mother's search. "She even learned Braille, became a transcriber and a teacher of Braille. Later she volunteered at Hospice."

"All that talent simmering, smoldering. Those women did everything they could to scratch that itch," Donna observes.

"And all that searching was fine as long as they managed to do it on their own time, but I remember the tension at home when my mother would transcribe Braille at night and later when she would teach at night. My father really resented it when she finally took a job. He couldn't accept that she found work she enjoyed, that she was good at it . . . or that she had some money she could spend without consulting him."

It's Wednesday evening—teacher research—and Bobbie has been sharing stories of reader response. I talk about my students' responses, including Donna's, to "The Story of an Hour." Bobbie, who has never read Chopin's story, is intrigued and asks to read it.

Later, during the break, she confesses, "I was right there with her. There are still too many women right there with her. She was living out all our fantasies. I wonder what part of Kate Chopin was in Louise Mallard?"

"A fair amount, I suspect," I offer.

"But Chopin must have had someone to talk to. Those ideas could only have come to her through conversations. You can tell, too, that Louise Mallard, like many women still, had no such group. She lived in a closed world . . . So did I. I always thought in the 60s when women were burning their bras, that I would be a liberated woman, but I'm not . . . and I hate to say this . . . but thirty years later I'm as liberated as I'm allowed to be, and that's only during the hours that I'm not accountable to him. Liberated women have had access to conversations that allow them to name their feelings. I still feel most free when I am with other women and explore those ideas."

"Like we do in here," Sharon suggests.

Bobbie agrees. "That's why I think it's so important for students to be exposed to literature and ideas and have opportunities to discuss. If someone had given me opportunities to read, to think, my life might have been different. But I never knew there was anything different . . . never knew I had options. I saw only June Cleaver."

When we've ventured into this territory in the past, Bobbie has always been quick to remind me how lucky I am that my husband "lets" me travel to conferences and generally do so many things. I remind her today that I let Kevin go to North Carolina this morning. "And I'm letting him spend the night," I add.

She responds with a knowing smile, her hands raised shoulder high in a shrug.

By Thursday the storm front has blown off to sea, and the day dawns clear and cool. We are all in the clutches of spring fever. Someone has opened the window, and a sweet breeze rustles the papers on my desk. At the previous meeting, I suggested that my students might want to share Mrs. Mallard's story with a parent or an older, married friend.

"Has anyone had a chance to reread the story or to share it with someone else?"

Jessica, one of the knuckleheads who, Donna lamented, just didn't "get it," raises her hand.

"Well, this is sort of strange," she admits, "because of what we've been talking about and all, but yesterday I was riding in a car with my mother and two of her friends. Gwen, one of my mother's friends, was saying that her parents have been married for over fifty years and her mother is completely dependent. She has never paid the bills, never written a check. . . she doesn't even drive. Gwen's father has always handled all their finances, and now she worries about what will happen if he dies before her mother does. She'll be lost."

"That's exactly what happened to my grandmother," Becky adds. "After my grandfather died, my mother had to show her how to do everything. She was clueless. But she learned."

"What does any of this have to do with Mrs. Mallard?" Carrie wonders.

"Well, hearing them talk just made me think," Jessica continues, "and I realized how terrible it would be to be totally dependent on your husband. Not to have the freedom or the knowledge to make any of your own decisions. When we got home, my mother and I talked. She reminded me that in our house she's the one who writes the checks and pays the bills. And all that got me thinking about the story, so I asked her to read it like you suggested. I just wondered what she'd think. . . ."

"Well . . ." Carrie prompts, as Jessica pauses to collect her thoughts.

"Well . . . after she read it, she looked up at me and smiled. Then she said something that really shocked me—'If anything like that ever happened to your father, I wouldn't remarry. For once, I'd like to do things on my own. Without having to discuss every decision, every choice. Of course, I'd be devastated if anything happened to him, because he's the love of my life. But if tragedy struck, I think I'd like to be my own person again.'"

"But your mother loves your father," Rachel is quick to point out, "and that's not the same as Mrs. Mallard wishing her husband was dead."

"Well, my mother thought Mrs. Mallard loved her husband too. She didn't wish him dead. Her wanting to be free had nothing to do with him. She didn't even realize that she wanted to be her own person until after she thought he was dead."

The others have been silent listening to Jessica. "What do the rest of you think?" I prompt after a moment or two, looking in Donna and Jane's direction again.

But Becky jumps in. "She used to live for other people and never for herself. It may have taken something terrible, but she did realize she was subject to another human being."

"I still think she was selfish," Rachel insists. "Why would you even get married if you didn't want to be subject to another human being? That's the point of marriage, isn't it?"

Jane, who has been taking this all in, begins now in the cool, deliberate tone of someone who has spent a great deal of time thinking about what she is about to say. "No, Rachel, that's not the point of marriage . . . and she wasn't being selfish. It took me a long time to realize that taking care to be myself is not being selfish. I lived for a long time in a situation in which my decisions weren't mine to make, and I felt incomplete . . . and owned . . . and I hope that's not what your marriage will be like. I finally realized that I had spent my whole life worrying about what other people would think of me.

Was I a good daughter? A good wife? A good mother? It was only when I started wondering what my daughter was learning from me that I knew I had to do something. I'd been sleepwalking through my marriage, through my one-and-only life. And it wasn't until I finally decided to come back to school that I woke up and found my old self waiting for me."

As Jane speaks, Donna leans into her every word, then reaches out to touch her hand as she finishes, and finally looks up at me, eyes glistening, a broad smile on her face.

My mother sailed through the Panama Canal yesterday. Last weekend, as I helped her pack, she once again marveled, as she so often does, at how I run through the paces of a life that includes a teaching career.

"I don't know how you do it all," she commented for what must have been the thousandth time.

"But I don't do it all," I protested yet again. "I certainly don't iron and cook, much less change the curtains and the slipcovers twice a year and vacuum and dust three times a week the way you did."

"Three times a week . . ." she repeated, remembering. "Busy work. What was I thinking?"

And, later, "You know, my father offered to send me to college, but I never thought I was much of a student, and back then all I wanted to do was get married. But you know," she paused, carefully folding, then handing me her white blazer, "I would have been a good nurse."

Women's lives: multiple voices, multiple perspectives. And I am left to consider how my classes of women have named and explored the problem, how reading the lives of women has complicated the way we think. None of us has found easy answers. Our epiphanies—Louise Mallard's looking out the window, Donna's scraping wax off the kitchen floor, mine walking across the campus at San Diego State, Jessica's hearing her mother's confession—each has cleared the path ahead at the same time promising to make the journey more challenging, but finally richer and more fully our own.

Works Cited

Friedan, Betty. 1983. *The Feminine Mystique*. New York: Dell Publishing Company.

5

Shoot-Out at the I'm OK, You're OK Corral

VICTOR VILLANUEVA JR.

An ethnography, better told as a day-in-the-life story.

It's the night before we begin discussion on *Ceremony*. The book, down.

This story hits too close to some part of home. Memories of the Army. Pride in ribbons, the medals worn, stripes on a sleeve, got by . . . I don't know. American. Spic. Tayo. Pieces of memory. I won't be able to talk much on this one. I'd just shove my way of reading down their throats. No dialectic that way.

Next day. Late afternoon. Spring. Bright sunshine streaming through waist-to-ceiling windows in the Chemistry Building (room assignments one of the great mysteries of college teaching). I lean against the chem room's sacrificial alter: the large wooden box in the front of all chem classrooms, black slab on top, a small sink, gooseneck faucet. Before me, a comfortable-sized classroom, fewer than twenty undergrads, a 300-level course, The Politics of Literacy. *Ceremony* was to be the practical application, the ways in which a fictional discourse carries political import. The hope was also that the story would prompt a demonstration of dialectical exchanges, that there would be points of contention within the book.

The students of the class, with one exception, look like just about any class. The exception, Tim Pequeñito, a huge fellow, at least two hundred pounds, but not much taller than five-five, too short to be in the football team. He looks Latino, has a Spanish surname, dark round face, thin mustache over thin lips, thick, dark eyebrows over almond-shaped black eyes. His hair, glossy black, prickly short on top, long behind the ears, loose curls cascading to the upper back. No neck. A width and thickness seldom seen outside

43

a superhero comic book. Small waist. He's not much of a participator in class. He won't be on this day either, though he'll end up playing a part in the drama. The students sit in neat rows, the desks bolted to the floor.

OK, they've been pretty good so far. Pretty good readers, ready to question. They sure enough questioned Pattison, and it was a crack up to see Ms. Outspoken jumping on the group when they asked who Burns and Allen were or why all the attention to Bob Dylan. They did a neat job on Heath, too: her apparent affection for "her own kind." Although I sure got talking when they agreed that stickin' to your own is just the way it is. "People stick to their own kind isn't good enough," I said. Maybe I should've kept my mouth shut. I will this time. Got angry when Mr. Slacks said "so what to the Townspeople's ways with words." I remember his saying something like "The politics of literacy are such that they're still going to have to know how to do things 'Right.'" Yep. Better choice of words than they realize. The politics of literacy. That's politics. At least Freire made some kind of sense to them: Start with where the students are at. Control the students. Give them what they want to succeed. Took some work to show that even though those things were really said in Literacy, they're not the whole meaning. Yeah, they're good, but those who speak sure are united. Consensus. Neat theory. The consensus is republican with this group—with a moral dose of liberalism.

What are they going to do with this book? This is their first from the perspective of people of color. And this one's local.

Opening gambit.

"OK, so what did you think about the book?"

Should I have said something outrageous? This is going to be death. Something about those guys in the book getting what they deserve or some such. And somebody's bound to say they couldn't follow it.

"I had a hard time following it. It goes like in circles," voiced by someone since gone from memory, though the sound remains: a constantly rising inflection, not quite a question, the sound students make to relay that they're unsure.

The very thin woman in the row closest to the windows, always about the third seat back, dry, dyed blonde hair, dry, sunken face, not unattractive, but that's a matter of study, of looking through the wear that tells of great worry, great hardship, sunken cheeks, skull-like. She's somewhat older than most of the class, mid-thirties, maybe, the most outspoken in the class, the one the students simply obey in group work.

Good, she'll get the republicans riled.

"No-o-o-o-o! I think that the way the story goes around is neat. It's like a movie twisting back on itself. It's like *Jacob's Ladder*...."

That look on student's faces that says they're thinking this one over, a nod in agreement—or two, maybe even three.

Skip it. Forget about mentioning James Joyce. Forget about American Indian conceptions of time as waves of sand or like tides with under-tows, things past intermingling with things present. Forget about the confusion that comes of war and mixed cultural heritage, no time for one puertorican's way of reading this, not the time to point to the way Silko has the narrative become more linear as Tayo becomes self-acknowledged. Jacob's Ladder will have to do. Smile and nod. They're talking, for chrissake.

First row to my left. About midway up. The young man who spoke often, fast, articulate. His manner speaks of New York, a privileged class, I figure. White shirt, unbuttoned at the top, sleeves neatly rolled up to midforearm, brown slacks in a classroom filled with 501 Jeans (including the instructor), expensive-seeming slacks, and soft, dark brown leather shoes, brush shine. He has dark skin, or at least not typically (stereotypically?) white, more the color of blonde wood, full lips, dark eyes, woolly brown hair, cut short, a round-seeming fellow, too fast-talking for the easier-going Southwest environment.

"Okay, *Jacob's Ladder*. But that guy in the movie's slipping. He's dying and doesn't know it. Right? That's not what's gone on here. This is Indian shit. I don't appreciate it. All that stuff about stealing the land that the Navajo guy talks about. You want it. You take it."

Is he looking at deDutch, the Navajo woman in the class with the Dutch name, a name given her by Dutch missionaries when they couldn't pronounce the name of her clan? I should have anticipated this, the way the student of color becomes the authority on all variations of cultures within some idea of race. She's going to get hurt here.

I'm panicking. She's cool. Looking down. Probably heard this kind of thing before. Somebody take him on!

"You sound just like that cowboy toward the end of the book who says that the 'goddamn Indians got to learn whose property this is!'" (Silko 1986, 202). This came from Outspoken.

Response: "No. I'm not that silly. Look at the Indians. They whine about

White People—Christians, it says in the book, as if we're all Christians—all this stuff about some witch messing with us and with the Navajos—"

Lakota! They're Lakota in Ceremony. *Only Old Betonie is Navajo, though he's the one who says the most about the stolen land. Mr. Slacks must've been in Flag long enough to have gathered the anti-Navajo bigotry.*

"—We're stealing? Hell, they're getting it all back by hitting on our tax dollars. All they do is go down to Camp Verde and sell blankets and junk jewelry. And still they all get new houses and fancy six-wheel pickup trucks. The Indians in Oklahoma all hit oil and their children are professors. And the Navajo are getting rich off of their uranium and all this guilt over what happened a long time before most of our ancestors ever got to this country. We act like, just because our skin is white, we're guilty. I don't buy it."

Too many heads nodding in agreement. Ms. deDutch! Speak up! Tim. Come on!

Front row. Directly in front of me. Maybe twenty years old. Huge blue eyes. Red hair in a coif, hair full, flipping up, none on her neck, though it might be shoulder length if not for the Stephanie Powers, decades-ago hairdo that somehow fits her and doesn't seem at all dated. She hasn't spoken a word in thirteen weeks, though her papers are publishable quality. It was she who had responded fully to Freire (1987), understood about *Literacy: Reading the Word and the World.* It was she who had written in her journal that Tayo is going through the process that Freire writes about—"where you sit in the world," in her words. She turns to Mr. Slacks.

"I used to think like you do. My father said that if the Navajo wanted more equity they should better themselves, become senators and judges, follow the example of black people like Chief Justice Thurman or even Jesse Jackson—"

Even? Not quite a liberal, a touch of the bigot maybe. Or maybe a real judgment after prejudging. And it sounds like she's going to speak against the idea that everyone can pick themselves up by their bootstraps. I'd better step out of the front of the class, away from the alter of science. Go sit on the radiator.

"—But it isn't that easy, is it? Have you ever been to Tuba City?"

"No shit!"

Who is that? Another of the silent ones. It's The Sleeper.

The sound had come from the young man in the back, by one of the exits, who was part of the local Mountain Bike Culture—walked in with his bicycle seat and one bicycle wheel every day; fingerless gloves, baggy shorts, tie-dyed T-shirt, short beard, long straight brown hair, always tousled. He had a friendly smile, would come in, smile, sit in the back row, look pensive, but within five minutes his eyes would swell and turn red, and he'd sit perfectly straight and perfectly asleep, only to awaken right as class closed, pack his backpack, smile, wave, leave. Every day.

"No shit! I used to think about the Navajos in the pickups. I even got a little pissed when I read in the book about getting gypped on pickup trucks."

Where did he get all this energy all of a sudden? I can't help but like him, like I can't help liking them all. But I never even figured he could get this animated.

He reads,

Tayo behind the wheel . . . . He searched the dashboard for the knob to turn on the headlights. When he pulled it, the knob came loose in his hands; he was too tired and sick to laugh at this truck, but he would have if Helen Jean had been there. Because she said it: gypped again. (Silko 1986, 167)

"Gypped again? What's with that? And then I thought about this guy I had to work with last summer. He had this Chevy pickup—all primered. So I, like, 'Smells like gas.' And he said it's a trick that White people play on Natives, that all the used trucks leak gas to kill off the last of the native Americans. Not funny. So I think that the only native Americans in new trucks are the ones with cowboy hats."

One more like this and I'll give up. I'll start directing the conversation. Maybe get back to writing.

"No. Wait a minute. He has something there." Source unknown.

"That's right." From Slacks. "The ones who make it are like *she* says," pointing to Even Jesse, "those who realize that the fight is over and it's time to do as in Rome."

"Wait a minute, man!" It's Sleeper. "That's not what I was getting at."

"Me neither." Even Jesse.

Outspoken: "Do you realize that children are dying from uranium poisoning on the rez. All that land is sold to the mining companies, then the Navajo rent out their bodies. Children are being born with radiation poisoning. And nobody on the rez gets rich," almost on her feet, red-faced at Slacks.

This is great! A real-live dialectic. Slacks is a wonderful bigot. He's smart.

"You've contradicted yourself, man." Another of the Silent Ones. "That's right." Even Jesse. "First you said the Indians got their new trucks from going to welfare. Now you say they got them by giving up their culture."

'Tis the way with bigots. Even smart ones. Don't say anything, though.

Slacks: "Both are true."
Groan from the class.
"Look. This is a win-win for Indians especially—and for all minorities. No offense." Looking at me. And looking at Tim Pequeñito. Tim looking at him, head tilted downward, a smile, shaking his head, an "I can't believe this" look. Me, corners of the mouth curled down, eyebrows up, something like "whatever." "If you decide to work, you get more than you're worth 'cause you're a minority; and if you decide not to, you get welfare because you're oh-pressed. And you never just join in like the rest of us have had to."

Okay, now for the question about why people on welfare eat Twinkies. This guy's a piece of work. But the class is taking care of him, looks like.

Sleeper: "I was getting at the same thing," chin pointing to Even Jesse. "The ones who have the new trucks have to give up everything. They're like Rocky in the book. Look at page fifty-one—"

God, I love this guy.

"—Listen to this."

They told him, "Nothing can stop you now except one thing: don't let the people at home hold you back." Rocky understood what he had to do to win in the white outside world . . . . Rocky deliberately avoided the old-time ways. (Silko 1986, 51)

"See what I mean. What did it get Rocky? He dies. That's got to be symbolic. He dies. Get it? It's like what Dr. V. said with that other thing. When the people of Roadville, right? Went to the town. They stopped being Roadville people. They lose something to get the truck. I don't think it's worth it."

Bless his heart. Bringing in Ways with Words.

Slacks.
"Symbols are something English majors make up. Rocky dies because people die in war. But he knew what he was. An American. Tayo can't make up his mind whether he's an American or an Indian."

"What!?" Shrill and loud, from Outspoken.

"I mean that he's uncomfortable with his identity as an Anglo. He doesn't seem to understand that even if he is a half-breed, he's still an American. He shouldn't feel pulled by two ways. We're all supposed to be one way. We've all had to let go of our original cultures to become American. Rocky is the one who got it right."

"Mix."

"What?"

"Mixed. We say 'mixed.'"

Whoa! Ms. deDutch.

Softly. But firmly. And there's a hush, an uncomfortable silence. "He was part Christian. But no Native is ever really American. We are the Navajo Nation. Dine'."

"Then why accept the charity of our government? And why not the Navajo Army?"

Outspoken up! Body faces Slacks. Both arms extended. In one hand is *Ceremony*, open. The other hand is poking at pages with an index figure. She reads,

Anyone can fight for America . . . even you boys. In a time of need, anyone can fight for her. (Silko 1986, 64)

She goes on. "It's there. Even the recruiter knew they weren't in some ways like us. That they did have their reservation, the Navajo Nation, if nothing else.

"And as far as those tax dollars go—have you ever been to the rez and Tuba City? Those are welfare houses, all right. And one supermarket. And a truck dealer. Those people are still herding sheep and living in mud hogans. So maybe some of it is cultural. But I know poverty. That's poverty. I know working to scratch your way out of the pit and no one helping, while folks think you've got it made 'cause you get food stamps.

"And—by the way—no one yet has mentioned that the book is written by a woman, a mixed-blood woman who's got to be writing some of this from experience."

"You mean she was a soldier captured by the Japanese?" From Slacks.

"Asshole."

And the class laughs and packs up. The fifty minutes have passed. I smile, say something about courtesy. But inside,

I have never ever had such success, confronting race, poverty, liberalism, the common saws that so many walked into the class with, confronted. Did it: the dialectic. Yes!

We meet again two days later. Slacks is silent. Discussion becomes decidedly text-centered. No more fireworks. Sleeper is asleep. Ms. deDutch stares down at her desk. Even Jesse turns around in her seat, wanting to take part in discussion. The next week I close the class, lecture for two days. An in-class essay. End of semester.

The semester ends. Then the mixed message. Slacks seeks me out for advice on future classes; he graduates, writes from his new home in New York, comes to visit when he passes through town. I don't know if he changed any, but he's more thoughtful, somehow.

Outspoken writes a scathing evaluation of the class instructor, complaining (most articulately) that the instructor had done nothing to put a bigot in his place. The discussion, she writes, was offensive, and the look of glee in my face added "insult to bigotry," her words.

Tim Pequeñito, the powerlifter, through a number of flukes becomes a longtime friend, his family my family's friends. He tells me one night that Outspoken had offered him $500 to "do something" about Slacks.

The lesson learned? I don't know. If at first you don't succeed. Or maybe ferret out the smartest bigot and find his button. Or maybe (and this was the real lesson for me) that texts can be presented to students in such a way that theory finds articulation in practice, that though there is anger and frustration, that is how the dialectic works. Race and class and gender struggles and coming to grips with those struggles means that there must be combat in the contact zone. And that persuasion in the sense of conversion is not likely in the few short weeks that we see students, but the *process* of change and reconsideration can surely be achieved, the dialectic entered into. And all that means is that once a foundation has been laid, students will carry the class pretty close to where you want it to go. Or—sometimes a class clicks and Lord knows why.

Works Cited

Freire, Paulo, and Donaldo Macedo. 1987. *Literacy: Reading the Word and the World*. South Hadley, MA: Bergin and Garvey.

Heath, Shirley Brice. 1983. *Ways with Words: Language, Life, and Work in Communities and Classrooms*. New York: Cambridge University Press.

Silko, Leslie Marmon. 1986. *Ceremony*. New York: Penguin.

6

Telling Stories About Stories

JOSEPH F. TRIMMER

It's Friday afternoon in English 205, Prose Fiction for Non-Majors. The students, trapped in their tablet-arm chairs, watch as I try to lead a discussion on "The Beast in the Jungle." They seem content with silence—the dead air they know will compel me, eventually, to start talking. And so once again, my voice fills the room—suggesting, hinting, speculating about how one might read the subtleties and ironies in the text. I catch myself, pause, and search a row of familiar faces, hoping.

"I don't get it."

"Pardon me, Tracy."

"I don't get it."

"What don't you understand?"

"The whole thing. It's a bore."

The class murmurs agreement. I am not surprised. I've been here before, and so I begin the standard defense.

"Well, students often have difficulty with Henry James because he writes in a complex style. But he writes that way on purpose to suggest how the mind works. 'The Beast in the Jungle' is a particularly difficult story because James is trying to show us a man, John Marcher, who is so obsessed with thinking about his life that he fails to live it. You may not see that the first time through; but once you've read the story several times, you begin to appreciate its subtleties and ironies."

"How many times have you read it?"

"Pardon me, Tracy."

"How many times have you read it?"

"Well, let's see. I read it first as an undergraduate, several times as a graduate student, and I suppose I've taught it two or three times a year since I started teaching. I guess I've read it—sixty, seventy times."

"You're kidding!"

"No, I read it every time I teach it. And I usually see something different."

"Well—if I had to read it another time, I'd start thinking about a different life!"

And I did—start thinking about a different life, my life as a reader before I knew how to talk to Tracy about subtleties and ironies.

I was eighteen and illiterate, or more precisely aliterate. I could read but preferred not to. My high school obsessions were football, cheerleaders, and rock'n'roll. But suddenly, by a process I still do not understand, I was transformed into a first-semester freshman at a prestigious all-male college. In orientation the faculty talked about art, science, the life of the mind. In the dormitory the students talked about Russian novels, biochemistry, European travel. My roommate, one of the ten national merit scholars on our floor, was completely at ease in his new home. Like everybody else, it seemed, he had attended an exclusive New England boarding school where he learned the code for choosing colleges, careers, and neckties. In fact, although they had attended different schools, all my classmates appeared to know each other or at least talk to each other in the same language. By contrast, I was lonesome, depressed, and out of my league. Then I met Holden.

Since it was the Sunday before classes started, the dorm was relatively quiet. My roommate was down the hall talking to some of his preppie friends. I sat in my lounge chair, mindlessly tapping the slender paperback that had been assigned for my Monday 8:00 A.M. class. The cover showed a guy wearing a strange red hat but otherwise offered no clues. I thumbed to the first page:

> If you really want to hear about it, the first thing you'll probably want to know is where I was born, and what my lousy childhood was like, and how my parents were occupied and all before they had me, and all that David Copperfield kind of crap, but I don't feel like going into it, if you want to know the truth. (Salinger 1951, 1)

The words, the voice, the person—Holden Caufield came alive. I knew this guy. He talked like me, thought like me, and more to the point, I realized as I read on, was trapped like me in a dorm full of phonies.

I don't remember much about the rest of that day. I skipped lunch, ate a quick dinner, and probably walked down to the john a couple of times, but mostly I sat in that lounge chair reading, listening, really, to Holden. He told me about Ackley's acne and Stradlater's conquests; about D. B.'s film scripts, Allie's baseball mitt, and Phoebe's journal; about the kid who straddled the curb, the kid who jumped out the window, and the kids who wanted to see the mummies; about the nuns in the cafeteria, the *fuck you's* on the wall, and the brass ring at the carousel. He even told me about the crazy things he did, such as telling Mrs. Morrow he had a brain tumor; telling Bernice, Marty, and Laverne that they had just missed seeing Gary Cooper; and pretending he would use an automatic to put six slugs into the fat-hairy belly of old Maurice. He was a terrific liar, but he could spot a phony in a minute. He really could. I didn't want the book to end. When it did, I felt like Holden was a friend of mine and wished I could call him up on the phone whenever I felt like it.

The next morning something else happened. In class, the professor started talking about a *bildungsroman*. For a minute, I thought I was in the wrong class until I realized he was talking about Holden. Then all those other phonies started in—talking about the subtleties of retrospective narration, the ironies of initiation, and the symbolism of the title. It was a damn conspiracy, if you want to know the truth.

I didn't know how to stop them. I wanted to talk about my friend Holden—this great guy who noticed that Jane Gallagher kept her kings in the back row or worried about where the ducks went in the winter. But I knew if I brought it up, all of them would probably do what the guys in Holden's speech class did when someone didn't stick to the point. They would yell, "DIGRESSION!" Like Holden says, "You can't unify and simplify something just because somebody wants you to" (185). But those guys sure could. And then it happened.

"Professor Stone? What about the significance of Holden's name?"

"Good point, Barrett. How do you read it?"

"Well, it's a pun. You know, 'hold' 'un' 'cau' 'field.' I think you could connect the name to the character's fantasy about being a catcher in the rye, his obsession with childhood. He wants to catch the kids before they fall off the cliff. You know, 'hold' 'them.'"

That did it. They not only ruined the story but they also murdered Holden. It killed me. It really did. I wanted to stand up and yell, "You lousy bunch of morons." But I knew it wouldn't do any good. Besides, it wasn't their fault. They were just playing the college game. Like Holden says, "If you want to stay alive, you have to say that stuff" (87).

As I kept reading, in college and then in graduate school, I got pretty good at saying that stuff. I didn't have to like the story, care about the characters, or even know anything about the author. All I had to do was read the text closely and collect clues for an explication. That was the major word I had to learn, *explication*. It meant to interpret or clarify a story by analyzing its images, paradoxes, and internal tensions. It was hard work, like trying to solve one of those story problems in math: "If character A exhibits the same qualities as character B, then how would you define his relationship to character C?"

Sometimes I couldn't solve the problem; other times I didn't know there was a problem. That's where the critics came in. I would read the story, pen in hand, confidently scoring the passages I thought were significant, and then I would check the critics to see if I was right. There were a lot of them. They explicated their readings in the small journals I found stacked along the shelves in periodicals. They would find hidden meanings in every story, and their footnotes rumbled about one another's misreadings. The stakes were high. This was serious business. All of us—scholars working on articles, graduate students wrestling with dissertations, and undergraduates churning out term papers—were supposedly accumulating evidence for the same thing: the definitive reading of a particular story. So I kept at it, reading and explicating, learning my craft, and only occasionally wondering what I had gained and what I had lost. Then I met the Compson family.

No apprenticeship in close reading could have prepared me for William Faulkner's *The Sound and the Fury*. I must have read the first two pages ten times. All the normal clues were missing. The scenes changed quickly but did not connect to one another. The characters—or more precisely, the names of characters—appeared and disappeared without explanation. Even the dialogue—often in dialect or, intermittently, in italics—did not help me picture what was happening. And I could not anticipate what might happen because I could not remember what had just happened. I capped my pen, closed the book, and conceded defeat.

But even in defeat, every close reader believes that somewhere in the stacks there are critics, expert readers, who have figured it all out. They assured me that the beginning was supposed to read like babble because it was a tale told by an idiot—the fragments of Benjy Compson's stream of consciousness. With charts, graphs, and time lines, they explained the significance of each scene and the logic that compelled it to drift into Benjy's mind. I uncapped my pen, opened the book, and used a ruler to mark and date the sixteen recurring scenes. Next, I reread the section, using my notes to sort through the clutter. I still needed help reading the three other sections, but Quentin, Jason, and Dilsey's stories seemed progressively more accessible. I was back in business, spotting images, tracking themes, nailing down my explication. Then I fell into the trap.

I had presumed that if I collected enough clues, read enough critics, I could "unify and simplify" the Compson's story. Each narrator told me more about the family history, more about Caddy, the beautiful, doomed woman at the center of the mess. But each narrator told the story so differently I had trouble finding reliable clues. If I started to form a clear-cut conclusion, I was suddenly undercut by contradictory information. I could not make it all cohere. That was the trap. The presumption that I could. The narrators fall into the same trap. Obsessed with order and stability, they find only confusion and flux. Mainly, they find but lose Caddy, the woman who haunts their memory, disturbs their lives, and escapes their control. *The Sound and the Fury* records their failure to read and explain her story.

But Faulkner does not fail. Or more precisely, I discovered that he is not bothered by failure. Unlike his narrators, he does not insist on certainty because "'living' is motion, and 'motion' is change and alteration and therefore the only alternative to motion is unmotion, stasis, death" (Faulkner 1955, preface). Like his narrators, Faulkner sees Caddy as his "heart's darling" (Gwynn and Blotner 1965, 6), but he wants to empower her, not to embalm her. In an appendix written fifteen years after the novel, he frees her to live other lives, inviting readers to speculate with him about the story of her continuous, contrary motion:

> Married 1920 to a minor moving picture magnate, Hollywood, California. Divorced by mutual agreement, Mexico 1925. Vanished in Paris with the German occupation, 1940, still beautiful and probably still wealthy too since she did not look within fifteen years of her actual forty eight, and not heard of again . . . [except for the] picture, a photograph in color clipped obviously from a slick magazine—a picture filled with luxury and money and sunlight—a Cannebiere backdrop of mountains and palms and cypresses and the sea, an open powerful expensive chromium trimmed sports car, the woman's face hatless between a rich scarf and a seal coat, ageless and beautiful, cold, serene and damned; beside her a handsome lean man of middle age in the ribbons and tabs of a German staff general. (413–15)

And so there they were. Two stories about my other life as a reader. I could tell hundreds, or course; stories about the power of first readings, stories about the revelation of additional readings, even a few stories about the insights of expert readers. But these two—one about loss, one about gain—suggested how reading had closed and opened stories for me before I taught Tracy. That was another story.

She sat in the front row with four other black women from her college sorority. Smart, chic—Claire Huxtable at eighteen. Except for her outburst on Henry James, she had been quiet for most of the term, allowing the rest of the class—mainly white, mainly male—to carry the discussion. But even on a good day there wasn't much of that. I'm not sure what I was doing wrong. I asked open-ended questions, hoping to promote personal response. I performed close readings, hoping to demonstrate formal analysis. Nothing happened. But something was happening in the front row. Tracy was scowling, shifting in her seat.

The story was Alice Walker's "Everyday Use," and for once the members of the class seemed mildly animated as they pondered my question: "Which sister should get Mama's quilt—Dee (Wangero), who will preserve it by hanging it on her wall, or Maggie, who will use it by putting it on her bed?"

A book slams shut.

"That's it! I've had it!"

Silence. Bewilderment.

"What's wrong, Tracy?"

"I been reading these stories all semester. Everytime black people show up, it's the same thing. They're either poor, ignorant fools, pickin' cotton and hiding from the Klan, or they're hyped-up street kids, preaching jive, pushing dope, shooting cops. Give me a break."

"Show us."

"Look, I know how *you* want me to read this story."

"How *Walker* wants you to read it."

"Same thing."

"Not necessarily."

"Whatever. Anyway, I know I'm supposed to root for bashful, backward Maggie. She's never had anything, so now Mama's going to give her an old quilt. Big deal. I also know I'm supposed to rag on Dee because she went off to college, got uppity, and changed her name to Wangero. But I don't want to read it that way. Dee did what her family wanted her to do—got educated, made something of herself. That's what I'm doing. I don't want to stay home and make quilts with Mama."

"Interesting reading."

"It's not just this story. It's all of them. We haven't read one story with a positive black character. In fact, we haven't read one with a positive woman character. They're all stupid, silly, or nuts. I don't like any of them."

"Now that you mention it, I don't think we've read a story with a positive male character. John Marcher's a beast."

"See."

"Are stories supposed to have positive characters? Is that why we read stories—to find people we like, people we want to be like?"

"I do."

"What about the rest of you?"

For a few minutes, my reticent readers turn into nonstop talkers.

First Jennifer. "It changes. When I was a kid, I loved Nancy Drew. I wanted to be just like her—perky, smart, solving all those crimes. Now that seems like kid's stuff. I can't read them anymore. I like stories about people different than me. Like this one."

Then Steve. "This one's OK. But it's like most of the stories we read. Sure, it's about black people. That's kinda different. For me, anyway. But it reads the same. You know—beginning, middle, end. I like stories with a gimmick. Something that confuses you at first. Makes you think."

Then Fred. "It depends. When I'm reading on my own, I look for stories with a lot of action. They don't have to be 'positive.' The more gore the better. Like Stephen King. Stories I can get lost in. When I'm reading for class, I just get lost. There's no action. Just description. I know I'm supposed to find some hidden meaning, but I never find it until you point it out. And then I never know where you got it."

Then Mary. "That's the problem with this class. You can't just read. You've got to analyze everything with those stupid terms. And even if you get that figured out, there's something else. Like stuff from the author's life or history or some style that only certain authors use. There's always something. How are you supposed to know that stuff, how are you supposed to enjoy the story? It's like that guy Marcher. You spend so much time analyzing everything, you miss the point."

Fred again. "What about those crazy ones. Like last week—you know, 'Lost in the Funhouse.' You said the point of that story was to make fun of stories that made a point. I was mixed up when I was reading it; but when you said that, I really got mad. I mean it. What's the point of reading the story without a point?"

Steve again. "See. That's the kinda story I like. It's a funhouse. You go down one hall, dead end. You come back, trapped again. And when you get out, you haven't been anywhere. That's a gimmick!"

Paul, a new voice. "Why do we have to like everything we read? What about Siskel and Ebert? They don't like every movie they see. They don't even like the same ones. But they talk about them, give you reasons. They don't just kiss them off."

Mary again. "They kiss off a lot of them. It's the way they talk to each other. Even when they both like the same one, they give you so many la-di-da reasons for liking it you don't want to go see it."

Back to Tracy. "You guys are missing the point. This ain't Siskel and Ebert. It's English 205. We don't choose the stories we read and nobody cares whether we like them—not really. They're in the book, so they're supposed to be good. Right? If we don't like one, we screwed up. We didn't read it right. Or missed something. Well I can read'm right—most of the time, anyway. I just don't like what I'm reading. I'm not staying home and making quilts with Mama. I want a different life."

Silence. Tracy's passion fills the air. I wait, searching familiar faces for a sign. Is that it? Is everybody talked out? Is it my turn, as always, to explain away, to unify and simplify? No. Mary is twisting over her tablet arm so she can see down the front row.

"You know, Tracy, I don't think the story is saying, 'go home and make quilts with Mama.' Mama's proud of Dee. She imagines their re-union on Johnny Carson. I just think she wants Dee to be proud of her and Maggie."

Then Steve, from the back row, talking into his book, avoiding the stares from the front row: "Tracy, I may be out of line—I know you're mad. But I'd be mad too if I made something for somebody and they just kissed it off. Dee could've had the quilt when she went off to college, but she told Mama she didn't want it. Said it was old-fashioned."

Then Jennifer, nervous, looking down her row for support and then vaguely toward the sorority sisters in the front: "Doesn't that bother you? I mean Dee was named after Grandma Dee and Mama's sister Big Dee. They helped Mama make the quilt. Dee said she didn't want it. Now she does. But she doesn't want her name. Calls it a slave name. That really bothers me."

"I'll tell you what bothers me," Tracy says, smiling politely at Jennifer. "Dee, Wangero—whatever—is the only character I've liked all semester. And now you guys are telling me how to read the story." Still smiling, she turns to-ward her sisters, gathers her courage, and then glares at me: "I told you. I know how I'm supposed to read it. I just don't want to read it that way. So what are you going to do about that?"

For once, I'm content with dead air. I avoid Tracy's eyes and stare at my copy of the text. The pages of Walker's story crawl with underlines and anno-tations in red and black ink. I know what I'm supposed to do. Smile kindly at Tracy and begin one of the standard defenses: "The author wrote this story for a purpose. You can't simply ignore her intentions." Or, "The text contains the meaning of the story. You can't simply disregard the evidence." Or, "A community of readers, scholars and students, have interpreted this story in a certain way. You can't simply dismiss their opinion." But I don't want to do it that way.

I watch the rows of silent faces watch me squirm. They know—oh, how well they know—that eventually I will start talking. Teacher talk. That's my job. I'm supposed to be in charge. And that's it. Or at least part of it, anyway. I'm tired of teacher talk, tired of hearing my own voice sorting it out, nailing it down, slapping it with a label. *Bildungsroman.*

"So what are you going to do about that?"

Tracy's question, unsettling, challenging, blossoms into other questions. Reader questions. What has my life as a reader taught me about reading stories? What have my students' lives as readers—each of them so different—taught them about reading stories? And what has our life together—liking different kinds of stories, reading the same stories differently—taught us about how we can talk together in the same class? Because no matter what else we do, we have to keep talking, telling each other stories about the stories we read. And each of those stories will be different—undercutting, confusing, revising the others. I can insist on coherence—on sanctioning one reading by suppressing others—but I won't settle anything. No matter what I say, what Walker says, what the text says, what the critics say, what Mary, Steve, and Jennifer say, or even what Tracey says next week on her examination or fifteen years from now when she is a mother, Tracy has had her reading.

"So what are you going to do about that?"

I catch Tracy's eyes. She knows something is happening. That this is a moment. For both of us. Her eyes flick anger. Then fear. Has she gone too far? Broken the rules? But that's the other part of it. It's not just the talk. It's those damn rules. Unspoken. Unbreakable. Unimpeachable. Teacher-student. Never reader-reader. Why not? That's not her question, but it's the question I see behind her question. So what are you going to do about that? I savor the silence, and, for once, give myself permission.

I stare into her flashing eyes, smile, and say, "Nothing."

"You're kidding?"

"Nope."

"I don't get it."

"What don't you understand?"

"You're supposed to tell me what to do. Tell me I can't read it that way. Show me how I messed up. You're the teacher."

"I want a different life. So what are you going to do about that?"

Works Cited

Faulkner, William. 1955. *The Mansion*. New York: Random House.

————. 1956. *The Sound and the Fury*. New York: Random House.

Gwynn, Frederick, and Joseph L. Blotner, eds. 1965. *Faulkner in the University*. New York: Random House.

Salinger, J. D. 1951. *The Catcher in the Rye*. Boston: Little Brown.

7

Beginnings

CHRIS M. ANSON

There was a situation which I had to decide if I was going to committ a serous crime on a family member.

I was well situated, I thought: happy to have "won" a teaching assistant-ship to support my graduate studies at a midsize private university. A mark of intellectual distinction, I supposed. But I was unprepared, at best, to stand in the front of a classroom and pretend I knew everything there was to know about good writing. I'd been assigned two sections of freshman composition, and we had been given no formal training—only a sample syllabus and an invitation to rummage through some old course files to see how our prede-cessors had survived. The files, located in a dusty alcove of a decrepit build-ing that housed the teaching assistants, were crammed with mimeographed handouts, old course plans, fragments of student papers. Bewildered and alone, I finally rolled the drawer shut, snapping off the tendril of a spider plant that had crept down from the top of the cabinet. Even the fear of de-signing an entire course and then explaining it, rationalizing it, to a class of eighteen-year-olds was nothing next to the thought of *me*, just a few years their senior, standing before them: the thought of my authority, my de-meanor. My control of the class.

That particular family member happen to be my oldest sister, she 36 years old. It all start when she come from DC to live with our family which was me my mother and my brother 21.

I started badly. I managed to struggle through the first two weeks of the class, mostly by lecturing nervously on grammar and principles of form.

61

There were occasions when two students would whisper to each other and smile, making me stumble and search for my ideas, or when, facing the class, I found myself gesticulating back toward the chalkboard and realizing to my horror that it was blank, that I had erased what I thought was still there.

Finally it came time for the students to turn in their first narrative papers. It was a Friday afternoon, and as I sauntered home with a satchel full of their essays, it never occurred to me that the panic and anxiety of the classroom would follow, like a shadow, into the cloistered quiet of my study. Of course, I'd heard the horror stories about teachers slowly sinking beneath the weight of hundreds of five-paragraph themes, the joists of their homes bowing and cracking under the strain. I was determined to be tough, organized, and quick about the whole messy business. And if that meant doing the job in one sustained effort, I was up to the task.

My sister has a mental problem which occured when she started dealing drugs ten years ago. I never did really get along with my oldest sister because I didn't like her personality.

The problem, I guessed, was sticking to the onerous task without getting distracted. On Saturday morning I got up early, made a pot of coffee, cleared the desk, rolled up my sleeves, and set to work.

She a mean person and don't care about no one beside herself. She also got a daughter who is 18 years of age I can't get along with her either so I stay away from her. She also got a daughter who 5 years old, she live with us most of the time.

In front of me, to my right, was the pile of essays the students had hurriedly turned in as they filed out of the room. To the left was a blank space where the papers would end up in a neat, finished stack in several hours. I reached for the package of five red, felt-tipped pens I had bought at the college bookstore the week before. Then, armed with a pen, I began to read the first essay, marking and commenting from the first sight of the first misspelled word in the first paragraph.

Like I say my sister a person who drink. She drink Wild irish rose everyday and then when she don't have it she get snotty with everone and I didnt like that at all.

I was also determined to be a good teacher. I figured that the more I wrote, the more my students would respect me. And if the administration ever happened to see one of my corrected papers, they would think me a diligent, conscientious assistant, someone worth appointing again and again until I had my degree. But the work also had to be done fast, or I wouldn't survive the Master's Program, no matter how well I taught.

So after awhile it started bothering me and I became upset.

Ten minutes later, I had produced a second, bright red layer of text over the neatly typed black letters of my first student. It was an essay typical of what I'd heard about first-year students' writing—banal, filled with generalizations, and topped with a smattering of errors and stylistic infelicities. Something about a car accident, his friends Jody and Kim and Tad. He'd learned a lesson. I wrote a hasty final comment and gave it a C. Then the second—ten minutes, and the same. And a third. And a fourth.

Me and my sister would argue (actually I don't claim my oldest sister). The more we argued the more I want to bust her brains apart.

Then something curious happened. As I began reading one of the papers, my hand fell to one side, the pen, for the moment, dormant. The paper was written by Shawn Brown, a young man who had grown up poor in the South Bronx. Although it was too soon in the course for me to see a clear face behind each name on the stack of papers, Shawn I knew—a loner, quiet, disengaged.

I read the paper avidly, in spite of the many grammatical errors. A *serious crime.* Strange family relations. Drunkenness. Drugs. The intrigue of a writer who confessed that he could kill—*had* he? And there was a kind of leanness to the descriptions that seemed almost deliberate—or was it the picture developing in my mind, a tenement, an old TV, a torn couch on a dirty floor, the echoes of raised voices, glass breaking? But what then to do about all the errors? I wondered whether I should grade this essay more harshly than the first four and remain true to my clear, objective criteria, or whether I should give Shawn credit for my engagement in his story, the engagement of being put inside his world, words and all.

My mother would tell me that I shouldn't argue with her because of what she been through but that wasn't no excuse for her to act the way she did to my family.

Fifteen minutes passed, then twenty, and still I hadn't graded the paper or written any comments on it. I kept seeing Shawn's living room, his estranged sister reeling around drunk on whiskey, her five-year-old sitting on the dirty floor, crying. I was also uncomfortable. I had the vague impression that I was making more out of Shawn than I should, more out of his essay than was plainly there. So *what* if the conditions of his life were not mine? Who was I to judge his writing on the basis of my own perverse interest in his depressing material conditions? After all, this wasn't Crane or Dreisser, for God's sake.

Finally, mostly out of frustration, I scribbled "D+" at the end of the paper, jotted down some marginal comments, corrected and circled as many errors as I could find, and turned it upside down on the left-hand stack of graded papers.

One night about 11:30 p.m. it was me and my mother at home and my so-call sister come in from a party and she was drunk.

But as the morning wore on, my problems only got worse. After a dozen papers, I began to feel weary and confused, nagged by the thought that I was no longer clearheadedly and objectively assessing the papers but falling prey to my subjective, shifting feelings as a reader. Here was John Charlesworth's paper, neatly narrated with almost no errors, but utterly without appeal. I didn't care about his grandmother, at least not as the person depicted in his text, and her death meant nothing to me. Still, it was clean: the suburban grandmother; the short, cropped sentences; the orderly yard; a certain lexical blandness, inauthentic, like fake lawn animals or carefully arranged cheap china figures on an Early American knickknack shelf.

Shawn's living room flashed into view, the worn chair, the TV with its bent antenna. Was John's paper really better than Shawn's? What did I like about Shawn's paper, anyway? So many errors . . . verb tenses, bad paragraphs. But that scene, that haunting bit about getting even. D+? My thoughts swirled in a confusion of impressions and tentative judgments. I began to feel as if I were losing my mind, ever so subtly, as I turned from one paper to the next. Halfway through the stack, this confusion became too much to bear.

She like to get violent when she drinks. I tried not to get upset because I know that I will kill when I highly upset and I try to prevent that, but in this situation my temper was boiling hot.

In exasperation, I turned back to the first few papers and began comparing them with the ones I had read in the middle of the stack. To my dismay, I soon found that I had graded the first essays more harshly than the fifteenth and sixteenth and seventeenth. Charlesworth's paper couldn't be as bad as Stanton's, with its atrocious, disconnected paragraphs. And as for Perachnek's. . . . The criteria had slipped from their moorings, and I was at sea.

Me and my mother was looking at television when she came in that night.

First I wondered whether I should grade the essays in the middle of the stack more harshly to make them conform to my grades at the beginning; then I thought that I might as well regrade the first essays more leniently to make them conform to my newer, looser standards. But no, the concentration had taxed me, I reasoned—drained me of sound judgment, made me soft. I would downgrade the later essays. Ripping open the desk drawer, I found a bottle of correction fluid and began painting over the little red grades I had assigned, neatly penning in new, harsher grades after the dollop of white had dried and cracked under the heat of the desk lamp.

So she decide to turn the t.v. from our view. And my mother she stood up and yelled at her severly.

But soon I was embroiled in a frenzy of whiteouts and re-whiteouts, of doubts and comparisons, until most of the essays I had graded were smeared with pinkish stains from the alcohol in the paint. In horror, I imagined my first class of twenty-five students on Monday afternoon, candling their essays against the bright neon lights in our classroom to see what I had really given their papers before some evil force had taken control of my spirit. I had visions of the students pulling the plastic tops from their Bic pens and scraping, scraping—all twenty-five of them—at the little white scabs until the truth emerged, triumphant, from the stains of my instructional ineptitude.

I was already in a bad mood and this just top it off. So I started yelling at her and my sister start crying. She then slapp my mother for no reason.

Suddenly I had a flash of insight. As I had been grading and regrading the papers, I found myself seeing some good where before I had only cringed, or bristling at some small infelicity I had overlooked. In short, there was an alternative: I could say anything I wanted, I could be as lenient or harsh as I pleased, above and beyond the dim consciousness of my students. A new, odd feeling of power came over me, demonlike. I was the expert. I was the expert! I could justify whatever grade I assigned.

So I got a butcher knife and threatened her with it so I told her that if she says anything I would cut her throat.

And so back I went, evening out my grades by writing nastier comments on the essays I thought I had graded too harshly and finding something, anything, to praise in the margins of those I had graded too softly.

She then got smart with me again and I just put the knife to her throat. Then I press the knife close and push it in to the skin a little my sister freeze right there and her throat make a gurling sound and her vein was beating.

Two days later, with half an hour to spare before the Monday class, I finished the last of the stack and, with a sense of determination, penned the grades into the little grade log supplied by the department. It struck me that there were far too many columns and boxes in the log for my course, and for a moment I wondered if there was something missing, something I should have been doing, some sort of testing or attendance records. But the single row of black letters also looked good and gave me a sense of completion and professionalism. A log book, a log of my judgments, my expert judgments.

As I walked across the campus, I felt confident for the first time about my lecture—a discussion of the ten most flagrant errors in the students' narratives. But my thoughts kept returning to my evaluations, lurking there in the darkness of my battered briefcase. All around me were students, laughing, talking, sharing stories and ideas and experiences. Then I thought of my class, the rows of students staring with glazed indifference as I lectured, their minds floating from the room as I droned on about thesis sentences and the passive voice.

But I just put the knife down because if I would have killed her then my mother would had to take care of her 5 yr old daughter and other things ran through my head.

By then I had reached the old, ivied building and recognized a couple of my students ahead of me, shuffling in silence toward the door, their thoughts probably turning to their grades. As I climbed the stairs in their wake, my legs suddenly felt weak beneath the weight of the briefcase, as if the papers themselves, airy with the unharried thoughts of young minds, had been turned to lead, soon to shackle their authors to their destinies as academic writers.

So that's why I made that decision.

For a moment I hesitated near the room, so unbearable was the thought of handing them back. I could say they got lost, maybe. Or that I forgot them. I could regrade them. The students would look at the grades immediately, they would ignore my copious comments, they would complain, they would despise me. . . .

But she still on my list.

But it was too late; more students came up from behind, and we all flowed together into the room. The satchel, like an old leather accordion, seemed to take up the entire surface of the front desk, and I turned quickly to the board.

I'm still going to get her because this is not the end yet.

At the end of the class period, I tried my first classroom joke. But there was no response.

"Come in, Shawn." It was my first real office visit.

Shawn sauntered in, wet from the afternoon drizzle, his rolled-up paper the only thing he carried. He moved gracefully but slowly, sizing up the basement room of the old building where I shared a group of 1930s wooden desks with ten other teaching assistants. Behind me, an enormous radiator clanked and hissed like a steam engine. It was late in the afternoon, and the other instructors had all left for home or the library.

Shawn sat down in the torn, overstuffed chair next to the desk. "What can I do for you?" I asked, acting as if I had been very busy before he arrived. I had a strong feeling he had come to contest his grade, and it had already set me on edge.

"Well, it's about. . . this paper," he said hesitantly, unrolling the essay and trying to flatten it out on the curved arms of the chair. I could see the film of red comments on his paper from my felt-tipped pen. A few of the comments had smeared across the page from the rain. "See, I don't get this. . . ." He turned to the second page and located my end comments and the grade. "This grade, a D+. D+. I mean, this paper. Ain't that bad. You know, not a D+. . . ."

Without letting him finish, I found myself beginning a kind of speech. I had dressed in a tie and an old blazer, and the image of myself as a university teacher overcame me, making me feel at once too young for the role and too stuffy to be genuine. "Now, the thing is, here, Shawn, you see, what I'm seeing here is that this is not the kind of academic writing that we expect, that is privileged here in college, you see. College writing is . . . ." Shawn was staring at me with a kind of indifference that made him look as if he wasn't taking it all in; yet I also felt that he was critiquing me somehow, calling my ideas into question as I was forming them.

"Well, let me put it this way," I went on. "Most high school students get the impression that they're pretty good writers, right?" I smiled, trying to spark some humorous self-deprecation in Shawn, but he sat emotionless, staring down at his paper. "But then you get to college, and things have really changed. Courses are hard. And other profs, well, they expect really good . . ." I hesitated, looking for the right word, ". . . really *clean* prose."

Shawn had fixed his gaze toward the iron grate that covered the basement window, and kept it there as he spoke. "Well, maybe I don't get what you want, what you wanted in this paper. A narra*t*ive," he said, emphasizing the *t* sound. "I wrote like you said, a story, a kind of personal story about my. . . ." He hesitated, as if suppressing an epithet. "About my stepsister. This woman, she crazy. She come in all hours of the night cussing and carrying on, drunk as hell. I wrote about her because she's crazy."

"Let me see your paper for a second if I could, Shawn," I said, extending my hand. Reluctantly, Shawn held the curled pages toward me and dropped them on the edge of the desk. I knew Shawn's paper well, and even the smeared, illegible comments were etched into my memory. But I exaggerated the time it took me to glance back over the paper, letting one, two minutes pass as the radiator hissed and clanked in the background, Shawn staring toward the gray afternoon beyond the window.

Finally I looked up. "OK, where do I begin?" I asked rhetorically. "First, we've talked about theses. A thesis, as you know, is a statement that organizes your paper, gives your reader a point or argument. Now, your paper doesn't really have a thesis, as I explained at some length in the margins here. What's it really about? What is. . . ."

"This about my sister, about me and my crazy stepsister," he interrupted. "I don't know what you talking about, about this . . . this *the*sis. I know how you explain it in class, but this paper, anyone can see this about me and my sister, that I didn't kill."

"Precisely, Shawn," I said. "The paper has a point, that you didn't kill your sister, but there's no thesis giving that point. We need to see that up front, I think."

Shawn looked agitated and confused. "So what that *look* like? I mean, you know, say what that *look* like."

I leaned back. "You mean compose one myself? Oh, well . . ." I chuckled. "Well, this isn't my paper, Shawn. I suppose I could . . ." I glanced through the paper again, skimming the first few paragraphs. "This first line here, where you talk about the situation, I mean, that could be a thesis of sorts. 'There was a situation in which . . .' Well, that's a point, isn't it. There's a situation, you make a choice, the choice is a good one, a moral one. OK, 'There was a situation in which I had to decide whether I was going to commit a serious crime against a member of my family.' You know, something also along the lines of, 'Everyone at some point in their familial history has the urge to harm a sibling or other relative out of the frustration of having to live in such proximity to them on a daily basis.' *Readers*—connect with your readers' experiences."

"So that's the thesis, then," Shawn said, looking at me as if I had discovered something good about his paper.

"Not ex*act*ly," I replied, sounding to myself as if I were acting the role of a professor in a bad movie. "The end. You don't really conclude here. This doesn't end conclusively, so whatever your point is in the beginning isn't, you know, rhetorically *wrapped up*, so to speak. You get my drift here?"

Shawn looked at me incredulously. "I thought you was talking about the beginning," he said.

"We was . . . we were. But you see, academic writing—it has a kind of, um, *sym*biotic relationship between introductions and conclusions, a kind of snake with its tail in its mouth, you know, it comes back to its point. At some point."

"Man," Shawn said, shaking his head. I couldn't tell if he was annoyed or sad. "I know I tried to write this like you said. This a story about me and my crazy stepsister, how I was gonna kill her and didn't that night. So, you know, I still don't get what's a D+ about this."

"OK, Shawn, let's focus on some more direct things here," I replied, shifting forward in my chair and concentrating on the curled pages before me. "Tense problems. Verb endings. Spelling errors. Capitalization. These are things that ought to be under relatively good control by now. Then there's the matter of your paragraph development. These short little paragraphs with no real detail. You see, academic writing—good academic writing—has paragraphs that are almost like little miniature essays, each one carefully developed with a beginning and an end." John's grandmother's house flashed into view—the knickknack shelf, the green shag rug.

"I got those," Shawn said, gesturing toward the paper. "Six paragraph. You know, the first one, number one, that's a long paragraph. So's the las' one."

"Sure enough, Shawn," I said. "But they're not connected, you see. Transitions. Remember the lecture on those transitional phrases that connect paragraphs? You remember that list, too, I bet—the *howevers* and *therefores* and *as a results* and *consequentlies*. Your readers need those to know where they're going, what's next in the paper."

"Look, I thought I did a good job on this paper assignment," Shawn said resolutely. "I tried to do like the assignment said. You know, I wrote a narrative about my crazy stepsister, I tried to have these paragraphs here, and I don't think I deserve this D+. You know, I'm trying . . . I tried to tell this *story*. What you wanted, a story about something that we decide to do or not to do, right in the assignment sheet."

I placed the paper on the edge of the desk where Shawn could reach it. "Well, you're partly there, Shawn," I said, softening a bit. "You've got a story, or parts of one. Now you need to work on some of these other matters, thesis development, paragraph development, having a point and a conclusion, grammar . . . and then I think your grade will improve."

"You mean do this, fix this?" he asked, pointing at the paper.

I felt a sudden burst of authority. "No, that's not what I mean, Shawn. We're moving on now and we have a whole lot to do on argument next, on fallacies and things like that. What I mean is in your next paper. Next time around."

There was a brief silence as Shawn considered my words. "OK," he said finally, "but I'm a ask you to do me a favor now. Could you take this paper, you know, take my paper and read it over again and see if this is really a D+? I mean, you know, just look at it again?"

Knowing full well that the number of errors in Shawn's draft could justify my D+ based on objective criteria alone, I nevertheless decided to take the paper home and bring it back to the next class session. Shawn seemed to relax a little, but as we ended the meeting and I watched him move slowly out of the room, I suddenly had the feeling that I had stumbled into the most distasteful profession on earth.

The next morning as I collected my thoughts for the class, I found Shawn's paper in my course folder and realized that I hadn't taken any time to reread it or reconsider his grade. I quickly glanced through the smudged pages, remembering my struggle putting a grade on it, remembering the images of Shawn's living room, his sister, the five-year-old on the floor, the TV, the whiskey, the butcher knife, the veins pulsing in his sister's throat, the blade pressed close. With minutes to spare before the class, I found six or seven more errors in Shawn's paper and circled these in black ink, then circled the D+ three times and added my initials to it. Shawn was at least trying to be an academic writer, I thought as I thrust the paper into my briefcase, but he had a long way to go.

So that's why I made that decision.

After I handed his paper back to him at the start of class, Shawn stared blankly at his desk while I lectured on comma splices, chalk dust on my hands, oblivious to the violence being done all around.

So after a while it started bothering me and I became upset.

After a while, it started bothering me.
This was not the end yet.

This is not the end.

8

Reading and Writing About Death, Disease, Dysfunction; or, How I've Spent My Summer Vacations

LAD TOBIN

When I was a first-semester freshman, I went with my roommate to see the dean of students. We had only been in college for eight weeks but we were convinced that we should be allowed to move off campus the next semester. We told the dean that we hated the dorms, the dorm food, the other dorm people. Looking back, I now realize that we were both so afflicted with an overwhelming cynicism, homesickness, and preoccupation with the relationships we left behind that we gave almost no chance to our new acquaintances and surroundings. All we knew was that we would be better off in an apartment in town.

I remember the dean looking sad. "I don't understand you kids. When I was a student here, we loved living on the campus. Those conversations we had in the dorm late at night, I'll tell you, those were the best times of my life. Now I see students, boys and girls, moving in together, I see them using drugs, refusing to get involved in campus life. When I was your age, whenever we were bored, we'd put on a fair or a talent show; or we'd organize a carnival. Whatever happened to good, clean fun?"

We both scoffed on cue.

"So," my friend Gary asked again, "can we move off campus now?"

A few years ago, I was hired to design and develop a new writing program for first-year students. I was brought in with a great deal of support and autonomy but also with what I feared were a great number of unrealistically high hopes by faculty across the curriculum: the new program should introduce students to academic discourse and intellectual life; teach them how to use the library, conduct research, and cite sources; and, most of all, make sure

71

that no professor on campus ever had to see another grammatical error or spelling mistake.

Given the high visibility of this sort of core program, I knew that the program I designed was going to be defined as much by what it wasn't as by what it was. And I knew that it wasn't a lot of things that a lot of my colleagues liked, including Great Books, essentials of English grammar and usage, critical thinking 101. It was instead a new-fashioned version of an old-fashioned "process" course built around revision, portfolios, workshops, conferences, and the simple notion that student writers should be treated as writers first and as students second.

My sense throughout that first year was that things were going reasonably well, at least as much as one person can sense anything that is happening to seventy-five instructors and two thousand students. Still, I felt pressure to produce some quick, tangible results, something to prove to everyone that the program was working. After all, the university had given me the resources to reduce class size, hire and train good faculty, and provide impressive pastries for our staff meetings.

I can't remember now whether it was me or Eileen Donovan-Kranz, the program's assistant director, who played Mickey Rooney to the other's Judy Garland, but I definitely recall that the scene had the feel of an Andy Hardy movie. The only difference was that we changed "I know how we'll get the money to save the school (or farm or family business): We'll put on a play!" to "I know how we'll raise the cultural capital for our writing program: We'll publish a book of student essays!" I do remember that we both felt a rush of naive optimism that somehow made us both believe the project would be a snap: We'd invite our first-year writers to submit personal narratives, textual criticism, political arguments, philosophical meditations, and researched essays; organize an editorial board; hire a first-rate art designer; find a publisher; and send out a memo announcing to the staff that the book—we would call it *Fresh Ink*—would be required the next fall in every section of the course.

When summer arrived and we started to read through the year's submissions, I was convinced that our optimism had been justified. The first one was called "Flow," and I was immediately engaged:

> This is not one story,
> but many stories which
> make up what I know of
> my family
When I was six or seven I lived in a small apartment complex in Acton. I only have a few clear memories from that place. One is a dented, faded red

tool box which my brother used as a container for his bottle cap collection. He would occasionally let me look at the caps and I remember how fascinated I was because no two caps were alike. One day I asked him why he had so many beer bottle caps. "Because Dad used to drink," he told me, "You were too young to remember."

That was the first time I became aware of alcoholism. (B.D. 1994, 39).

The student author went on to explain how he first became aware of the pattern of drinking and abuse that characterized his father's relationship with his grandfather and, to some extent, his own relationship with his own father.

The second essay I read was by a student writing in heartbreaking detail about her own eating disorder. The third, a eulogy to a loving grandparent who had recently died. I was excited—this writing was engaging, intense, alive. Now assuming that the quality of the other kinds of essays—essays about literary texts, political issues, philosophical ideas—was as good, *Fresh Ink* was going to be a breathtaking success. It would win awards. I would win awards. I would field fan letters from envious writing program directors asking for guidance and advice. I'd go on NPR's "Fresh Air" to talk *Fresh Ink* with Terri Gross.

But as I read through the pile, my anxiety started to grow; there were no essays about literary texts, political issues, philosophical ideas. Or, at least, there were not many. Instead, there were dozens, even hundreds, of personal narratives about loss, anger, confusion, and grief. There were suicidal friends and maimed pets, abusive relationships and date rapes, eating disorders, and acts of delinquency. There were heartbreaking accounts of growing up in some way different—African American, Latino, Asian American, Jewish, nonathletic, nerdy, fat, four-eyed, a victim of divorce, anything—and feeling forever out of place and sorts. There were summer jobs from hell; there were sadistic high school teachers, substitutes, coaches, and administrators (these at least introduced a hint of humor and comic relief); and there was citation-filled page after citation-filled page of research papers on AIDS, HIV, ADD, autism, cancer, Alzheimer's, schizophrenia, obsessive compulsive disorder. What next? I wondered. Scoliosis? Osteoporosis?

All of these essays about pain and suffering—friends who had moved away, broken down, even done themselves in. Relatives who had died slowly or suddenly, usually not allowing the student enough time to say good-bye. Classmates who had been cruel, vicious, insensitive, bigoted, racist, homophobic, anti-Semitic. Reading all these essays, one after another, felt overwhelming, ominous, even apocalyptic.

Whatever happened, I wondered, to good clean fun?

In the summer before I started college, my parents' marriage fell apart. It wasn't the first or the last time—their whole relationship was predicated on melodramatic, near-divorce experiences followed by euphoric, post-near-divorce reconciliations—but that summer my mother's anger reached new heights, her despair sunk to new depths. That summer my parents' marriage imploded in a way that was more extreme than what had come before and less predictable than what would eventually follow.

As the tension escalated, my mother's mood and health grew worse. She began spending more and more time in bed—reading, sleeping, watching TV, and plotting strategy. Sometimes she would call us up to her room to tell us what her lawyer had advised or to ask us to speak with my father about his behavior. It was important, she would say, for us to get him to change. While she spoke, I would stare at the pattern of the carpet or the bedspread, trying to disappear, waiting to leave.

Over the years I've grown used to arguments against requiring or even allowing students to write personal essays in a Freshman Comp course. Critics say that personal narratives are too easy because students have already learned to write autobiographically in high school or that they are too hard because students so young should not be expected to have a perspective yet on their own life. Or they point out that personal narrative has too little to do with the writing of the workplace or, on the other hand, that it has all too much to do with the bourgeois goal of selling oneself or commodifying one's experience.

How can you still ask students to write personally, a postmodern colleague asked me recently, when we all know that the very notion of a single, unified self is hopelessly naive and retrograde? When she realized that she was speaking to one of those hopelessly naive, retro selves, she proceeded to tell me that it was outrageously insensitive "to coerce students into personal revelation in public space"—a rule that applies apparently even if that personal revealer is only a myth, a mask, or a socially-constructed representation.

According to the critics of personal writing, our students desperately need all sorts of things: training in literary criticism, the tropes and conventions of academic discourse, cultural studies, postmodern theory, multiculturalism, grammar, usage, critical thinking, library skills. The last thing first-year students need, apparently, is an invitation to tell us or themselves who they were (or who they may still think they are) outside of our classroom.

Even if I granted this point—that we have little to learn from our students or their stories, that they are deficient in so many ways that we can't afford to squander any time encouraging them to talk about their families and friends, their failures and accomplishments, their worst experiences and most nagging doubts—even if I believed all that, I still would wonder how we could expect adolescents, many away from home for the very first time, to move seamlessly from past to present, from parents and siblings and boyfriends and girlfriends and old familiar teachers to unfamiliarity and loneliness and homesickness. Even if I believed that they really did need to know right away about Foucault or syllogisms or socially constructed selves, I'd worry that until they cleared out at least a few of their earlier memories, fears, and fantasies there just wouldn't be enough room left in their brains.

In the summer before I started college, I received a letter from the Selective Service telling me that I was 1A. The letter should not have been completely unexpected; after all I was a basically healthy male who unfortunately happened to turn eighteen in that small space of time when the student deferment exemption had ended but the Vietnam War had not. Still, this was not supposed to happen. In communities with money and power—and I am still a little ashamed to admit that my hometown had much more than its share of both—getting out of the war was like getting out of jury duty. In fact, I did not at that time know a single person who had gone to Vietnam.

Still, I was not sure I wanted to rely on my luck in the lottery, and so I spent part of my summer trying to come up with a fallback plan. I made some inquiries about the possibility of gaining conscientious objector status, but the lawyer I spoke with at the American Friends Service organization advised me that as a nonpracticing, nonbelieving secular Jew, my chances were pretty slim; apparently he was not impressed that I had organized a successful student demonstration in my high school cafeteria, had waited in line three hours to attend the trial of the Chicago Seven, had passed out leaflets for Eugene McCarthy, and knew every word and inflection in every antiwar song by Bob Dylan, Country Joe McDonald, and Phil Ochs. My attempt to get a psychiatric exemption was equally unsuccessful: the psychiatrist I consulted told me, in true Yossarian fashion, that the people *he* was worried about were the ones who *weren't* trying to get out.

Going to war was out of the question but going to jail or to Canada seemed almost as impossible to a nice suburban kid with a room of his own, an acceptance letter from a liberal arts college, and tickets in hand to see Neil Young and The Who over Christmas break, not to mention a fear of guns, bugs, haircuts, and authority. Still, for some reason—I think it was the fact that I was eighteen—I was irrationally calm about the whole thing. And, sure enough, the week before I left for college, I found help from an unlikely source: I called my allergist to tell him that I needed a letter for the infirmary at college so that I could continue to get shots for my hay fever.

"Do you need a letter for your draft board too?"

"Would you write one?"

"Sure," responded my seventy-five-year-old antiwar allergist. "But do me a favor: When you come in for your next appointment, I want you to jog here. No, actually, I want you to run here. And if you have any trouble breathing, don't stop. And don't use your inhaler."

His plan, of course, was to induce an asthma attack, which he would then witness for the sake of the accuracy of the draft board letter. And it worked like a charm. I ran, I had the asthma attack (or something that he led me to believe was an asthma attack), and he wrote such a strong letter unrecommending me for service that even when the members of my dorm gathered in the lobby to listen to the 1971 selective service lottery, even when January 6, 1953, my birthday, came up #36, I figured I was home free.

For that reason, I was more than a little shocked when I received a letter in my college mailbox notifying me to report in three weeks for an induction physical.

Last year, the second year of *Fresh Ink*, we published an essay from a student who had witnessed his best friend die in a gang fight, another from a woman who had been beaten up by her boyfriend, another from a student who grew up in Cambodian refugee camps, and still another from a student whose family escaped Vietnam on a makeshift boat:

> After a week of traveling we were still out on the water. Many got seasick. Children cried with hunger. Mothers breast-fed their babies. Siblings held each other the way they never did before. Men tried to be calm and brave. Suddenly, we discovered that there was a small boat within fifty meters of us. We were very afraid. We were stopped by Thai pirates. They were mean and nasty and had weapons on them. Several women immediately hid their gold and jewels in their mouths. My mother had a stomachache but she had to hold back the pain or those pirates might have gotten angry and killed her. All the pirates wanted were gold and jewels. They were very greedy. One girl was raped. One woman got her lips ripped almost in half because she tried to hide her wedding ring and jewels in her mouth. One man got injured badly because he had a gold tooth and a pirate tried to pull it out. We felt lucky that no one was killed.(Ngo 1995, 37)

While very few of the submissions to *Fresh Ink* describe such physical violence, a great many are explorations of emotional trauma. And while an essay about a student's struggle with bulimia or a broken home or a dying grandparent is certainly not the same as being attacked by Thai pirates, it hardly offers much relief.

I don't remember much about my courses my first semester at college, though I do recall that in Freshman English we had to read a book and write a critical essay each week. The first was about Thucydes' *The Pelopynesian War*; I think we were given a choice of three questions. The second was a comparison of *Antigone* and *The Trial of the Catonsville Nine,* a transcript of the trial of nine people, including Catholic priests Daniel and Philip Berrigan, accused of breaking into a selective service office and burning and destroying files during the Vietnam War. The professor wanted us to think about the relevance of Antigone's appeal that "the laws of god take precedence over the laws of man."

Although my now-active selective service file had been transferred from my hometown to the draft board closer to my college, I was never asked to think—by my professor or by myself—if Antigone's philosophy might shed some light on the decision I was now struggling with or whether my struggle might shed some light on the play. As far as I can recall, my college writing course was my college writing course and my life was my life. And even when my life might have impinged on the text under discussion or the text might have impinged on my life, even, in fact, when we read and discussed Huck Finn, the philosophy remained the same: Never the twain shall meet.

I remember feeling surprised and a little horrified that the students who submitted pieces to *Fresh Ink* identified more phases of death and dying than Doctors Kevorkian and Kubler-Ross knew existed in their universes. I wonder now why I didn't expect it. After all, we had asked students in our classes to write what mattered, to take risks, to search for significance, to explore topics about which they still had questions. And what could be more significant and mysterious and risky than death, dying, disease, and dysfunction? So why was I surprised to read so many stories of loss and lack? What did I expect? And what did I crave? I know that I did not crave happy talk about functional families for, as Tolstoy taught us, those families are all boringly alike. It is in the dirt of the details about our common and uncommon suffering that we approach interest and insight. But did so many of these students have to be so sad, so serious?

Did so many have to write about friends who died in car wrecks or committed suicide? About visits to nursing homes to see grandparents and godparents deteriorating with Alzheimer's and cancer? Did so many really have wicked stepmothers, bigoted and insensitive teachers, siblings with autism or AIDS or anorexia?

The irony of all this is not lost on me: Here I am asking the same questions of first-year student writers that they are often ridiculed for asking their high school or college teachers after reading *Oedipus Rex* or *Hamlet* or

Beloved. Why all this writing about suffering and loss, ambivalence and confusion? Can't we read some happy stories about successful people?

Yeah, why *can't* we? I think. Screw Tolstoy, I could stand a happy family or two myself.

Since textbook companies and core committees have taken to publishing their plans to celebrate diversity and embrace multiculturalism, it was no great surprise to see how many students submitted essays to *Fresh Ink* about their ethnicity and identity. The surprising and distressing part was that so many of these students view their ethnic background as a serious problem, an albatross that has held them back from social or educational success. A Costa Rican woman complained about friends who innocently told her jokes about Hispanics. A Chinese American woman who has never felt as if she fully belonged in America wrote about a trip to China to see her grandparents who she could barely understand and who referred to her throughout the visit as "the American." A Jewish student described the anger and disorientation he felt on a predominantly Christian campus.

There were a few exceptions: A Puerto Rican woman wrote proudly and nostalgically of her childhood memories of San Juan. A black woman wrote to explain why she resented the mass media's narrow definitions of beauty and why she was proud of her "nappy, natural hair." But, for the most part, students wrote about ethnicity only to describe the pain of feeling foreign in a country in which they were born and the still-greater pain of feeling even more foreign when they have visited the country in which their parents were born.

Like many Jews in Russia and eastern Europe early in this century, my grandparents came to America to escape poverty and pogroms; like many Jews growing up in the 1930s and 1940s in urban America, my parents watched their families go from destitution to a comfortable middle-class life; and like many other Jews of my generation, I grew up rich enough to support my romanticized ideas about poverty (not to mention assimilated enough to support my cynical attitudes about Judaism). By the time I reached adolescence in the 1960s, our family tree had been firmly replanted in one of Chicago's leafiest and most desirable suburbs.

Those romantic ideas about poverty kept me from sitting up when I rode in my parents' car (I actually crouched down in the back seat so no one would see me riding in that Cadillac), but they did not keep me from amassing a huge record collection or from choosing to attend a private, expensive college. And these ideas did not seem all that romantic when my father told me that he did not have the money to pay all of my tuition for the second semester. He told me to tell the business office that he needed "to move some money around" and that he would pay them in a few weeks. This came as something of a shock; after all, he was a doctor who made a great deal of money. But, as it turned out, he was also an investor in experimental drug companies and South American diamond mines. And during my first semester of college, drugs and diamonds, at least the ones my father chose, were down. Way down.

Not all of the *Fresh Ink* submissions were meant to be depressing or negative. In fact, one of the most common genres was the highly sentimental eulogy for a beloved grandparent. I don't mean to suggest that these pieces were upbeat: In most cases the grandparent in question was quickly deteriorating or, more commonly, recently deceased. But these Nanny or Papa pieces were rarely meant to be tragic or even sad; they were meant instead to be sweet and touching tributes to the one adult who had provided the author with unqualified love and a model of how to live.

It has the feel for me of a bad dream: My parents had gone out of town for the weekend and left the four of us—my three brothers and me—in the city with my grandmother. We were not happy about this: My grandmother has always been frantic, controlling, ill-tempered, and, since she speaks in her own hybrid of part-Yiddish, part-English, part-mutter, part-yell, she is almost impossible to understand. When my mother was around to translate, deflect, and defend, seeing Nana was fine. But without our buffer, in that small city apartment, it was almost too much for my small suburban sensibility to bear.

Thankfully I've repressed most of it, but I do remember her up at the crack of dawn, turning on lights and muttering, "Enough with the sleeping. Up, the Jeffrey Bus, crowded later, a sale Eva told me at Carson's. . . ." And I remember hours of being dragged from store to store, being implored to keep up, being scolded for sitting down on a department store floor. I remember her looking for bargains, crossing items off a list, arguing with salesclerks. And I remember her telling us that if we were good we would get a treat. The treat turned out to be lunch at The Blackstone, an imposing-looking restaurant that had the look of a men's club with heavy mahogany tables and chairs, waiters in white starched aprons and black bow ties. But we were there because from 12:00 P.M. to 2:00 P.M. The Blackstone had a special children's meal and price. Though we would have all preferred a hot dog and fries from a street corner stand, Nana was set on the good deal at The Blackstone, and so there we were being told "Boys, presentable, tuck in your shirt tails, *again* I have to tell you?"

The meal was a disaster. We ordered hamburgers, expecting skinny

McDonald's-like patties, but getting instead four-inch-thick ground sirloin. My two younger brothers refused to eat it, sending my grandmother into a fit. But just when it looked bleakest, the maitre d' came by, sussed out the situation, and came to the rescue. "Here at The Blackstone, we have a policy: If a child finishes his meal, we give him a special prize, a toy. But if he doesn't, no prize." And so Jeff and Dan fought their way through those monstrous ground sirloins in search of their treasure. When the meal mercifully ended, the maitre d' returned with the gifts. But just as he reached out to give them to the victors, my grandmother's hand suddenly reached out, snatching them out of the air. "These treats," she told my now tearful little brothers, "for these, you eat dinner tonight."

Though the sweetness of the grandparent submissions to *Fresh Ink* should have provided some relief in an otherwise bleak landscape, I found the opposite to be true. Of all the submissions, these bothered me most of all. I found myself immediately impatient and dismissive as soon as I read about Poppy's favorite stuffed chair or Grammy's apple turnovers. I found myself doubting that Nanny's eyes always twinkled like a starry night or that Pappa always smelled like peppermint.

During her second open-heart surgery, my mother almost died. In fact, three hours into the operation, one of the surgical nurses came out to tell us—my father, aunt, two of my three brothers, my grandmother, and me—that we should prepare for the worst. For a moment, we all just sat there stunned. "Someone should call Dan." My younger brother had been unable to come to Chicago for the surgery and sat thousands of miles away awaiting some word. Since I was closest to him or maybe just to the telephone, the task fell to me. "Things look really bad, Dan. Mom might not make it through the surgery," I managed to stammer. Miraculously, though, just an hour later, the nurse was back. "Good news: Things went much better than we expected. She's going to make it." This time I jumped for the phone: "Dan, Mom is going to be OK!" In the jubilation of the moment, I noticed the frown on my ninety-year-old Russian Jewish grandmother's face.

"Who is Lad talking to?" she demanded.

"He's talking to Dan, Nana," my aunt said gently.

"*Again* with the long distance calls?" she responded in disgust.

My own stories all have anticlimactic endings: My grandmother, even as she approaches one hundred, continues to inspire some of my strongest feelings of frustration and ambivalence. My parents did not divorce. The market for diamonds and drugs picked up.

And I did not go to Vietnam. Before my induction physical, my parents were able to get my allergist, my pediatrician, and an ears, nose, and throat specialist to write letters testifying to the severity of my asthma (not mentioning of course that it was not so severe as to keep me off the wrestling and cross-country teams). When I arrived at the physical, I could not get anyone to tell me if these letters were in my file or to look at my copies. As the physical and psychological examinations proceeded, I got more and more frantic because, except for the text in which we had to match pictures of tools with their functions, I seemed to be passing with ease.

In fact, I seemed to be frighteningly healthy. Unfortunately, many of the men there that day were not nearly so unlucky. One guy next to me in line was sent home with a dangerously high fever; his physical was rescheduled for a later date. "Each time before I come here I drink some of my own urine," he whispered to me. "As long as I keep it up, they can't get me." Another unfortunate member of my cohorts was sent home when the chest X-rays revealed a spot on his lungs. "That's terrible," I stammered. "No, man, it's great. They said they can't take me because it might be malignant. They want me to have it biopsied, but if it's benign, they'll take me then. Well, I'm not playing their game: I just won't have the biopsy."

At the end of the day, an officer gathered all of us who had passed our physicals. "When you men come back here next month, it will be for induction. Please do not bring any of your own weapons." A few men around me cursed. Others were not about to give up so easily. "What about a pistol?" "What about a bowie knife?" "What about a blackjack?" The officer waved them off. "Men, please, we will supply all weapons." More cursing.

Finally, at the very end of the day, I waited in line to meet with an army doctor. "You have passed all the exams," he told me, "and will be inducted into the U.S. Army next month. Is there any information that you have that would disqualify you for military duty?" With desperate gratitude for the question, I handed him the letters and began to tell him about how useless I'd be in the jungle, about how long it takes me to catch me breath after a jog, about. . . . He waved me off impatiently, read the first paragraph of the first letter, and looked up. "Why haven't you notified the army about your condition before this?"

"I have. I've sent you several letters."

He opened the folder on his desk and thumbed through the papers. Then: "Yes, I see it here. You are 4-F and are not medically fit to serve in the U.S. Military. Do you understand?" And he handed me a suitable-for-framing document stating that I could never enlist in the American armed services and told me that I could leave.

By the time the bus dropped me off in town, it was after midnight. I remember feeling that I should feel relieved but all I felt was numb. It was freezing cold, I was four miles from campus, and there were no cabs anywhere in sight. I can't remember how I got back to my dorm but I do remember standing in a phone booth, suddenly feeling overwhelmed with homesickness for a place I no longer considered home.

We often wonder why students hardly ever submit textual criticism for publication in *Fresh Ink*. After all, students in our program often write about poems or stories or films or music or art exhibits. And yet the few submissions that deal with texts seem teacher-based, half-hearted, flat.

I don't remember much more about my first semester except that the last three books in my Freshman English course were *Civilization and Its Discontents, No Exit,* and *A Good Man is Hard to Find.* I remember those three because I somehow convinced the professor that I was being hampered as a writer by the paper-per-week constraint and that, since I had done well on the weekly themes, I should now be allowed to write one longer essay combining all three books. Though I've mercifully managed to repress the details of that composition, I do remember that I put it off until the last moment and then stayed up all night frantically trying to finish. My last foggy memory of that first semester is of getting the paper back covered with corrections and a final note from the professor apologizing; "I'm afraid I let you get yourself in over your head on this one."

I still gasp when I come across a student essay about sexual abuse or date rape, but, on the whole, I have grown harder to shock. I find myself reading more like an ethnographer, noting new patterns and trends. Last year I noted a run of narratives about dying grandparents and lonely first-generation immigrants, while this year's batch seemed heavy on weekend fishing trips with divorced dads and pregnancy scares after drunken unprotected sex.

Still, one trend has not changed: Almost all of the student submissions have happy endings. At least, that's how they are intended. After detailing a hundred ways that they have been damaged and dissed, scared and scarred, these student authors usually try in the end to put on a happy face. "Now I've learned never to take life for granted." "It's all for the best; you only learn through suffering." "But I know he's in a better place." "I'm glad my father was not like the other fathers; he's special."

Maybe they say such things because they feel guilty about having exposed family secrets. Or maybe because they think we expect essays to have clear resolutions. Or maybe they say these things because this is what they actually believe.

In any case, it is one more problematic feature of the confessional student essay, one more reason that critics often find this form so unsatisfactory. As a group, we academics crave ambiguity, sophistication, doubt, even cynicism. According to some of my colleagues, recounting a tragic tale and then invoking a pat resolution—"I'm sure it all worked out this way for a reason"—is the stuff of daytime talk shows, not rigorous academic work. I see their point, I suppose. And yet dismissing all of these narratives simply by invoking Oprah or Geraldo seems a lot like a pat resolution to me, too.

The more I remember my own adolescence, the more I watch the world through the eyes of my own teenage daughters, the more I read about mental and physical illness, violence, and tragic loss in Shakespeare and Toni Morrison and the daily newspaper, the less I wonder why so many first-year students choose, first, to write about death, disease, and dysfunction and, second, to repress in the end what they have just written. In fact, I've grown so used to these essays that my question is no longer "Why do they write about these things?" but "How could they *not* write about them?"

Still, this knowledge doesn't make these essays any easier to read. Each summer Eileen Donovan-Kranz, my coeditor, flips frantically through the pile of submissions to *Fresh Ink* and pleads, "This year, can we please find in here at least one piece about a *functional* family?" And after that, I think, maybe we could organize a carnival or put on a fair.

Works Cited

B. D. 1994. *Fresh Ink I: Essays From Boston College's First-Year Writing Seminar.* Chestnut Hill, MA: Boston College Press.

Ngo, Anna Hang. 1995. *Fresh Ink II: Essays From Boston College's First-Year Writing Seminar.* New York: McGraw-Hill.

9

Telling Stories and
Writing Truths

TOBY FULWILER

I want to tell the story of the best writing class I've ever taught. By "best" I don't mean these students produced the best papers, either individually or collectively, because they didn't. And I don't mean they developed the best ever attitude about writing, because I'm not sure they did. What I do mean is that teaching this class gave me—and many of the students—the most satisfying classroom experience. And I want to tell an honest story, so that its truth serves both my needs and yours. It is only later, after the first telling, that I find these needs in conflict.

I. Telling a Teaching Story

The following narrative is composed of excerpts from informal student writing collected from an advanced composition class called "Personal Voice" at the University of Vermont. Sources include journals, letters, exercises, freewrites, and anonymous evaluations. My own narrative stitches these fragments together.

Silence. On the first day of class, I enter quietly, say nothing, and write instructions on the overhead projector: "Welcome to 'Personal Voice.' For the next seventy-five minutes, get to know each other and me by writing, not talking." For the rest of the period we talk on paper—passing notes, reading the syllabus, writing questions, laughing quietly, and, finally, taking silent attendance.

Sarah: I walk in early (I'm always early) only to find "SILENCE" written on the blackboard. Class fills up with new and familiar faces. Never had this Toby guy before. Instead of saying anything he uses the overhead projector and tells us to write to others in the class. It's silent chaos (I get in trouble for whispering). Not a word, the whole class. Toby's way of showing us the importance of voice? Weird . . . not one word.

Brian: The first meeting with this class is a complete shock. A strange and chaotic world in which everyone writes, no one speaks. Silent. Erie.

Andrew: I arrive 10 minutes late. No one is speaking, everyone is writing. I get reprimanded for asking the girl next to me what's going on. I get reprimanded for asking the teacher what's going on. I leave class partially humored and partially annoyed.

Emily: I know absolutely no one, and I am not happy about being here. I think that I am a terrible writer and I question why I chose this class. To make matters worse, no talking is allowed on the first day. We can only write notes to one another. I leave thinking that I am never going to survive English 112.

Trouble. The registrar's computer has overenrolled "Personal Voice" by seven, so I'm looking out at thirty-two juniors and seniors who refuse to drop, switch, or do anything to make the class smaller. They all want personal attention to their personal voices. On the second day of class, everyone is relieved to discover that I can talk and they can too.

Halley: Today he greets us with words (he can talk!) and a smile, telling us seven need to drop. Everybody laughs. He starts with me, my admit slip still unsigned: Please oh please let me in? I'm graduating . . . I just have to . . . I'm not leaving.

Sarah: At the beginning of the second class Toby tries to scare us into dropping the course, tells us this will be the hardest most bad-ass college class we've ever had. Instead of being scared, we laugh. Nobody drops the class.

Strategy. I try to keep eager and jaded, experienced and inexperienced writers alike off balance. In signing up for this class, many expect to write in only their most personal voices, so my first assignment asks, instead, for their best academic voices, me believing that knowing one is how one knows the other. In fact, every week, in every assignment, I ask for different voices.

Karyn: As an English major I have written many essays for professors, yet I have never ever written six drafts of one essay—and each one in a different voice. These eccentric techniques actually work and spark my interest.

Rachel: What is Voice? What does it mean? How does it get there?

Scott: I'm willing to try four voices: Me at four. Me applying for college admission. Me mountain climbing. Me lovesick.

Dialogue. I guarantee some dialogue with each student in this overenrolled class by asking them to write me letters each Tuesday (Dear Toby). I write a composite letter back each Thursday (Dear Classmates). Most students seem to write candidly of concerns about reading, writing, style, and voice. In my letters back, I quote from their letters, making public their concerns and insights, attempting to use shared dialogue to create a larger community.

Brian: It's easy for you to say your writing never comes out right the first time. What if your writing never comes out right at all? I cannot get any of the ideas I have in my head on to a piece of paper . . . I feel like I am watching a TV that never comes in quite right. The more I play around with it, the fuzzier it gets . . . I want the crisp picture.

Toby: So, classmates, what do you think? Does Brian write like a man who can't get ideas from his head to paper? How many of you feel like Brian? Is Brian doomed or fixable? If fixable, how?

Emily: The voice in your last letter was sorta laid back and a little silly. Like the syllabus, it was definitely serious about writing and our job in your class, but not without a bit of humor.

Toby: Thanks, Emily. Rather silly than too serious, I'd say. Can you be any more specific about the quality of "laid backness" you find in my voice? Which words or passages project that laid back feeling?

Grades. I teach writing classes by putting grades in the background, allowing students to try out new ideas, forms, voices, and not be penalized when something doesn't work—which, when you're experimenting, is quite often. Instead, I want to reward risk taking, so cumulative portfolios graded at midterm and endterm make the most sense.

Melissa: The workshop structure of the class stimulates my writing. I forget about A's, B's, and C's and concentrate on drafts. There's always room for improvement—I like that. We get no grades until it's over.

Scott: We respect each other & help each other out & talk all the time & nobody seems to worry about grades. I say an "A" for writing courses.

Papers. In Thursday paper drafts students try out, expand, and examine various writing voices. Most end up writing with some combination of enthusiasm and frustration in response to my three assignments: (1) a research report; (2) a reflective essay; and (3) a language autobiography. In truth, none of these assignments accomplishes exactly what I intend—are my assignments too murky or are their efforts too lazy? I never resolve this, but console myself that the writing seems to serve their purposes even as it misses mine—in the end, a more important goal.

Rachel: I still don't know if it was me or the assignment, but it took me five different drafts, using a number of different styles and approaches, to finally write a paper that worked—at least it worked for me.

Andrew: Draft on top of draft. Do we ever stop writing and rewriting? No. Our class is one continuous rewriting class. We talk, discuss, produce (sort of), but whatever we say, it's in one examined voice or another.

Sarah: By concentrating on a few papers, I learn to write multiple drafts. Other classes had not challenged me to do this, to take notes, try new things, and push myself further. There is little emphasis on grades; instead it's on doing the work on time, making the writing work, and getting it right.

Collaboration. On days when drafts are due, people divide into groups (self-selected) and read to each other, share ideas, make suggestions. I sense these groups work well, but don't join in unless invited; by midterm I've managed to participate in each group at least once. The noise and laughter in other groups tell me these are good—though not all the time and not for every student.

Halley: Under the shade of the University Heights trees is where the action is. Sitting cross-legged, in circles, the pages of *Major Modern Essayists . . .* [Muller and Crooks 1994] flapping in the breeze. That's where it all came out.

Adam: I realize it is important for the group members to see the progression in the paper from draft to draft. But oftentimes the members get bored of hearing the same ideas rephrased.

Toby: I, too, would "get bored . . . hearing the same ideas rephrased." So what's the answer—or did I already answer it in my letter last week?

Andrew: Listen, how many English students does it take to write a paper? I don't know, but right now I can't think of anything. Emily, tell me what you think, no better yet, write it down for me . . . OK, now let me expand on what you said . . . You gave me the idea, but I made it better, right? So who's idea is it now? Listen . . . .

Teacher presentations. On days when I return a set of drafts, I make transparencies of selected passages from half a dozen different papers to project to the whole class—which on even the nicest fall days dictates we stay inside. I ask students to read their passages, then I explain why I found the passage especially interesting; I've noticed something working and believe everyone can profit from witnessing it. Sometimes, in addition to being "interesting," a sample will reveal a problem that needs solving.

Rachel: I was a little disappointed my paper didn't make it to the big screen last week. It's my best effort so far and I was sure he'd agree.

Lauren: I hope it's not my paper. He'll just wreck it. I don't like it. In fact, I hate it. Why should the class have to see it. I silently pray, no, no, no. Plastic hits the overhead. Unfamiliar font. Thank you.

Student presentations. Teams of two students each take turns presenting published essays from *Major Modern Essays* to demonstrate different voices. The greatest hits prove to be Margaret Atwood ("The Female Body"), Joan Didion ("In Bed" and "Marrying Absurd"), and, much to my surprise, E. B. White ("The Ring of Time"). Nobody wants to dwell on content; instead, everyone steals ideas about form, style, and voice.

Melissa: Let's go outside, it's sunny, it's so warm out. Where's Toby? Whose turn is it to teach today?

Sarah: My presentation. Our presentation. Something different. So let's reread "The Female Body" and different groups rewrite different parts. Then each group write their own version of "the male body."

Talk about a collective voice. Look at Atwood's voice, then at your own!

Lauren: I am instructing the class today on Lewis Thomas. I am nervous as hell, but had you told me that I would have been doing this eight weeks ago, I would have said "no way." Public speaking is not one of my stronger assets and plus, who was I to interpret someone else's writing style?

Karyn: My favorite class was the one I presented with other members of the class. I enjoyed it because I felt the rest of the class was having a good time while actually learning something.

Adam: I enjoyed teaching the class, even though our lesson flopped.

Ambiguity and Confusion. [No comment.]

Sarah: This class was probably the most unorganized English class I've ever taken—a free-for-all. But that made no difference in what I learned, in fact, I think it helped me learn more. I had to straighten things out for myself, so I concentrated more on the written material and other students' work plus my own.

Emily: A lot of work and still one of the most fun classes to attend—but at times it became difficult to understand exactly what Toby wanted for assignments. I guess that is the nature of writing classes, as it is a more subjective discipline than most.

Rachel: Some of the instructions were not so clear, but as a class we overcame the adversity. The class was a free-for-all in creative thought, which I enjoyed.

Class Books. Class consensus is that we publish four different class books, with teams of two editors each collecting essays from class members to demonstrate the different essays written during the term. Four themes are chosen: "Experimental Voices," "Autobiographical Voices," "Research Voices," and "Collective Voices." We each submit to the book most likely to publish our piece. The "Experimental" editors reject my essay, but the "Autobiographical" editors accept it.

Scott: Mayhem. Everyone's yelling. "No, four separate books!" "No, only one!" "How much is this going to cost?" "What's group one again?" "I don't know which category my paper falls under." "Can I get central attention?" (That's Toby.) "All right, what are the categories?" One voice shouts, "Number one is weird," over and over again. Toby says, "Okay, weird." He spells it wrong on the board—w-i-e-r-d.

Melissa: How many books? Can we submit two? What are they about? Color covers? How many pages? Anymore questions?

Adam: Toward the end of the term things got a little out of control with multiple options and new ideas popping up and the editors changing the themes of their books. How were we supposed to know where to publish our essays?

Class Crots. Tell the story of "Personal Voice" through snapshots or "crots" (Winston Weathers' [1980] term for brief prose stanzas). Look for highlights, skip the transitions, and we'll let the readers fill in the rest. So everybody writes a brief (fifty words) prose snapshot of the class to capture what each remembers best—some, including me, write more than one. This collection of forty-four anonymous snapshots is published in the fourth class book as "Collective Voices."

Anon: Crot, crot, crot. After thirteen weeks of reading, writing, revising, writing about writing, reading about revising, writing about reading it all comes down to the truth of a single crot.

Anon: My personal voice in a single crot? Why not? Get to the point. Teach, learn, amuse—that's what it's all about. Be yourself, be someone else, let it all work out of you.

Portfolios. Near the end of the term, I invite students to edit selections from drafts, essays, journals, and letters that tell of their journey through "Personal Voice" and to call these "story portfolios." These final projects end up telling as much about the writer's failures as successes—the honesty is riveting and these semester interpretations reveal some of the best writing I read all term. I enjoy these portfolios more than the conventional "comprehensive" ones and vow, from now on, to require them.

Community. My own journal writing from week seven captures my feeling about this class: "It happens often, especially when I'm late, that when I get to class it's already happening, that in some ways (and I haven't exactly tested this yet), the class would go on without me and that possibly (and I don't want to test this) I wouldn't even be missed." As every writing teacher knows, it's the regular sharing of the writing that makes this communal difference—and sitting outside on the grass doesn't hurt.

Halley: The sky is blue, the leaves bright orange, yellow, and red. As we walk out the south door, the eyes of another class watch us woefully—we're going outside again. Unfair they say. Gets our minds going we say. Three of us wander across the street. Sit under a tree, breeze in our hair. Share words, ideas, papers. Love the writing, love the day.

Andrew: Sitting outside in a lopsided circle talking about voice. Some of us light cigarettes ("Smoke 'em if you got 'em!"). Others play with the grass and dirt and try to remain focused on the task of the day. English 112. Personal Voice. Public bonding.

Karyn: After one month, everyone laughs and swears, talks to each other, talks to Toby, who even talks to us. I actually look forward to class— learning with comedy is such a novel idea.

Melissa: This week in class I'm ten minutes late and have no paper to hand in. A friend stops me in front of the library. I explain my predicament. "Why are you bothering to go?" he asks. Because "I have to see my buddies."

Lauren: I bitched and moaned my way through this class, but what I realize, now at the end, is that there was room to bitch and moan.

Student Evaluations. I don't read these until a month into the spring term— grades done, students dispersed (some graduated), new classes begun. I read the anonymous course evaluations and am pleased with what I find; my instincts were right, it was an exceptional class:

> This class rocked! It was frustrating, time consuming, nerve-wracking but *never* boring, slow or uninteresting. . . This class really was "personal." . . . There is no doubt that Toby worked us hard—but we *needed* that.

> I used to hate critical thinking about literature and stuff like that so I thought I would hate critical thinking about anything. But no . . . critical thinking about the range of my own voice has been great! I guess what it boils down to is that this class has helped me discover me.

> Well, this class has been a *great* struggle throughout this semester, I have complained, cried, laughed, and thrown things, and in the bargain I've learned that writing is at once simple and complicated.

Hey! You might want to try some different assignments next time though. And how about letting people revise old drafts more instead of writing all new papers every week?

Almost done. Study break, then finals. No problem. Oh, yeah the portfolio. Revisions, more drafts. Did I find it? Did I obtain personal voice?! I sure as hell hope so.

I survived Personal Voice. I am not sure if I can still define voice, but I now have a better understanding of how complicated it is—something that comes both from within and without. Both nature and nurture.

II. Complicating a Hero Story

My first telling of the 112 story was inevitably the kind of narrative Joe Trimmer calls a teacher-hero story—the kind he did not want us to write for this collection. But my ego is fragile enough and my clear-cut victories few enough that I needed to tell the story and imply—if not state outright—that I was the agent who caused this special class to happen. In telling the story, I wanted the world—at least the world of writing teachers—to celebrate with me the richness, variety, energy, and spirit of this teaching experience.

However, to be both honest and celebratory, I need also to understand—and much of the preceding narrative, even to me, is more summary than interpretation—more *what* than *why*. Since I teach all my writing classes pretty much the same—starting in one place with first-year students, another with advanced students—I'm not yet sure what made this 112 class more satisfying than, say, my first-year composition class or my senior seminar. In all these classes I make variations of the same assignments: voluntary journals, weekly letters, a few formal papers in many drafts, collaborative local research projects, class books, and portfolio assessment. So, if I taught this class as I always teach my classes, what made the difference? Why did it "rock"? If it wasn't a new approach or a better design or a more charming style—all of which the preceding narrative pretty accurately rules out—what was it?

While I'd like to take much of the credit for the variety and power of learning that I believe happened in this "Personal Voice" class, the writer in me admits that the story is more complex, less certain, and no doubt less heroic than the one the teacher just told you.

Qualifications Need to Be Made

In retrospect, at least two of the most powerful elements that made this class satisfying were either accidental or out of my control—circumstances and chemistry—which substantially diminishes my claims to heroic leadership.

Note that this class met during the fall term, on Tuesday and Thursday afternoons, from 2:00 P.M. to 3:15 P.M., in a first-floor classroom in a small building adjacent to quiet campus lawns during an exceptionally warm Vermont fall, allowing us to move outside whenever the overhead projector wasn't needed—at least once and sometimes twice a week during September and October. The circumstances of fall-semester meetings, outdoors, after lunch, in pleasant weather appealed to every possible student fantasy about good learning conditions, adding a warm and, perhaps, superficial glow to whatever else happened during those seventy-five minutes.

Note, too, that the chemistry of this and every other class is a crapshoot. I got lucky here. "Personal Voice" turned out to be a mix of just enough students who knew each other to create initial comfort and just enough new faces to avoid cliques and promote the excitement of new friend making. All were juniors and seniors, most were English majors, and the course was elective, so motivation was not an issue. Twenty were female, twelve male—a gender balance I kept intact as I told the class story—though I'm not sure what difference this balance made. I do know that if there is heroism in this narrative, it has to be collective, the agency shared by the chemistry of compatible and motivated classmates.

Of course, in any one-chapter portrait of a complex entity such as a college class, the whole is bound to emerge as greater than the sum of its parts. However, in telling about the telling of the story, the fair, accurate, and honest "whole" gets increasingly more complicated, since the case for the whole is an edited selection of parts—which means featuring the right details, forgetting the wrong ones. Furthermore, in a class of thirty-three individuals, over a time span of fifteen weeks, far more complex happenings, insights, and stories take place than any single central consciousness can collect, understand, explain, or narrate, as any book-length ethnographic study will demonstrate.

It is at this point that I see more clearly a real conflict between the two most important intentions of this narrative—a conflict between my role as teacher and my role as writer. To feel good about myself as a teacher, I need to feel knowledgeable, imaginative, resourceful, and relevant. And I need to believe in and celebrate (narrate) my classroom successes as much to affirm my own identity as to inform and enlighten others.

At the same time, to feel good about myself as a writer, I need to be accurate, truthful, insightful, and vulnerable. I need to share with my audience things that don't always make me look good. For instance, I can't tell one-dimensional teacher-as-hero stories about myself and expect to keep my audience interested or involved. We've all heard or told too many such stories to accept them at face value. If there are heroic events—and I believe there are—so too are there mundane, accidental, and cowardly ones. The writer in me knows that to tell celebratory stories as I have just done is to tell half-truths only. To tell better stories, I need to uncover the ordinary along with the exceptional, the dark along with the light, and admit to complications in my narrative.

III. Telling a Writer Story

Because this chapter is a story, not an ethnography, simplification is the rule, generalization a given, and some fictionalization a fact. For example, to compose the original story, I quoted only eleven of thirty-two students; had I quoted a different eleven, I would have told a different story. In addition, while all of the student names and quotations are real, the quotations credited to Karyn are composites of three different students, combined to simplify the cast of characters. And, only after completing the story did I realize that I never quoted the best writer in the class, Kristina. Why? Was her informal writing so mediocre? Or did I ignore her because she had nothing celebratory to say? In any event, to make this a better writer story, there are more things you need to know. (If this were an ethnography, the following would be footnotes.)

Silence. For some years now I've started all my fall classes in silence; I don't start classes this way spring semester since I don't want word to get out and become predictable. This fall, it caused me real problems. Since I didn't take attendance until the end of class, only then confirming the overenrollment of seven students, how could I kick out students who had suffered through seventy-five minutes of forced silence?

Trouble. Entering the second class, I already knew nobody would leave voluntarily. The Vermont English Department has too many majors, not enough instructors, and too few upper-level classes; once students manage to get into an advanced class of any kind they never drop it. Seven extra students in a writing class matters. In 112 it contributed to some of the assignment confusion that resulted when I didn't individualize enough instruction. For example, instead of holding individual conferences, I usually passed around sign-up sheets to schedule small-group conferences, when three or four students would meet with me at one time to discuss their drafts. The gain was that students got to know each other and each other's writing better and that many of my comments to one student helped the others as well—but I did this initially to save me time and slighted some individual writers in the bargain.

Strategy. Some of these students, such as seniors Andrew and Emily, enjoyed being in the class, seldom missed, and ended up completing all the assignments—but never on time and never in the voice-stretching manner I requested. They wrote late and safe, refusing to experiment or take risks, arguing something like "This is my voice, don't mess with it, that's the way it is." Though I enjoyed these students personally—and Andrew continues to write me long e-mail letters since his graduation—in refusing to value my assignments, they learned less than they should have.

Dialogue. I think I assigned these weekly letter exchanges as much for me as for my students. The letters forced me to wrestle, regularly, with the direction and purpose of my instruction. One week I asked everyone to write their letter as an e-mail—to me or to the class listserv—which had the positive effect of coercing some students to explore this medium for the first time. But this exchange proved more time consuming for me, as everyone wrote to me personally, not to the rest of the class, and I felt compelled to answer individually, which I always resisted with paper letters collected and read at one sitting.

Grades. I'm actually embarrassed to talk about the grades: While my advanced writing classes are usually A/B classes, with the B's outnumbering the A's, here I gave nineteen A's, thirteen B's, and nothing lower. Whew! I don't ever remember giving grades that high in an undergraduate class. And in reviewing my grade book, I noticed, too, that every 112 student received a higher grade at term's end than at midterm—guaranteeing each an upward learning curve. Was it the writing or good vibrations that justified nineteen A's?

Papers. In the end, we settled on two (not three) finished papers of any kind on any topic (!) from each student. I dropped the request that they necessarily be "researched" or "reflective" or "autobiographical." I caved in here, in part, because I'd done a poor job explaining and justifying my initial assignments and, in part, because I began to believe (or their lobbying persuaded me) that they'd learn more about their voices without my limits and restrictions—which happened for some, but not for most. And where I really felt I'd lost here was in reading the class books: No paper, including Kristina's, was as careful and finished as it could have been. While individual insights and passages were often dazzling, no writer edited, to my satisfaction, for rhythm, balance, precision, or emphasis. The final products always fell short.

Teacher Presentations. Though I vowed to celebrate rather than critique the student texts that I put on the overhead projector, I often forgot this and focused instead on the problems. No wonder that Lauren, among others, was relieved not to see her text featured before the whole class.

Student Presentations. In spite of building in time for students to lead the class, I remained always at the center, even when I didn't seem to be. For instance, I required students to rehearse their presentation strategies with me before leading the class. And I was always keeping time, moving things along—sometimes trying to slow things down—never as unobtrusive as I wished to appear. And few students focused on the specific passages or language of the texts they presented, confirming my suspicion that most students prefer the easier tasks of generalization and summary to the more difficult tasks of interpretation and analysis.

Ambiguity and Confusion. My initial writing assignments proved terrific in theory, but weak in practice—something I was especially slow to figure out. I was singularly unsuccessful in separating "research" from the category of "research paper"—an assignment they seemed to loathe. Nor was I any more successful in defining or explaining or illustrating how to write a "reflective" essay. It really threw students for a loop when I tried to *require* essays based on real information rather than top-of-the-head speculation. My singular failure here lead directly to my compromise on the assignments. Without question, it would have been a better class with clearer assignments.

Class Books. The class did publish the four books the editors brought to the last class meeting—the last one arriving only after the period was half over. Every student was published in at least one book, so each bought one book; I bought all four. Each one proved a mixed production, with insightful introductions and clever author biographies offset by poor proofreading and inconsistent voices.

Story Portfolio. I added the idea of story portfolios with only three weeks left in the term, encouraging everyone to try one in place of the more conventional, comprehensive one requested on my initial syllabus, but only three students—Sarah, Rachel, and Emily—wrote them; they were delightful to read, but the small sample disappointed me.

Community. In a class that celebrated community and togetherness, you would think the teacher would know all of the students personally—especially with a paper draft or letter due each week. Wrong. Even at term's end I still could not tell Amanda from Amy or remember Adam's name when seeking to hand his paper back. I think they forgave me this, since many of their teachers never even try to learn names—but I never forgave myself or, apparently, took the time to improve my memory.

Student Evaluations. To tell this teaching story, I actually edited out many references that praised my teaching, used my name, called me a "fearless leader," or claimed this the best class ever taken—and, actually, there were quite a few of these. But in a chapter such as this, committed to a candid accounting of classroom life, overly positive testimonies seem to exaggerate rather than support the story's credibility, making for yet another layer of complication.

Coda. In the end, I've so analyzed, tested, and qualified my original narration as to make me doubt it *was*, in fact, the best class I ever taught. It makes me doubt, in fact, that I've ever had a fully satisfying class—for if it were not to be found in the narrative with which this paper began, when then? I distinctly remember feeling satisfied at semester's end and again when, several months later, I reviewed class documents to write this story. But since few parts of my original narrative withstood cross-examination, I'm less satisfied now than then.

Both the teacher and writer in me understands the value and necessity of clarifying and complicating my initial 112 story for the benefit of my students, my readers, and myself. In the next offering of "Personal Voice," my students will benefit if I control enrollment, explain assignments, and make all requirements clear at the start. You, dear reader, will benefit since this revised story humanizes rather than glorifies the teaching of writing—allowing as much to be learned from what didn't work as what did. For myself, well, knowing the truth—at least more dimensions of it—should free me from illusions about myself as a teacher-hero and maybe about the very existence of teacher-heroes in the educational universe.

However, even as this final telling goes to press, doubts remain. In the end, the writer has persuaded the teacher in me that true stories cannot be conveyed in single or simple tellings—that the truth of examined narrative will always be complicated, compromised, and uncertain. So, why does the teacher in me resist this liberation? Why doesn't this truth make the planning of my next syllabus or the meeting of my next class a little easier? Why, in other words, do I still need the illusion that "Once-upon-a-time" stories are true?

Works Cited

Muller, G. H., and A. F. Crooks. 1994. *Major Modern Essayists.* New York: Prentice Hall.

Weathers, W. 1980. *An Alternate Style.* Rochelle Park, NJ: Hayden.

10

Nancy's Promise

SHARON J. HAMILTON

No one spoke.

It was 7:30 P.M. Eyes avoided contact with each other; bodies restrained themselves around the large table that filled the small classroom. We were just starting the second half of my Advanced Expository Writing class, and I was concerned. Where was the curiosity, the analysis, the comfortable camaraderie of the first half of the class? The players were the same: my students and me. The task was the same: reading and responding to an early draft. The only difference was that this time, for the first time, the text was mine. It was the opening page of the first complete draft of *My Name's Not Susie: A Life Transformed by Literacy*. My editor had returned it for revision, just as I had returned my students' drafts for revision. I wanted to include my students in the process of writing for publication. Moreover, I wanted the same kind of helpful assistance that the class provided for each other in their discussion groups, especially since this particular class seemed comfortable speaking constructively about each other's work. I specifically wanted assistance with the first page, which currently pleased neither my editor nor me (though I was happier with it than he was). He had said to me, "Get into the classroom right away." I thought I had achieved that, but it still wasn't right.

The class was not accustomed to silence. The students had worked collaboratively from the first day and were used to expressing their opinions about each other's writing. They were not, however, accustomed to critiquing the writing of their instructor. We were all uncomfortable, they with the unfamiliar task and me with my growing sense of their discomfort. I could see them searching for "the right thing to say" about my writing, just as I often searched for "the right thing to say" about their work.

"Someone's got to start. It might as well be me." Relief registered briefly on each face. Whenever Nancy initiated a conversation, it inevitably ricocheted into the unpredictable, often outrageous. With one breath, we braced ourselves.

"The tone's all wrong. You sound superior, and I don't think you want to or intend to."

"What? Where?"

Denise picked up on Nancy's observation. "You always suggest we read early drafts out loud. Didn't you say that reading aloud captures tone? Why don't you read the first page out loud? Then maybe you—and the rest of us—will hear what Nancy heard when she read it by herself." There was a slight twinkle in her eye, reminding me of her initial discomfort with reading her own work aloud. I could tell she was beginning to enjoy this opportunity.

Seeing most of the rest of the class nod in agreement, I began reading the first page:

"Dr. Hamilton, I'm having a party on Saturday night to celebrate my divorce. Will you come?"

Pale blue eyes just learning again to sparkle darted around the classroom. "And you come too, Stephanie. And you, John. And you and you. All of you. You've all been so encouraging the past few weeks while I've been writing myself through this mess."

Fading bruises from Angie's last altercation with her now ex-husband, documented with an eerie emotional detachment in her most recent essay, accused me in advance of my response. "I'd love to, Angie, but I can't. I've already made arrangements for Saturday night." I should probably have stopped there, but anticipation of an evening of Prokofiev's masterworks loosened my tongue. "I'm going out for dinner and then to the symphony."

"Hold it. Stop right there!" Nancy commanded. "Why say, 'I should probably have stopped there'?"

"I thought that I was giving too much information." And suddenly I had an inkling of what Nancy was getting at. "I don't mean too much information for a student. I just thought . . ."

"Well, I think it sounds exactly as though you mean that. It makes you sound elitist, as though you think it's really none of the student's business."

Elitist! I had deliberately tried to sound anything but! "No, I really was thinking that we shouldn't spend time talking about what I was doing on Saturday night."

"But you thought it was OK to spend class time on what Angie was doing on Saturday night."

Now that perspective had not occurred to me. I reread the offending sentences, and understood what Nancy was saying, while still knowing that my writer's intentions had been nowhere near that interpretation. "How many of you had responses similar to Nancy's when I first read those lines?" I asked.

"It flashed through my mind for just a moment, but then I thought you probably wouldn't mean that," said James, "so I didn't really think any more about it."

"I could see what Nancy was getting at after she said it," added Jo-Ellen, "but not when you first read it."

"I can see room for both interpretations," said Dan.

"So, what should I do?"

"Leave it out," quipped Nancy. "Even if you didn't intend it, 'Prokofiev's Masterpieces' is just as elitist in its own way as 'I should probably have stopped there' is. And what's all that business about her bruises accusing you? That makes no sense, unless you really are feeling guilty for the elitist comment you're about to make. Just leave the whole thing out."

"The whole thing? From where to where? The part about 'dinner and the symphony' is very important because of what follows."

"How about, 'I've already made arrangements for Saturday night. I'm going out for dinner and to the symphony'," offered Denise.

"That sounds good to me," I replied.

"But does it sound *better*?" asked Nancy, with an edge of worry in her voice. I was beginning to realize just how much courage it had taken for her to speak.

"Do you think it resolves the problem?" I asked her.

"I think it does, but do you? I mean, I didn't mean to change what you wrote. I just wanted to point out my response."

"It reads differently. Whether or not it reads *better* will depend on the other changes we make. How about if I mark it down, and we keep working through the page? Then, when we're done, we'll see how it all sounds."

I marked the suggestion with my pencil and then prepared to continue with my reading. "What do you think of my just going all the way to the end of the first page, so you'll have the whole piece in context, and then we'll go through whatever responses you have?" I suggested, realizing almost immediately that once again I was jumping the gun on decisions I had intended to leave up to the class. As might have been expected, they nodded in agreement, making me realize once again how difficult it is to share power in the classroom. Even so, I felt their approval and hoped that they would come up with more suggestions.

"Dinner and the symphony?" echoed Stephanie, another student in this writing class who had also recently escaped from an abusive marriage. "Out for dinner and to the symphony," she repeated, as though tasting each word. "I know people do that. I know there are people who go out for dinner and to the symphony, but I've never actually known anyone who does that. It must be wonderful."

The chasm, the space between who we are and who we wish to be, between how we live and how we want to live, is always there, sometimes a crack, sometimes a gaping hole, but always, always there. The chasm gaped with Stephanie's remark as she stood less than three feet away from me, yet seemingly a whole world away. I thought of the first essay she had written in this evening writing class, detailing how she had lived for two days in the New York subway with three children, one still a tiny baby, and with fearful memories of the vicious fishing rod her husband had used to discipline her and their children. I thought of her most recent essay, about smashing a cockroach crawling across her mirror with much more violent force than needed, and her exploration of the sources of that violence. I thought of the other student writers in this class, each with a story to tell, all trying, in their writing in particular, and in their pursuit of higher education in general, to reach across that chasm to a different, better life. Given the option to call me "Sharon" or "Dr. Hamilton," most of them chose "Dr. Hamilton," and uttered it with a kind of reverence, not for me, whom they met only once a week and therefore scarcely knew, but for the educational level it proclaims and for the life and background it implies. It conserves the chasm.

I stopped, sensing that something was a little off. "Now that last bit, about what students call me, perhaps I should leave that out for the same reason as the other bit. If anything sounds elitist, that does. I didn't intend it to. I kept revising it, but I'm still not altogether happy with it."

"It doesn't strike me as elitist," said Nancy.

I was suddenly silent, waiting for elaboration.

"I think it's something we can all identify with," said Tamla, who, until this moment, had not participated in the discussion. All heads turned in her direction. "You told us on the first night that we could address you as 'Dr. Hamilton' or as 'Sharon,' whichever made us feel more comfortable. I don't know if you've noticed, but I don't address you at all. Some people in the class call you 'Sharon,' but I don't feel comfortable with that. At the same time, I don't want to be the only one who calls you 'Dr. Hamilton.' So I know exactly what you are saying there."

Déjà vu in spades! These students were confirming the very tensions I had been trying to capture in the text we were working on. I could scarcely contain my excitement as the conversation veered directly in the path of ideas about literacy.

"Didn't you tell us that names and naming are related to power, and that what we call someone establishes the power relationship?" asked Dan. "If you're going to be talking about power relationships, then that part is important, isn't it?"

"That's it!" Nancy hurtled once again into the discussion. "That's the problem in a nutshell! You say we should know very early on why what we are writing is being written. I don't know from this first page why it is being written. It's interesting, but I don't know whether that's because you're our teacher or whether it's because, because—oh, shoot, I've lost it. What was I going to say? Oh, yes, of course, or whether the topic is of interest to me, because, while I know that it's about you, I don't know *why* it's about you. Does that make any sense? To any of you? It just barely makes sense to me."

Denise crossed her arms in thought, and we waited while she formulated what she wanted to say. "We've talked a lot this semester about leads and opening paragraphs. About whether dialogue or some dramatic image can propel the reader right smack into the narrative. About whether that's better than some sort of thesis statement or topical statement—no, wait a minute, not just a statement, that sounds too much like what we did in Freshman Comp, but a sort of topical context—would that be the right phrase?"

"Like what?" asked Jo-Ellen.

Looks passed around the table, but nobody was ready to speak.

Like my students, I was discovering connections between Denise's questions and questions others had raised about the opening part of the book. "I think I know what you're getting at, Denise. I mean, of course I remember those conversations we had, and I deliberately chose to begin with dialogue. I wonder if what you're suggesting is based on the same concern that my editor had."

"What was that?" asked Dan.

"He wanted me to get into the classroom immediately. I used dialogue, but that didn't seem to be what he had expected. I wonder whether he might have wanted to know *why* we were in the classroom, and what the classroom was really all about."

"That makes sense to me," replied Denise.

"I think it makes sense to me, too" added Nancy, "but what do you do about it?"

"Ah, that's the question," I said, although I was already getting a very strong sense of the answer. "That is indeed the question, and you are all in a perfect position to help me with it."

"Really? Oh good," said Denise, smiling and clasping her hands in front of her, in anticipation of how this help would be asked for and given.

"This is a classroom very like the classroom in my narrative. In fact, the issues of power and authority, of motivation and participation that the text explores in this passage have been playing themselves out tonight while we have been working on it. Here's how you can help. I know you all know each other quite well by now, but I would really appreciate it if you would tell each other why you are here, what you hope to accomplish, where you've come from, and where you see yourselves headed."

"Whew," said Nancy in mock concern, "that's a tall order." And then she settled into a more serious tone. "Most times I feel I'm going nowhere, and I don't think you want to know where I've come from. Problems. Disasters. Failures. You name it. I've been there."

"But Nancy," interjected Denise, "we've talked. You know where you want to go, what you want to do. Tell the class."

"I'm so far from being ready. I'm so far from it, it seems ridiculous to tell it. I'd be tempting the fates to send me another disaster."

But Denise would not let her go. "No, Nancy, you're not far from it. We all feel the way you do from time to time, as though life takes us from one problem to another, in directions farther away from where we want to go. But we know, from this class, but also from others, that we are gathering, garnering, getting the kinds of knowledge that can get us there. I don't know if I am saying this right. But what we've learned from this class, specifically, is that by talking and writing about our goals and dreams, we can make something of ourselves. So tell us, Nancy. Because if you won't, I will."

I had no idea how Nancy would react. She stared at Denise with widening eyes that began to swell, but never quite overflowed, with tears. Then she turned toward me and pushed out each word. "I want to write. I want to be a published writer. I want to do something with all the ideas that race through my mind. No, not race through, because they don't leave. They pester me until I write them down. But for all sorts of reasons, I've been resisting. Excuses. It's all excuses. Yes, I want to write. And I promise all of you tonight, I will— no, forget that. I've made promises in the past. I'll promise myself first, and then I'll let you know. But yes, that's why I'm here. I want to write. And I want what I write to help other people, just as this text we're working on tonight has helped me. And that's where I'm headed, however it works out."

And round we went, from Nancy to Denise to Dan to James to Jo-Ellen to Tamla and to all the rest. Stories of dreams and challenges, fears and hopes, successes and disasters. My head whirled with all that they had overcome to get to my classroom and with all they hoped to accomplish in the ensuing years. I went home and rewrote the part I had read to them.

They come to a world where increase in literacy offers promise and hope for a better life. They come from home, from work, from families, from worlds they want to escape to worlds they want to understand. The cramped classroom accepts its continuous ebb and flow of students with the seeming neutrality of shadowless florescence. By five forty-five in the evening they arrive exhausted from the day's demands, sinking tiredly one by one into the haphazard circle of desks. Their energy sinks with them until someone—sometimes it's me, sometimes a fellow student—galvanizes them to discuss a common concern.

Tonight it's Angie, who arrives with an announcement and an invitation. "Dr. Hamilton, I'm having a party on Saturday night to celebrate my divorce. Will you come? And you come too, Stephanie. And you, John. And you and you. All of you. You've all been so encouraging the past few weeks while I've been writing myself through this mess."

'This mess' is the process of escaping her brutal husband, source of the still visible bruises on her face and even more brutal bruises on her soul, evident in every one of the essays and journals she has written this semester.

"I'd love to, Angie," I reply, but I've already made arrangements for Saturday night. I'm going out for dinner and to the symphony."

"Dinner and the symphony?" echoes Stephanie. "Out for dinner and to the symphony," she repeats slowly, as though tasting each word. "I know there are people who go out for dinner and to the symphony, but I've never actually known anyone who does that. I wonder what it would be like."

The gap between who we are and who we wish to be, between how we live and how we want to live is always there, sometimes a crack, sometimes a chasm. Crossing it is a ceaseless human challenge. Those who make the attempt choose from an array of means, depending upon how they perceive and define the nature of the gap. Some define it in terms of happiness, or money, or power, or love. All the students in this class, though very different one from another, share one common determination: they have all decided that education, specifically a literacy-based liberal arts education, will be their means of crossing the gap.

Stephanie's first essay in this class described living for two days in the New York City subway with three children, one still a tiny baby, escaping from the beatings with the fishing rod her husband had used on her and on their children. A later essay anguished over too violently smashing a cockroach crawling across her mirror, and explored the sources of that violence. Stephanie, Angie, and all the other student writers in this class are learning that they have a story to tell, and that telling it may become an impetus to some sort of understanding, insight, and even action.

They are all trying, in their writing in particular and in their pursuit of higher education in general, to reach across their respective gaps to a different, better life. Given the option to call me Sharon or Dr. Hamilton, most of them choose Dr. Hamilton, and utter it with a kind of awe, not of me, whom they meet only one evening a week for four months and therefore scarcely know, but for the educational level the title proclaims, and for the life and background it implies. (Hamilton 1995, 1–2)

I could hardly wait until the next week to show my class the revisions. Their participation in my writing process had played such a crucial role in the most important part of my story—its opening words. But a week is a long time in the life of our modern day commuter students, and by the following class, their attention and passions had turned to different concerns, to another biographical narrative, by Maxine Hong Kingston, that had been their reading assignment.

My editor was pleased with the changes I made in my narrative, and so, silently, they became part of the published version of the text. Last week, almost eighteen months after the class I just described, and more than a year after the publication of the book, Nancy called.

"I'm working in the office of the Public Defender. I'm a paralegal now."

"That's terrific, Nancy."

"I have your book."

"What do you think of the first page?"

"Awesome."

"You know where it came from. Do you remember? Do you see your ideas in there?"

"Of course. That's why I called. In part, that's why I'm where I am."

I smiled as I thought to myself, "And that, Nancy, is why I'm where I am. Because students like you help me learn about teaching and writing." And then I remembered Nancy's promise. "And what about your writing, Nancy?"

"Well, that's how it all happened. I won't bore you with all the details, but I had a couple of friends who were about to lose their kids because they were involved in a lesbian relationship. Their lawyer asked them to present their case in writing, and they asked me to help them with it. The lawyer structured her case on what I had written. Suddenly, I felt what you used to call the power of writing. I used writing to make a difference, just as I had always wanted. And then, something happened. It was probably just a coincidence, but I'm sure it was destiny. I found a flyer from Continuing Studies in the Sunday paper. My eyes fell immediately on the paralegal writing course. I enrolled, loved it, completed the rest of the requirements, and now have my certificate. I write all the time in ways quite different from what I envisioned in your class, but it achieves the same end. What I write makes a difference every day in someone's life."

As the conversation continued, I hoped she could tell how pleased I was for her. I remembered beginning *My Name's Not Susie* many times and giving it up because it seemed more self-indulgent than purposeful. When I began to realize how literacy had transformed my life, how telling my story might make a difference for students seeking to transform their lives, I was able to continue and finish. Like me, Nancy was discovering that writing does not always work the way we envision, but it takes us down new paths and often reveals new purposes. She was now living the text I had been writing. She told me a little more about her job and then asked, "What are you going to write next?"

I paused for a moment, remembering her in my classroom, imagining her now in her new office.

"I don't know, Nancy. Perhaps I'll write about you."

Works Cited

Hamilton, Sharon J. 1995. *My Name's Not Susie: A Life Transformed by Literacy*. Portsmouth, NH: Heinemann.

11

No Secrets

NEAL BOWERS

The poet in the classroom is one of the curiosities of contemporary education. Obliged to bring a solitary occupation into the sputtering fluorescence of public view, the poet is instantly at odds with himself. He knows what he knows about poetry because he is a poet (though he often wonders if he really is). Such are his credentials. In his heart, he realizes he can impart almost nothing of what he knows to anyone else and privately believes himself to know very little. The poetry, after all, is the matter of central importance and says whatever needs to be said. Nonetheless, there he is, in a room aswirl with chalk dust, listening to students read their poems, trying his hardest to encourage creativity.

After a recent graduate poetry workshop session, in which I made my usual effort to shun authority and become just another voice in the circle of writers, I received the following e-mail message from one of my best students:

> I think that, as a class, we're underestimating the importance of artistic vision. What is missing, I think, in many of our works including my own, is a coherent understanding of the world and therefore a meaningful comment on it. Interesting, fresh images and nice language do not make a poem—in my opinion. In the poetry that matters to me, something behind the words is at work making the images and phrases more than they would be in a vacuum. And I don't mean the reader, either.
>
> The artist who will have something to say is asking who she is. Whether she really wants to know. What all this stuff means, at this moment, to her. Not just "what am I hearing buzzing in my ears?"—write down what

buzzes or tweaks, and there's my poem. I've read some of your work, and I don't believe for one minute that that's what you consider poetry to be.

In an age of relativity, political correctness, and diversity, heaven forbid you should impose a rigid definition, i.e., any definition of poetry on your students! Yikes, you might just hurt one of our feelings or discourage a budding genius. But if we were poets, we'd write what we felt compelled to, no matter what you said. Some students would write exactly the type of poetry that I don't appreciate, and do it brilliantly, and I'd be glad to bow to their right to do it, and to their vision.

But at least let's talk about what poetry may and may not be, and what we're trying to accomplish through ours.

Because I insist from the outset of each workshop that my views are far from definitive and that other perspectives are equally valid, I knew my student's remarks were offered as a way to contribute to the class. She, in turn, knew I would not dismiss her advice out of hand but would give her a respectful hearing. That her forthrightness still required conviction and courage should be obvious to anyone who has ever been a student, even in a very open and democratic class.

What surprised me was her bluntness. Perhaps the informality of e-mail emboldened her, or perhaps she had simply held back as long as she could. As an older student with a graduate degree in English, she had enrolled on special status just to take the poetry writing class, squeezing it into her busy life as a full-time editor at a local agricultural business. Privately, I regarded her as one of my most promising poetry writing students in years. Her life experience gave her abundant material for poems, and she was verbally talented. Moreover, she seemed to know exactly what a poem was and what she wanted it to do. Possibly, she was hoping to test her notions of poetry against mine, but it seemed more likely that she was determined to extract from me the "secret of poetry."

Teaching poetry writing seems deceptively simple: All the instructor has to do is read and comment on student poems. Anyone observing one of my workshops might think my approach the easiest of all. Because I refuse to be the final authority, choosing instead to add my voice to the general discussion of each poem, I am seldom heard holding forth and try never to dominate any evaluation. Sometimes it is difficult to hold my tongue; and I occasionally think the sessions would be less demanding of me if I simply insisted that everyone write a certain kind of poem—no arcane allusions, no foreign expressions, no abstractions, and absolutely no poems about poetry. Being proscriptive or prescriptive would simplify everything and save me from having to follow a new and unpredictable trail through each workshop meeting.

Mindful that "poetry" has never been adequately defined and that practitioners of the art have represented it in an extraordinary range of styles, I feel that stepping forward with a single view and insisting that my students adopt it would be limiting and misrepresentative. Still, it is not easy for members of the class to take charge. As soon as the discussion of student poems begins, the poet-teacher is out in the open. Slouched in his seat in the circle, he may try to be just the facilitator; but everyone knows he's the designated expert and waits for his opinion or judgment or whatever it is the guru at such a gathering is expected to dispense—wisdom, I suppose.

All of us who teach begin with the understanding that we cannot know everything. Hard though it may be to admit, knowledge is limited for even the most expert of teachers. For the workshop instructor, whose field of knowledge is marked by divergent views of the very nature of poetry and whose discipline has no clearly defined pedagogy, knowledge can be a dangerous thing if it is too certain. Strong views are not off-limits, of course, but they must be represented in their proper place among a great many other strong views. What my graduate student wanted from me was something I could not in good faith provide.

Moreover, her letter evoked all my self-doubts. Just writing poems seems presumptuous to me, and I am often haunted by the fear that whatever I have to say in my own work is of little consequence. The dense shadow of literature, the collective work of those writers regarded as important, is chilling. How can I presume to shoulder in among them? In the classroom, I sometimes feel like an impostor; and my anxiety keeps me from presenting myself as an authority or, heaven help me, as a poetic genius. Essentially, my personal challenge in the workshop is to hide in the open.

My demanding student refused to let me get away with my usual evasions. Because she had been forthright with me in her e-mail message, I felt a responsibility to be so in return when I sent the following e-mail reply, believing myself at the time to be entering into a dialogue:

Dear Anne:

Thanks for your thoughtful letter. Because I regard your work so highly (yes, your poetry) and value your participation in the workshop, I'm keenly interested in anything you have to say about what we're doing and/or saying about the process of writing poems.

After a great many years spent in the company of bright, often verbally gifted students, I've decided that not very many of them will ever make a place for themselves in the world of poetry. You might say they lack artistic vision; I might say they lack the true poetic gift. This doesn't mean that they can't write respectable poems or that their work isn't important to them. It does mean that most will never attain the status of Marianne Moore or Robert Lowell. Should I bring this reality to the center of our weekly discussions, it would have a deadening effect; so I leave it to each workshop member to grapple with this demon privately. All of us who write are obliged to cope with the vacillations of self-regard—feeling like a genius one day and a fool the next. Personally, I cannot represent myself to my students as a genius or even as someone with poetic vision. Whatever I think of myself as a poet, on the good days and the bad, is something best kept to myself, I suspect.

Actually, I have no rigid, formal definition of poetry to offer. Privately, I know what a poem is to me; and I have strong opinions about what constitutes good and bad poetry and about individual poets. To impose my quirky views on the class would be to foreclose the process of discovery I believe to be essential to each poet's development. Encumbering a young writer with a view of poetry I've worked out for my own purposes over the past twenty-five years would be like loading her backpack with my own provisions and then telling her to hike wherever she chooses. Anyhow, by this point in the term, you must have come to know how loath I am to be autocratic. I hate people who think they have the answer to anything, and I refuse to be one of them. So it's not that I'm cringing under the shadow of political correctness, diversity, or some kind of relativity; I'm simply expressing my personality.

Everything anyone wants to know about what I think about poetry is, by now, on the page somewhere. My critical books and articles are in the library, as are my collections of poems and my poems in various journals. Every word I write as a scholar and as a poet says, "This is what I think poetry is." Doubtless, every word I utter in class, regardless of my wish to give my students as much space as possible, says the same thing. But the message is implicit rather than overt.

Definitely, I think we should talk about what poetry may or may not be and what each workshop member is trying to accomplish through poetry; but I don't think it's my place to act as the judge in such a discussion. My job is to give up all my secrets, scant as they are, and to say, "Here's my reaction to your poem and to your work overall, but it is only *my* reaction. You must find your own way."

Just between you and me, I don't think anyone under the age of forty can expect to write powerful poetry. It takes at least four decades for the world to worry an individual into the proper understanding and receptivity to be a poet. Poets over forty may not have any more answers than their younger counterparts, but they've had to ask the questions for a longer time. That's often what shows up behind the lines of poetry that we admire and value, that thing that transcends voice. Call it experience or even vision, if you like. Consequently, the message I could deliver to my poetry writing students, but don't, is simply this: "Bear down for a long apprenticeship."

Thanks for sharing your thoughts with me. I'd be pleased to continue this discussion via e-mail or personal conference.

Looking back at this electronic communication from the distance of a year, I wonder if I was perhaps too direct. I sound to myself much stricter than I meant to be; and the letter seems, in its laying down of the law-according-to-Bowers, to contradict my disavowal of authority. I certainly didn't mean to have the last word on the subject and hoped my invitation to continue the exchange would be accepted. When I next saw the student, I asked if she had received my message and urged her to respond in whatever way she wished. She indicated that she would be in touch with another e-mail letter, but nothing came until after the term was over—a complimentary thank-you for the course. Apparently, I foreclosed the discussion by sounding too much like the dogmatic instructor I was working hard not to be. I fear that what I really said to her was, "I decline to be authoritative, and that's the final word on the subject."

In addition, I probably confirmed her suspicion that I could, indeed, tell everyone what a poem is and separate the contenders from the also-rans, if I wanted. In effect, I passed judgment on everyone in the class and found all of them wanting. A note of condescension, the very last thing I intended, bleeds through my words; and a reasonable person could conclude that I do not set precise standards and use them to evaluate student poems simply because no student could measure up. So much for my noble intentions.

What continues to trouble me is the realization that I have no better response for my student than the one I gave. However I try to express it, my view of the workshop is inherently ambivalent. I continue to teach it, even though I worry that workshops in general have corrupted poetry, and even though I personally disliked the few workshops I took when I was in graduate school. Sitting around, trying to think of something bright to say about a fellow student's poem, was not my idea of how to become a poet. I preferred, instead, to be off on my own, reading and writing. Moreover, I never believed that anyone could be taught how to write poetry because I regarded poetry as a calling rather than as a profession. Poets do not choose their craft; it chooses them; and no amount of talk within a classroom will make the difference. Privately, I've always thought the best service I could provide to my workshop students would be to send them off to their separate lives to read, write, and think about poetry.

Even so, most of my students enjoy the workshop and many seem to need it for the stimulation and support that are otherwise lacking. I assume that few of them imagine a future in which they are the poet laureate, although the majority have ambition enough to want to publish. In most respects, they remind me of myself when I was in my mid-twenties, driven by an almost idealistic need to be artistic and to say something powerful and memorable. Balancing my misgivings about the workshop with a desire to facilitate and to honor the impulse that brings students into a poetry writing class, I do my best to teach them what I know. That I withhold from them my strong belief that only a small fraction of them will ever write well enough to publish books and that none of them will become poets of note within the literary world at large is a product of kindness or cowardice, maybe of both. To pass such judgments openly, I would first have to identify myself either as a failed poet or as one of the chosen few. Otherwise, I would have no position of authority from which to issue proclamations. Understandably, I think, I am reluctant to strike either pose.

My student e-mailer simply identified me as someone with insider information. Perhaps the climber who fails to reach the summit possesses as much knowledge as the one who stamps the imprint of his shoes in the pure snow at the top. What the novice wants from either one is the benefit of his experience. The problem for me is that I consider myself still to be climbing. Having not yet come off the mountain, in victory or defeat, I do not have a whole story to tell. Perhaps this incompleteness was what my apprentice poet sensed. If so, the information she felt I was withholding from the class was not about poetry but about myself. My almost testy reply to her letter certainly makes sense in this more personal context, as I reacted the way a person might when his privacy has been invaded.

Hearing in my own voice a mixture of self-defensiveness and professional formality, I realize how untenable the creative writing teacher's position is. Obliged by the job to be a practitioner of the genre he teaches, the workshop instructor must first be a writer. But being a writer and teaching writing are far from the same thing. I would write poetry if I were a linguistics teacher or if I were in some line of work outside the university, because poetry is an intensely personal and necessary part of my life. While I certainly don't mind letting my students know this, I am less willing to share with them my ambitions, doubts, frustrations, and rationalizations. In fact, I try to keep most of these things hidden even from myself. Like the climber who has trained himself not to look down for fear of falling, I keep my focus on the immediate hand- or toehold.

My assertion that I give up all my poetry secrets to my students is true only by default. There are no secrets to confide, at least not about poetry, which remains mysterious, even to its most ardent devotees, and everything that is to be learned about it must be found in the process of writing it. Apart from a little practical advice about such matters as form and diction or titles and endings, I cannot reveal to anyone the secret of writing a good or even a passable poem. My tinkering during workshop discussions always focuses on mechanical things, and I try never to judge a poem a success or a failure, preferring instead to comment on what works and what doesn't, sticking close to the particulars without backing up to look at the whole construction and assess its worth.

Nonetheless, I recognize that my student's request for a more judgmental approach is reasonable. If I oblige her, however, and begin labeling the elect and the damned, I will have to tell a truth that may be destructive for all of us. This is the door behind which I have locked my secrets, the door she rattled with her request. Suppose I open it to expose the strutting ego, the supremely self-assured extreme of myself that can draw only unfavorable comparisons between my work and anyone else's. How would this insufferable fraction of me contribute to the education of my students? Or say we bring out of the shadows the whimpering other who has convinced himself that all poetry, including his own, is a sham. His ranking of every poem as dead-last probably wouldn't be inspirational.

A less-polarized version of myself seems a better choice as the workshop instructor. Perhaps my student drew the same conclusion, after having a whiff of the other options that arose between the lines of my e-mail text. This, too, would account for her silence after our initial exchange of letters. While I have whimsically thought of teaching my next poetry workshop as if I were possessed of multiple personalities—five weeks for the egotist, five for the pragmatist, and five for the more user-friendly Neal Bowers—I don't think I could. Anyhow, I feel certain my student wasn't asking for such a sideshow.

At odd moments I worry that I missed her point entirely. Maybe she would have been satisfied with my old glib responses: If you have to ask what a poem is, you will never appreciate poetry; and if you need someone else to tell you whether your own poems are good or bad, then you're not cut out to be a poet. Possibly a little sententiousness would have done the trick, and I wouldn't have had to offer any kind of apologia for my teaching strategies. That it took so little to set me to babbling, like a crook with a ready alibi, makes me question my own comfort level within the workshop.

Signs of my discomfort are nowhere more apparent than in the following poem, which I handed out at the first meeting of my graduate workshop the semester before my e-mailing correspondent appeared on the scene:

THE MUSE TAKES OFF HER GLOVES

To speak for the great silence,
it is not necessary first to take notes
or make an outline or rehearse anything.

As an emissary out of nowhere,
with blank portfolio,
you are fully qualified.

The sovereign emptiness you represent
is older than any place
and has no boundaries.

Because the word is also the breath,
everything you say
is expiration.

Each page, a monument
to language,
displays its epitaph.

Nothing you say
can equal the eloquence
of wordlessness.

Now, write.

I distributed the poem without comment, and my students never mentioned it. Like a shared wound, we kept it to ourselves, although I don't know how we managed to conduct workshop business with such a manifesto of loneliness and uselessness foregrounding everything we did. At the time I wrote the poem, I had my students and myself as their teacher clearly in mind. In fact, the poem's original title was "For the Workshop," but I decided to credit (or blame) the muse rather than myself for such a bleak credo. I suppose the poem was intended, in part, to diminish expectations that I would be a brilliant guide to the wonderful realm of poetic vision. Primarily, it was meant as the bluntest and hardest challenge I could put to my students—my way of saying, "This is no parlor game we're playing."

Year by year, writing poems becomes harder for me, and teaching poetry writing seems more and more like a pretense. The attempt to transform such an exquisitely difficult and private obsession into a public undertaking must inevitably lead to discrepancies between student expectations and the instructor's ability and willingness to deliver the goods. Nowhere else in the English curriculum is the relationship between the personal and the professional more complicated, and I can think of no other area within which a simple request for definitions and judgments would provoke in the instructor such resistance and argumentation. This essay itself is testament to my uneasiness.

For my students in upcoming classes, perhaps I should create a home page on the Internet, a site that I could update daily to reflect the changes in my personal life as a poet. Anyone curious to know how things are going for me in my continuing struggle to utter the ineffable could visit my page and find out. I imagine their faces lit by the glow of their video display screens, gray-white or queasy green, staring into some portion of the hideous secret. I'll bet I could even get a small grant from the university to undertake such a project.

What I prefer, though, is to have my students read my poetry. Everything I know about writing can be found there, along with a few truths that transcend the temporal shiftings of my ego. My poetry is infinitely smarter than I am. That's my worst-kept secret, as anyone who knows both me and my poetry will attest. To understand this seeming contradiction, it is perhaps necessary to be a poet or at least to have a poet's sensibility. Therein may lie a useful shibboleth.

At my best in the poetry writing classroom I am irrelevant, as my students build their own supportive local network. At my worst, I am a partial source of wisdom, inadvertently implying that I could be wholly wise and give up the secrets of poetry. Conflicted as I am, students like Anne give me hope that I will not do serious damage to the best writers who enroll in my classes. I often think of her assertion of creative autonomy—"if we were poets, we'd write what we felt compelled to, no matter what you said"—and it gives me faith in my students when faith in myself continues to vacillate. Anne already knows the secret—she doesn't need me.

12

Subverting the
Academic Master Plot

LYNN Z. BLOOM

Teachers' Tales—The Master Plots

Teachers' tales out of school, the stories we love to hear, seem to have two basic master plots, both with happy endings. Plot One shows the teacher-as-practitioner playing the role of what North calls "television doctor." In this "miracle-cure scenario" (46) the teacher is confronted with a new, or chronic, problem that defies solution. This mystery malady infects the entire class or individual students, who for unfathomable reasons can't master the requisite skills or learn the lessons du jour. The tortured teacher, who has previously leapt all problems with a single bound, is stymied. She paces and ponders, buttonholing colleagues with the Problem That Will Not Die.

Picture, for example, Mina Shaughnessy "sitting alone in the worn urban classroom" where her "severely underprepared" freshmen have "just written their first essays." In astonishment and despair, the Master Teacher ponders their "stunningly unskilled" writing. However, unable even to "define the task" or "sort out the difficulties," she can "only sit there, reading and rereading the alien papers, wondering what had gone wrong and trying to understand what [she] at this eleventh hour of [her] students' academic lives could do about it" (vii).

The universe is out of step until the teacher through accident or intention stumbles on a solution, trying first one, then another remedy until fortune favors the prepared mind and—voila! The miracle cure is at hand. *Errors and Expectations* metamorphoses into *Great Expectations*; Shaughnessy now has "no difficulty assessing the work to be done nor believing that it *can* be done" (vii). The students' problems are solved; "Oh, Dr. [Shaugh-

116

nessy], this is so much better! How can I ever thank you'" (North, 46). Other teachers are inspired; Shaughnessy's ragtime band marches on in triumph.

Although Plot Two might be considered a variation of Plot One, for it too ultimately has a miracle cure, this version is inspired by the Book of Job instead of the Book of Mina. In this story, for whatever reasons, the class begins to deteriorate; students and teacher are either marching to different drummers or else not marching at all. Unless a Dramatic Change happens in a hurry—prompted by the teacher's agonizing reappraisal, the students' spontaneous turnaround, or some form of deus ex machina—the class is doomed to entropic disaster. The teacher, formerly arrogant in her confidence that she can work miracles, has been thoroughly humbled by forces greater than she. The dark night of the soul infects students and teacher alike; Dostoyevsky reigns in a Kafkaesque universe.

But wait! The Dramatic Change does in fact happen, and redemption, resurrection are at hand. Teacher and students have learned An Important Lesson together and, sadder but much much wiser, have achieved Victory Against Great Odds. Praise the Lord; the beat goes on. I myself have structured "Finding a Family, Finding a Voice" according to this plot, which tells how my course in "Teaching Composition" for new TAs had become an unstructured, off-balance response to a crisis (no textbooks, students who themselves were not teaching). In this weekly guerrilla theater, by sharing my own risk-taking writing-in-progress (a very personal, very exploratory version of "Why I Write"), I and the students "effected a paradigm shift. Within two months' time," I wrote, "my class had changed from students in the process of learning about teaching in order to teach writing, to students in the process of becoming writers in order to teach writing" (62, 64).

We live by these master plots; they exalt every valley and make the rough places plain. These are the success stories that, in one form or another, teachers love to hear, and live to tell. But the story I am finally able to disclose to you here, nearly two decades after the dismal events, fits neither of these ultimately exhilarating plots. It is the story of the worst course I ever taught, the worst teaching I've ever done, the most students who didn't stay the course—and right they were. Since even the greatest of teachers must have dwelt in Disaster City on occasion, I assume that such stories are legion, buried in the secret files of our minds. Like accounts of illegal abortions, these seldom attain the public status of lore or legend—and when they do, they happen to someone else.

Well, this one happened to me, with my unwitting—indeed eager—complicity. It is, at best, a cautionary tale of some of the bad things that can go wrong when a course and a teacher and a class and a curriculum inadvertently conspire to subvert the academic rhythm of a semester, flexible and forgiving, by trying to cram what should have occurred over fifteen weeks into a five-day summer session. Six months ago, when I began to write this, I continued to attribute all the difficulties to the course's truncated time frame. But no longer. As I have been pondering this debacle I have come to understand that yes, the compressed format provided insurmountable constraints, but these were exacerbated by my own ignorance. I was a stranger in strange lands, in a university new to me, in an unfamiliar school (of Education) with its own (and to this English professor) strange culture, trying to introduce new doctoral students to a new discipline that neither they nor I could have mastered in a week's time. The redemption from this disaster lies in the warning I offer here.

Academic Rhythm

I live by the generous rhythm of the academic year. Martin and I, already wedded to the semester system, were married during the shimmering legato of a summer vacation between master's and doctoral study. Our children were born during summer vacations. We've always moved—for new academic jobs—during summer vacations. Indeed vacations, particularly summer's three capacious months and the punctuation of Christmas break, which always moves presto, no matter how many calendar days are actually allocated, serve a myriad of academic purposes. For vacations make possible the time out of time—an increasingly rare luxury in today's downsized, outsourced, overstressed workaday world—that provides the steady heartbeat for the entire academic year: the opportunity to read, write, do research, reinvent old courses and create new ones.

Summer school courses disrupt two sets of natural academic rhythms, the summer's stately pace and the semester's measured tempo. Attempts to adapt the semester's customary pace to summer school's double, or triple, time may work in courses that consist primarily of reading as the way of learning—students can read more, or read faster. Or they can read less. Or teachers can expect less, although I am in Shaughnessy's camp and teach with great expectations, in all seasons.

Indeed, I've found that the summer school mode most conducive to student learning without compromise on my part is the intensive workshop format, such as that used in the numerous sites of the National Writing Project, and in the Martha's Vineyard Summer Workshops. The long days, happy nights in which students can get to know and work (and yes, play) with one another, the built-in two-to-three-day breaks (good for library or field work and major writing), are supplemented by an extra month after the course ends so the students can complete an extensive term project. This schedule gives the students, mostly full-time teachers themselves, ample time to read widely, to reflect, to engage in various modes of research, to write, and to revise—maybe even more than an ordinary semester would allow.

Perhaps it was three satisfying summers of teaching in a National Writing Project's five-week intensive workshop format that led me to accept an invitation from Prestige U to teach a summer school course, "Research I, Introduction to Research Methods." Those summers of team teaching with an Ed School colleague and a veteran high school English curriculum supervisor—as well as the Writing Project participants, smart and energetic—had led me to believe I understood, even shared, the schoolteachers' view of the composition studies universe.

"You can use whatever time frame you want," offered the dean's henchperson, "three times a week for the entire summer, every day for six or eight weeks, half-days for two weeks, or," when I still did not answer, "full days plus some evenings for a week." Even the anemic salary, scrunched into a single week, appeared robust. So I leapt like a trout at the one-week format—the one most congruent with our family's summer plans. That this format proved totally uncongenial to every principle of teaching and learning that works well in a semester format should have been no surprise to me or to the sponsoring institution, for that matter, especially in the bailiwick—devoted to the study of education—where I was to teach.

A similar—so I believed—course had been the capstone of my own formal doctoral study at another even more prestigious university—required of all students not the moment they entered the program but after they'd passed the doctoral prelims. Its virtue lay in the enforced opportunity to write one's dissertation prospectus, and to rewrite it dramatically, under supervision, every week for fifteen weeks until we got it right. As a consequence of innumerable visions and revisions the project, always intellectually interesting, became doable, elegant, and refined—and of course refined and adapted again many times during the actual research. "No problem to condense that course," I thought, for at the time I had never met a course I couldn't teach, "as long as I can plan it thoroughly in advance." A meticulous syllabus would see me through.

Alien Nation

I had come, fresh from the country, to the holy city of Byzantium on a blazing July Sunday afternoon loaded, I thought, for bear. I had already sent ahead a syllabus, detailed hour by hour, and a stack of journal articles to be photocopied as the required reading.

My underventilated undergraduate dorm room, windows sealed shut and accessible only by elevator and a fistful of keys, was home away from home. It reeked of eau de Big Mac and throbbed around the clock with heavy-metal pulsations. When I finally fell asleep, they even penetrated the anxiety dream that reliably precedes each semester. This one differed from the usual in which I'd forgotten my books, or syllabus, or a critical article of clothing—only to discover its absence when I faced the students and opened my book bag—or took off my coat. In this one, however, the dean called me the night before class was to start to say that he'd changed my assignment. Instead of teaching composition I was to teach calculus. "But I don't know anything about teaching calculus," I responded. "You can *read*, can't you?" he thundered. "Just pick up the book and go to class and read faster than the students."

On Monday morning I arrived a half hour early at the frigid seminar room where the class was to meet from 8:00 A.M. to 5:00 P.M. for the next five days. Several students were there already. Greying and grave, they eyed my cotton shift and sandals with calculated impassivity. I began to shiver despite the fact that here, too, the windows were sealed shut.

The early arrivals' not-so-casual conversation made their agenda very clear. "Our own schools have recently let out. We're glad to be here for only a week; it won't interrupt the rest of the summer very much," said a woman in a twin sweater set and pearls. "With Prestige's evening and summer courses we can teach full-time and still work on our degrees. And of course we expect A's." This was spoken with a smile. "We're entitled to A's," quickly added another, whose navy suit and pumps signaled a person accustomed to Being in Charge—whether of a classroom, a department, or an entire school didn't matter. "Admission to the doctoral program automatically guarantees this." There was no smile. What did an A here mean? I wondered. Were A's in fact a doctoral entitlement? Well, they'd have to do the work, and then we'd see.

By 8:00 A.M. the room, designed for twenty, was crowded with forty around the seminar table—an astonishing enrollment even for a required course. "Let's get acquainted," I chirped. "You don't know me" (I had no reputation at that school as a teacher, nor anywhere as a researcher in the field of education). "You can call me Lynn, and I'd like to call you by your first names."

"Here we call our professors by their titles and they call us by ours," shot a slender, bearded young man in jeans. His glittering eye fixed on mine. "You *are Doctor*, aren't you?"

Ordinarily I'd have joked, "Not a *real* doctor." That morning I simply said, "Yes. A Ph.D."

"My name is Mister Barber, *A.B.D.*, and I want to know why you don't have an Ed.D. This is a School of Education, and an Ed.D. is our normative degree."

"What's the difference?"

"*You* should know."

Even though he shouldn't have asked, he was right. I should have known that because I was the creation of an English Department, my understanding of the meaning of research was very different from that of the Ed School faculty and students. Research in English—at least in the research institution from which I had come—was theoretical rather than applied; text-oriented, not classroom-based; qualitative rather than quantitative; analytic rather than descriptive. When I'd taught a comparable course to English grad students we always skipped the math to cut to the humanities chase—theory; philosophy; rhetorical analysis; case studies replete with character, plot, and resolution. I recognized that *CCC* and *RTE* of the time revealed very different research paradigms, but since I'd never had a doctoral student in Education before, I'd never had to figure out why.

As I distributed Xerox after Xerox, I tried to introduce the course. Most of the students, I had been told before I came, were newly admitted to the doctoral program. All that I knew about Prestige's expectations of the course came from the catalog description. I told them, "Research I will be, as the catalog explains, your introduction to the specialized professional literature and to the methodology of composition studies research. Because the scope of this course, like many that focus on the state of the art in any field, exceeds that of the existing textbooks, I—and you—will have to tell each other stories about how our teaching experiences connect with those journal articles."

I ventured a smile at the noncommittal faces. "As you can see by the syllabus"—I felt as if I were droning on, even though the class had been in session less than five minutes—"we'll be spending half-day segments on overviews of some of the major methodologies of composition studies research, as represented by well-known, well-regarded studies in the field. We'll look at methods ranging from teacher lore and teacher-as-researcher to case histories; to clinical research emphasizing small and large group studies, short- and long-term; to assessment of reading and writing. Because the field, new as it is, is changing so fast, these methods are exemplified primarily in the journal articles I'm giving you."

This scheme anticipated a combination of the topic areas and procedures later discussed in North's *The Making of Knowledge in Composition* and White's *Teaching and Assessing Writing*. Had these books been available at the time—along with Lauer and Asher's *Composition Research: Empirical Designs*; Tate's bibliographic overview; and alternative paradigms to North, such as Kirsch and Sullivan's *Methods and Methodology in Composition Research* and Gere's *Into the Field*—the course, even in a one-week format, might have been manageable.

It occurred to me as I was talking that I should have asked a Prestige faculty member what the course usually covered. Now, even if the map I had prepared was inadequate to navigate this unknown territory, it was already too late to change. So I soldiered on. "As you can see from the syllabus, this course, short though it is, will culminate in a term project that requires you to conceptualize and design a research project. With luck, it will prove to be a model for your dissertation research."

The class erupted with questions. "How much time do we have after this week is up to turn in our papers?" "Would three months be enough—by mid-October?" I replied. "I'd like to allow some turnaround time so I can comment on a preliminary draft." "Our annual bonuses depend on the grades being turned in before Labor Day"—what I saw by then would be all I'd get. "How long do the papers have to be?" My usual answer, "Write until you've said what you have to say and then stop" would hardly suffice. "How many outside sources do we have to use?" How could I answer that when I didn't know what they were writing on? "Where can we find these sources?" "What are the summer library hours? Is it open on Sundays?" I didn't even know where the library was. "What else will our grades be based on?" Attendance and class participation seemed too juvenile for this obviously mature group. There would be no time for them to prepare reading-response notebooks or literature reviews during the week we were meeting, and it would be hard—in these days B.C.E. (Before Computer Email)—to collect and respond to such work once we left campus. I said, "I'll. . . I'll have to let you know."

During these preliminaries I became aware of considerable rolling of the eyes among Mr. Barber and two other bluejeaned peers. And then it hit me. What was an A.B.D. doing in this course for new doctoral students? I could have asked, but the answer—any answer—would only create complications. We were going to stick to the syllabus, by God, so that I, at least, could stay afloat for the week.

And so we did, at least on Day One. Contrary to my preferred format of interactive class discussion interspersed with smaller groups that focus on particular issues, I did most of the talking—all morning about writing process research, all afternoon about issues of language teaching and linguistic research. The strict constructionists, ardent champions of current traditional grammar, listened with distant politeness to my stories of other systems of grammar—structural, transformational, formal, and informal. Then they asked, "But how can the pupils do sentence combining properly if they don't label the parts of speech?" "Why should we bother with deep structure when the students already have trouble diagramming the surface structure?"

"You'll be better able to answer those questions tomorrow morning," I said, wondering if my own sentences were still coherent after eight hours of practically nonstop speech. I continued, "After you've read the Chomsky material tonight."

The class jerked to attention. "What reading tonight?" asked Mrs. Sanders, a woman whose take-charge manner pegged her as a principal.

"What's on the syllabus, of course."

"Doctor Bloom," she enunciated with precision, "You need to understand that most of us have a long drive to get here in the morning, and we'll be going home in the rush hour. We have other responsibilities once we're there. There's no way we can read a dozen articles a night, let alone absorb them. Especially," she added, "when we already have a backlog of today's articles that no one could read in advance."

She added, "Just tell us the two most important ones and we can at least skim those."

"Every single reading is important." I replied. "Every single reading deals with a different aspect of the field, and every single hour of the day's lectures is predicated on your knowledge of the readings. Except," I paused, trying to calm down, "Wednesday afternoon, when another lecturer will run all of us through the boot camp basics of statistics." These were concepts I barely remembered from the single undergraduate course I'd taken fifteen years earlier: ANOVA, Beta weights, Chi squares, Likert scales, multiple correlation, one- and two-tailed statistical tests, threats to internal validity, and Type I and Type II errors. "You won't need to be able to do the actual math at this stage," I offered, "but knowing the terminology will help you read the research articles." Which they weren't about to do.

"Well," I finally said, "if you have to choose, start with Elliot Mishler's 'Meaning In Context: Is There Any Other Kind?' It's just come out and it will help to make sense of everything else you read. And the Xeroxed section of Emig's *The Composing Process of Twelfth Graders*. We'll be discussing narrative research methods in the afternoon."

"Such as. . . " asked Mr. Barber.

"Oh, teacher stories focusing on practical wisdom and teacher-as-researcher, some interviews and case histories, mostly."

"Anything else?" he persisted, his gaze unflinching.

What was he driving at? "We'll take it up tomorrow." The students talked among themselves—but not to me—and surged into the steaming summer sunset.

The Cooked and the Raw

The next morning I began with, "What are good research questions?" in hopes of warming up the room, which was even colder than the preceding day. "How do we know they're good?" "How could a question be translated into a workable research design—say, for your term papers?"

"Excuse me," offered a middle-aged woman who had taken notes non-stop on Monday. "My name is Mrs. Miller. This is my first doctoral course. You just gave us the syllabus yesterday, and we haven't had a chance to read much." She looked embarrassed. "I'm sorry, but I can't answer your question responsibly until I've done more reading and thinking. At the moment I haven't a clue about what would be a good question to ask—or a bad one. Until now I'd never thought about research designs, ever. How can I invent one out of thin air?"

"You're right," I began, ignoring the groans of Mr. Barber and his two pals. "It's not possible for someone new to research, no matter how experienced you are as a teacher or writer to understand at the outset the research issues and models that you're here to learn about." I smiled and she smiled back. "This five-day seminar will just scratch the surface."

As I spoke, the import of these words began to sink in. How, indeed, in this brief span of time could the students even learn enough terminology, let alone the research literature in their chosen area—whatever that was to be— well enough to join in the ongoing dialogue in the academic parlor, as Kenneth Burke envisioned? Even when they did find a research focus, they'd need to let the ideas marinate long enough to make them their own. Would it be possible to devise a workable research design at this stage of their graduate study? Any design would predictably require a number of revisions, and consultations in connection with each one. Even with express mail this would be a stretch to accomplish from a distance. But the entire course was built around this task.

"I'll try to confer individually with everyone this week, and we can at least map the terrain." Where would the extra twenty-five hours come from in the next three days to make good on this desperate promise?

"Well, I know what I'm going to do," announced a pretty peroxide blonde. "In my experience, rule-oriented grammar drill is the best way to teach students to write well. My students always ace the SATs, and their newspaper—I'm the advisor—has won state awards three years in a row." Her crimson smile was triumphant. "In fact," she asserted, "Drilling the rules is the *only* good way to ensure that students will write properly. My term paper will prove I'm right. That paper will be the basis of the thesis that my dissertation research will prove." Several of her peers nodded in approval. "What a wonderful subject," said one, ignoring my surprised silence.

I couldn't imagine that Prestige would let its students investigate an issue that even at the time had been thoroughly discredited. However, there were already so many things I hadn't anticipated at Prestige that I asked, "So what else do you think would be good term paper topics?"

"What about an ethnographic study?" interposed Mr. Barber.

My hesitation did not escape his notice. What was "ethnography"? I was as startled to hear this unfamiliar term as I had been when someone complimented me at a professional meeting for having done "a pioneering study in protocol analysis"—a method so unusual at the time that it had no label. Mr. Barber had me exactly where he wanted—up against the wall. With no context, I hadn't a clue. I took a deep breath and said, "What's ethnography?"

"You don't know what ethnography is? Well, let me tell you. We've"—he gestured toward his two companions—"just finished a research course in ethnographic methodology with Shirley Brice Heath"—whose early innovations and methodological sophistication had yet to appear in *Ways With Words*, the transformative work that would make ethnographic research as standard a tool in schools of education as it was in anthropology and that would later win her a MacArthur "genius" award. "We can't do our doctoral research with her because she's moving to Stanford. But we signed up for this course to lay out the groundwork for our dissertations. If we get the methodology worked out this summer we can do our classroom fieldwork in the fall. But you," his face reddened with anger, "you don't even know what ethnography is. I didn't pay eight hundred fifty dollars in tuition for this course to listen to low-level grammar projects. I know how to do statistics. And I can't stand your silly stories." Even then, telling stories was for me as natural as telling the truth.

"Why don't you drop the course?" I could hardly get the words out.

"I've tried. There's some rule that the registrar won't waive."

"I'm sure if you hold your ground you'll get a refund." Mr. Barber and his two colleagues quickly stuffed the day's Xeroxes into their bookbags and marched out. "If anyone else wishes to leave, please go now." My words reverberated in the frozen air.

No one moved, but I knew that from then on the course was irredeemable. I would never be able to regain the authority that for Mr. Barber and his associates I had never held in the first place. I would like to be able to say that with the malcontents' departure the course immediately shifted into the overdrive I work for in all my classes—high energy, low friction, full speed ahead. But when I try to recollect the particulars of the rest of that very long week it is as if I had been anesthetized. Through memory's translucent scrim the course topics, the visiting statistician, and the students pass in slow motion, with the sound turned off. I am giving lectures no one can hear, holding soundless conferences with every student before class, during lunch, late in the afternoon, throughout each exhausting evening. But this class has shattered into discrete fragments at the utterance of "ethnography," and its members float off into space—some beyond reach, the rest to alternative universes, from which they send me term papers better than they should be. The best is on teaching writing by teaching grammar.

Works Cited

Bloom, Lynn Z. 1990. "Finding a Family, Finding a Voice: A Writing Teacher Teaches Writing Teachers." *Journal of Basic Writing* 9(2): 3–14. Reprinted in *Writer's Craft, Teacher's Art: Teaching What We Know,* edited by Mimi Schwartz. Portsmouth, NH: Boynton-Cook.

Chomsky, Noam. 1957. *Syntactic Structures.* The Hague, Netherlands: Mouton.

Emig, Janet. 1971. *The Composing Processes of Twelfth Graders.* Research Report #13. Urbana, IL: National Council of Teachers of English.

Gere, Anne Ruggles, ed. 1993. *Into the Field: Sites of Composition Studies.* New York: Modern Language Association.

Heath, Shirley Brice. 1983. *Ways with Words: Language, Life, and Work in Communities and Classrooms.* Cambridge, England: Cambridge University Press.

Kirsch, Gesa, and Patricia A. Sullivan, eds. 1992. *Methods and Methodology in Composition Research.* Carbondale, IL: Southern Illinois University Press.

Lauer, Janice, and J. William Asher. 1988. *Composition Research: Empirical Designs.* Oxford University Press.

Mishler, Eliot. 1979. "Meaning in Context: Is There Any Other Kind?" *Harvard Educational Review* 49(1): 1-19.

North, Stephen M. 1987. *The Making of Knowledge in Composition: Portrait of an Emerging Field.* Portsmouth, NH: Boynton-Cook.

Shaughnessy, Mina. 1977. *Errors and Expectations: A Guide for the Teacher of Basic Writing.* New York: Oxford University Press.

Tate, Gary, and Edward P.J. Corbett, eds. 1981. *The Writing Teacher's Sourcebook.* New York: Oxford University Press.

White, Edward M. *Teaching and Assessing Writing.* 1985. San Francisco: Jossey-Bass.

13

You Can't Tame a Polecat
by Caging It

RUTH VINZ

Sarah Lynn leans hard over the podium at the front of the classroom. She's reading from a story she's written: *"Death comes knockin' on everybody's door. Night or day. Summer or winter. Slippin' through the window, cracks in the floor, movin' right through the walls, death stands over everybody sometime and bends down."*

I am sitting at Sarah's desk listening when Dane Watkins walks into the room twenty minutes late. Dane has returned to finish his senior year in high school fresh from an Army dishonorable discharge. Rumor has it he raped a local girl near Fort Bragg. He's one year younger than I, in this, my first year of teaching. Sarah pauses, cheeks flushed, hoping to hear the applause that signals approval for her performance. Dane begins a slow clap against his right thigh. The room is silent as he continues—clap, clap, clap—his white shirt brilliant against a too-dark tan. Coins jingle in his pocket in synch with his swaying hips. I suspect he developed the loose hips from long nights of dancing with southern girls or God knows what else. "Good mornin' Ma'am," he singsongs as he nods my way. "Lovely sweater."

His hair is growing curly on the ends, nearly defiant of what until recently was the telltale buzz cut of a young recruit. Hearing the slow gurgle of his voice, feeling the rhythm of his movements across the room, I'm thinking about jumping right up and putting my fingers around his too-muscular neck and strangling him. *I catch him off guard, a strangle hold until he's gasping for mercy, then I repeat Sarah's last phrase: "Death stands over everybody sometime and bends down."*

What I do instead, heart pounding, is suggest to Dane Watkins, "We're wasting time. Sarah's reading—not you." I manage to slip these words through my chattering teeth. Dane slumps behind his desk, looks left, then right. I angle my eyes and catch his glance. He doubles over in his desk and holds his gut, "I got a bat bite; that's why I'm late." He shows bruises on his left arm and on the white flesh of his stomach. "Fourteen days. Fourteen shots. Late every day for the next two weeks, Ma'am." He waves the yellow admit slip and waits for a reaction. Most of the girls sit with their heads bowed, looking at the floor. Sarah stands frozen at the front of the room. Tamara, loose lipped and with a similar reputation, snickers and shouts, "So, do you drop your pants for all those shots? You think some nurse believes she got it lucky?"

"Stomach," he says to Tamara, "the shot's in the stomach, stupid. You wanna' see for the thrill of your life?" He lifts his shirt and teases at his belt buckle.

"OK. OK. Let's get on with the stories. Sorry, Sarah. Finish or start again? Whatever you think. We're wasting time." I walk toward my own desk, feeling more anchored when I sit down. Out past the row of trees by the edge of the road, a group of girls play softball on a makeshift diamond. One girl swings a bat back and forth. Each hit at the phantom ball causes her to lose her balance. Ms. Allan, a first-year PE teacher, puts hands on her. She reposi-tions the bat, moves the girl's shoulders to a different angle, shadows her through the swing. I think how easy it must be to coach. There is always a goal—the girl wants to hit the ball. She listens intently to Ms. Allan's instruc-tions.

Jealousy creeps in, settling as if it belongs. I'm trying to get my students to write. If they write, I'm thinking, they'll learn about themselves, imagine the world differently, appreciate other writers' craft when they read literature. I'm teaching in spaces I've never been as a student. I don't think I ever wrote a story or poem for school. I know I didn't read aloud in front of the class. A nagging sense of loneliness overtakes me. I look at Ms. Allan again. "I'll bet she sleeps nights," I say aloud.

"What?" It's Sarah asking. "Do you want me to start over? I don't want to read it ALL again. What do YOU want?"

I feel my shoulder blades tighten. I don't know what I want or even how to do what I'm trying to do. I turn away from the window and ease myself back into *my* classroom. "Sarah, do whatever. I'm sorry. The interruption. Who's reading next? Let's get going here."

Dane becomes the center ring attraction each day through his antics. One day he interrupts Jefferson's story to tell us that he has the bat's wing hanging from his bedroom ceiling, says he tore it right off the bat when its teeth sank into his arm. Jefferson Chambers has the courage to say it isn't true. He challenges Dane to produce it. "No wing; no story," Jefferson rocks his head back and forth. Dane isn't daunted—says it's private, tells us the spell cast over the bat might be broken if he takes it down. With a wry smile, he invites all the girls in class over to his apartment to take a look. Says the bat flew right in the window. "It circled with no hesitation and sunk itself into my right arm. I killed it though, bare-handed," Dane brags. "Ripped the wing right off." We have our doubts.

Jefferson, dressed all in black, the look of the 1960s, picks up again with his story about a runaway kid, Jasper, who is hanging out in the Haight telling tall tales to the drunks on the street. *"Yeah, yeah, yeah,"* Jefferson continues, *"I coulda' gone to Berkeley but after the fire our band, well, sorta had a string of bad luck. We attributed it to Zelda. She was this old gal up into her fifties whose body was covered with tattoos of dragons and snakes. She just started followin' us around and our luck turned down. She told fortunes and ours wasn't pretty. Peter Pan, I never knew his real name, died a couple of nights ago after Zelda told us that one of us was done for. So here I am now, out of luck and money and hanging on the streets—I just had to get away from Zelda. No family, no money. Zelda, she must be a witch or somethin'."*

"Ya need to cast a spell." It's Dane who interrupts. "Your Jasper don't know how to frighten the old winos." By now, I'm facing Dane. "It's Jefferson's story. You'll get your turn."

"Just tryin' to offer advice to the fledglings," he looks me in the eye of my breasts. "Could give you a little advice too, Ma'am," he reaches for my hand. "Enough," I say, moving back awkwardly before he can touch me. I trip on Brent Tate's book bag and stumble. The heat of embarrassment rises like flames into my cheeks.

Another day. Jennie Lynn walks in the door, sits down hard at her desk. "I'd kill Dane if I could get my fingers around his fat neck. He is full of it. Says the doctor says he's going to die and maybe I should help him out 'cause he doesn't want to die a virgin. The bat had rabies and the shots didn't work. He's such a liar." That morning Jennie reads a story to the class that she's written about her grandmother. "Everybody has a story about their grandmother," she prefaces. "I'm no exception."

"Not me," Dane twists his tongue to his right cheek and closes his eyes. "No grannie to cry at my funeral or me at hers. Just think of it. Me all alone in that coffin and all you so glad about it." I stand a safe distance from Dane, my body bent away from him. "Come on, Dane. End it." I raise my eyes and trace his outline right down to the tip of his toes. I stare into his eyes. He stares back, searing right through my insecurities.

"What you gonna' do about me, Ma'am?" he drolls, peering over his shoulder, left then right, to see who is watching.

"Go ahead, Jennie," I stand facing Dane for a moment longer. Jennie begins to read: *"In the beginning we thought it was a temporary craving she had. Now it's gone on for a full year. She's taken to eating junk food. She calls me every afternoon to pick up stuff for her. About halfway to her apartment I cut diagonally toward 1st Avenue, round the corner and into the Delessandro market. I dig in my pocket for eight cents change to give myself time to explain to the checkout girl that I'm buying this not so decent food on somebody else's orders. Then, I set a fast pace over the two blocks south to grandma's place, run up the steep stairway and take a right down the hall on fifth floor and plaster a smile on my face before she opens the door. Grandma lifts her arms up to my arms. One hug. Then another. I'm juggling the bag. 'Hello sweetheart,' she says. I watch her chew away at breaded fish fillets with mayo piled on top. She'll eat those down and start on the can of Van Camp's pork and beans by the time I take the garbage out to the chute and open a window or two to get the stale smell of last night's fried onions out of the air. Funny how things change. She fiddles with her hair when she talks to me these days. She even paints up her face. I notice the cobalt over her eyes and the round spots of cherry red on her cheekbones. In spite of this effort, she's turning doughy and looks pale."*

"Death and more death. Does everybody haf'ta write about death? Nothin' else to write about around here," Dane cries out.

"Not again," I sound more exhausted than I'd like. "Maybe you could just sit this one out in the principal's office." I walk toward him, hoping he will agree to keep quiet. Instead, Dane laughs. "OK, Ma'am," he rolls his tongue clockwise on his lips, "only if you'll take me down." I notice for the first time a small scar, like a quarter moon, rising from his upper lip toward his cheek as if someone's fingernail had dug in deep. I turn away and ease toward an empty desk. Jennie breaks the silence. "So where's your story, Dane? We haven't heard from you yet."

"Well, you will," says Dane, "oh, you will."

I'm burning Dane's thumbs with my cigarette. I burn his left cheek and his right breast. Sizzle, sizzle, sizzle goes his skin against the red coal. As the dream ends, I wake, pull an old oxford shirt tight around my breasts, and head for the bathtub. Make Dane submissive—that's my goal. All I need is the principal's help. I've written everything down, from Dane's insults to his innuendoes, to his off-the-cuff request that if I am in my right mind I'll want to skinny-dip with him. "I'll talk to the principal today," I say aloud to bolster my resolve.

I close my eyes as I go underwater. I want to dream something other than school and Dane. "I am visiting Sorrento and taking a trip to the Blue Grotto," I say in a whisper, as a mantra to prod me into dream. The water soaks into my bones and brain. Steam rises toward the skylight where clouds mottle like cottage cheese in the haze of sunrise. "Grotto. Water. Forget Dane. Tiberius. Blue Grotto. Start a story, Ruth," I say, sinking lower into the tub. Tiberius comes out of the too-turquoise water toward me. He is tan-as-the-bark-of-tree; he lives in water. He calls me. Nothing else in the world moves except him—toward me. Light in the grotto rises in wisps like smoke from an underground chimney. I hear his breathing; I hear the beat, beat of my heart keeping time with his step toward me. I stare at his solid line of black eyebrow. I take both hands to lead him back to the water, coaxing him gently to come swim. Shadows. Shadows, dark and dusty crisscross his face. I strain to see him, the way you strain to see a boat in the fog when you hear its mournful whistle. He appears again, caught by a narrow band of light. It's Dane's face, his black eyebrows, his eyes staring straight into mine. I push him into the water and watch him go under, the new curl of his hair spreads out like fine lichen. The sweat that trickles down my scalp awakens me. The morning sun hits the skylight above, making bars across the water in the tub, caging my body. "What am I to do about Dane?" I say aloud, jolting myself fully awake as I slide out of the water.

"Marie. I want you to tell him." I give Mr. Godfrey's secretary an earful about Dane. Twenty minutes before first period Godfrey shows up in my classroom. "He's just testing you," says this longtime principal with a condescending edge in his voice. "You're a first-year teacher and a girl"—*a girl, did he say a girl?*— "and he just knows how vulnerable you are." *Knows, he knows how vulnerable I am?* The image overtakes me in waves. I see myself as I must look to all of them and to Dane. Me, only three or four years older than they—too eager, finishing most sentences on a high note that makes everything I say sound like a tentative question. *Vulnerable;* the word tears through the air and echoes off the blackboard before it trickles off the wall. *How vulnerable I am. I'm trying to keep from bursting into tears here.* Godfrey shrugs and, as he turns to leave, lays the palm of his right hand across my shoulder and collarbone. I'm close enough to feel his warm breath against my face. "Ah, listen, honey, we have word from the school board to keep Dane here. I mean, his father. . . . " *Honey, is it honey?* "They'll protect Dane no matter what he does. His daddy is a big executive in a lumber company." I look straight at Godfrey. He stands grinning and the electricity in his hair shows his boyish cowlicks. I step back from the weight of his hand on my shoulder. I think that a man who was once a teacher himself could do better than this. Then, I wonder about my own easy belief that it should be so. The door creaks to a close as Godfrey leaves. "He's probably right," I tell myself. "I'm making a big deal here." In another breath I think, "bull." The first bell rings sooner than I'd like.

"Oh, come on, Dane, please, let's not get into this. How about let's just leave other people to tell their stories. You'll get your turn. Maybe, tomorrow? You ready to entertain us?" *Mister, big shot, big man—see just how you do after your bravado.*

"Nah. You want me to write the story of what my dad says after his AA meeting, or how he was a kid whose dad got killed in a car crash when he was drinking and that equals an excuse?" Dane pushes up his shirt sleeve as he says this, exposing jagged crossbones tattooed in a blue and red blur. "It's a crummy life, full of crummy people trying to convince each other they're all sane. What's this story shit anyway? Don't you think we're all tired enough of living this life let alone make-believing about a bunch of messed-up psychos or stirring our own psycho messes? You know? You know what I'm sayin'?"

It will take another thirty minutes through silvery morning rain, the windshield wipers keeping time to Rimsky-Korsakov, before I reach my mother's house. I turn onto Lincoln Lane. The street rises sharply before the Walnut intersection and curves past Elm near the corner park where, as kids, we played at baseball or hung upside down on monkey bars, the boys taunting Eva Carlson to relieve their boredom. I still see Eva standing on the curb, red splotches blossoming on her cheeks from the crying. I see her face rapt in sorrow, Sears Roebuck oxfords and cable-knit stockings splattered with the mud Tom Jeppesen flung at her. I remember that I was happy that it wasn't me they'd chosen to torment.

When we were seniors in high school rumor had it that a circle of boys led by Dike Lowder closed in on Eva when she ran from them, making the fatal decision to take a shortcut along the river bank. They left her lying among waist-high willows—Eva stunned and sobbing quietly, while semen, like egg white, dried on her sweater and skirt. Eva didn't come back to school after that March day, and she received a diploma absentia at the graduation ceremony. When her name was read, Dike and his friends made snorts by drawing air into their noses. All the girls remained silent, terrified and thankful at the same time.

Chills dart across my shoulder blades. March, already. The first year waning to its end. I'm thinking about next year without Dane. Eva must have felt this way, looking forward to graduation and years of future peace. I suspect she watched carefully and rehearsed her escape route. But, she was caught short, couldn't have imagined what the boys might actually do.

The road narrows into a trestle bridge and I turn right into the long drive that winds toward the house where I spent the first eighteen years of my life. I haven't visited in the past several weeks—too many papers, too little pride, some agonizing guilt about failing with Dane. This is a small town.

"They're talking about you," my mother says, noticing I've eased through the front door. The air smells with her scent. I can't remember when this room didn't smell of her—China lily emits from her pores with each steady breath. Suddenly I remember sleeping with her as a child, the need to press my nose against the softness of her flannel gown and breathe in China's best lily. I could use that softness now.

"What do they say?" I set my most stubborn jaw.

"Too much," she twists her mouth into a pucker that turns into laughter. But in a moment she is serious again. "You can't handle the Watkins' kid?"

"He's not a kid, Mom," I hear the edge of a plea in my voice. "Who's talking anyway?"

"Old Man Watkins is bragging around town how his boy has you intimidated, how you can't handle it."

"Mr. Watkins is a drunk and his kid, well . . . he isn't a kid and shouldn't be in school with kids. It's about that simple, and I have nothing more to say." I move away from her as if she's betrayed me. I'm tired of Dane. I can't wait until graduation. I imagine Dane walking across the stage in his cap and gown smiling and jeering at the same time. I just want him away from me and out of the classroom and away from all the girls. I want to move on— make new plans, buy new posters, get ready for next year without Dane.

"Byron has a new sorrel saddled for you. He's in the East Barn," my mother says with a smile that strains the wrinkles over her cheekbones. Her eyes trace the paths of sadness or some kind of grief on my face. "Byron's a handsome man now." Her face softens into mild. "Ever thought about that?" Her mouth trembles and tightens against what she feels.

"Dane . . . I can't get to him, Mom. I'm failing myself and everybody else in that class. I don't know how to do it better. I just can't get through to him. One minute I don't care what Godfrey or the town thinks. I just want to throw him out. The next second I know I can't. If he didn't leave on his own, what could I do? Even if he did leave his dad would have him back in class the next day. What would that accomplish? It just isn't working with him. He does just what he has to in order to keep himself in the class. But he frightens the other students and me."

Mom's voice strains as if she doesn't fully believe what she's saying. "Sometimes it's just patience, dear. A little gentleness. Try to make a connection somehow. He know he frightens you. He works by intimidation. He had a good teacher in his father. You need to hold out until June. Just keep him in control. Maybe he won't love your class. Maybe you can't get him interested in something you're doing. Hold out and don't be too hard on yourself."

When she says this I realize her face is thinner than I remember, but the skin still radiates olive. Age does not apologize for what it is taking away. I walk to the bay window, stinging with the knowledge that I can't figure out what to do. *Vulnerable. Failure. Honey. Girl. Patience. Connection. Hold out.* As tears well in my eyes, the trees burst into tiny rainbows through the blur. Down the road the pond, cradled in birches, comes into view when I blink. Beyond, a slope rises into a wooded hillside. "A ride's what I need." My mother takes me by the hand and leads me into the den.

Very carefully, she opens the closet and goes through the ritual of laying out my riding clothes—smoothing the pant legs, stretching the collar of the coat straight, rubbing a speck of dust off the boot. "Trouble with you," she says, holding the jacket open for me, "you can't let anything rest. Do what you can for this kid and move on to the others. You're a good teacher for most of them, you know." I look stupidly at her.

"Why not admit that you sometimes lose one? You've never liked to lose at anything. Couldn't ever admit you weren't in complete control of everything. You can't change the world for this kid. Lots of people are responsible for who he's become."

She tugs at the collar of the coat again and opens the French doors facing the barn. "Button up. There's still a mist of rain. And I'm still giving advice."

"Where do you think the island is located?" I ask the class.

Dane laughs. "Everywhere and nowhere. Evil's all over the place just waiting to lure us all in. We're such easy targets, you know. All of us have weaknesses and somebody's just out there waiting, waiting for each one of us. Like Rachel here." He reaches over with both hands and grabs Rachel's arm. She nearly jumps out of her skin.

"Let her go," I say quietly. He pulls his hands away and shows his palms in the gesture of surrender. Rachel's eyes turn dark with fear or contempt.

He laughs. "And now—now who will die a terrible death in this story? It's only a matter of time."

Of course he is right. By the end of the week Simon and Piggy are dead. After the students finish mapping their versions of the island, Dane has his say about *Lord of the Flies* I feel the cold burden of his presence when he starts to talk. A scant breeze from an open window ripples the maps that have just been taped to the wall. He uses the maps as a backdrop as he holds up a copy of *The Rise and Fall of The Third Reich.* "This is ultimate power," he nods toward the book in his hand. "I think Jack and Ralph, just like Hitler, are crazed by power. We all are, underneath. I saw it every day in the Army. We're all Ralph and Jack if we have the chance. Ralph's no saint as some of you are thinkin'. He wants to control, to lead. It's a fatal weakness. We're Piggy if we're weak. You can't let down your guard and go soft. And we're all like these islands," he swats at the maps. Air currents set the papers dancing. The veins on his neck spring out as he laughs. "What will become of all the little islands we are?" No one moves. I remind myself to breathe.

"Well," I hear myself saying. "There's one interpretation. What do some of the rest of you think?" *If anybody else had said what Dane said, I'd take it in, listen, entertain the idea. With Dane it sounds so sinister. Is it me interpreting him or his interpretation that disturbs me? Is it my reading of him, my fear of . . . what? Is it the intensity with which he says it? What do I do now? Validate him. Come on, Ruth. Give him something for his efforts. Maybe I'm implicated in making him the outcast in this room.* "Well," I say again. "Dane's given us a place to start. Do some of you have other impressions of Ralph? Is Piggy's weakness a weakness in all of us? Does Golding create a symbolic island that is representative of the islands that each of us are? *Slow down, Ruth, you're tripping over your own questions. Too many questions. Vulnerable. Afraid. How do I get this discussion going? Uncertain. Why doesn't somebody talk? Young, too young.*

Dane answers, "I'm not askin' for people to agree or not, I'm just giving my personal opinion. Sayin' what I've got on my mind. So, we got a war on this little island that's sorta like the war within each of us—I'm speaking for myself here—and something from inside is going to win out as this little war is played out. Now, which side wins," Dane touches Rachel's arm again, "depends on who influences . . ." I motion for him to take his hand off Rachel.

"We only have about ten minutes, so let's take time to look at each map. Take your notebooks and jot down what you notice in everyone's interpretation. How have others seen this island—literally, or more figuratively as Dane suggests? We'll start discussion there tomorrow." As if all in the room are collecting themselves, they sit motionless and silent at first, talk and movement creeping in slowly like the beginning of a storm.

"I'm suggesting," Dane raises his voice above the low murmur, "that the desire for power's got the upper hand in all of us. We should be facing up to that instead of talkin' or writin' stories and drawin' maps." He laughs and the awkwardness passes. I note the exchange of looks as students collect their notebooks and begin to move toward the maps. I take a deep breath to clear my head. *What's next here? I feel confusion somewhere deep in my bones about what I'm teaching and why. He's right; he's probably right.* "We'll continue this tomorrow," I murmur. "Let's see what we come up with." *Tonight I'll try to figure out what it is I think I'm doing here.*

At the YMCA pool, I finish a series of laps after school. I pull myself up beside a starting block and struggle to catch my breath before kicking off again. A bus rumbles along the street outside, shaking the window glass and sending tiny waves rippling across the water. A lone swimmer, goggles covering eyes beyond recognition, comes up in the lane next to me. He stops near the block. I notice the jagged crossbones first. Then the voice. "Hi, Ma'am," an air of gentleness to the voice in the cushion of water.

"Hello, Dane." The only motion is the kick of our legs, keeping us buoyant.

"Wow!" he says after a minute. "How many laps you do each day?"

"Nothing set," I tell him. "Whatever energy I have left after teaching."

"You're good, you know," he's lifting his goggles to his forehead and wiping his eyes.

"What?" I'm asking.

"You got the teaching figured out," he whispers as he puts the goggles in place and pushes off, quick as a bird moves from limb to air.

I bob in the water left from his plunge and feel the cold splash against my bare back. I don't know whether to be mad or happy or angry or embarrassed. I swim like it's a matter of life or death until I look in the next lane and see that he's gone. I stop to take air into my lungs. The pool is empty. I catch a glimpse of Dane, dressed now, talking to the girl who works the front desk. He heads out the doorway without looking back.

After turning the desk light out, I often sit in darkness until the house settles itself in. In my head, I replay the five class periods from each day, the kids' talk and actions circling around like stars and planets do in the night sky overhead. I relive the day until I numb myself for sleep. During the night I have rigorous dreams of the next day's classes. Less often than in September, I wake up in a sweat, having just confronted Dane again.

Typical teachers' dreams for the most part—of not being able to get the class's attention or about the principal walking in when *nothing* is going on. I dream how a lesson might go, rehearsing over and again, say, how to open a conversation on *Hamlet:* "What would you do if you suspected a relative had killed your father?" *No, too direct. Try again:* "Imagine that you were called home from college. . . ." *The college idea might get some interest. Try another:* "What if you've made a promise to someone and. . . ." *Too serious, too revealing. Hook them with the ghost thing:* "Imagine you're outside, it's nearly midnight, and you see a ghost. That's how this play *Hamlet* begins. Let's read the opening scene together. Any volunteers? *But, the language is difficult. Will they even know this is a ghost scene?* Then I dream that we start by seeing the opening scene in movie version. (Remember, no VHS, just 16mm reel-to-reel of Lawrence Olivier with the buxom, braided, big-boned Ophelia. Where was Mel Gibson when I needed him?)

The naked teacher dream exemplifies it best. Me, walking down the

main hall without clothes. A second version finds me in the classroom frantically looking in the closet for an old coat or some odds and ends of costumes
with which I could cover, well, at least the most obviously naked parts. In
some ways I feel like Alice, having fallen through a rabbit hole, who lost her
solid footing in a world she had learned to read. This Wonderland (read it
school)—with its weird and colorful cast of characters, actions, motivations,
dress, attitude, and language—has become a world alien, nonsensical, sometimes threatening, unpredictable, and not always readable.

I'm looking out the window at an after-school crowd. Unusual for Dane to
hang around on the baseball diamond with the younger boys. Simon Jeffers
throws a curveball at Dane. Dane swings through air and winds himself
around himself. Simon raises his fist, a sure sign of his pleasure. The baseball
diamond shines in the slant of afternoon light. Leslie, the senior class president, is in the room telling me about her growing exasperation with Dane.

"We've tolerated his rude comments all year. I can't get anyone to do
anything. He won't keep his hands off me. I can't wait for school to end. He's
always asking questions about where I live and what I'm doing on the weekend. He makes me cringe." Patches of red swell around her cheeks.

I watch the other Jeffers kid take a swing. His arms are solid and he
moves the bat deliberately through the air. I catch the instant when the ball
makes contact with bat. Leslie's into another conversation with herself, "I'm
thinking all the girls should get together and do something. Maybe if we
complain to the school board. We've talked to Godfrey, and you'd think it's
our fault: 'Oh, honey, Dane's just teasing you girls!' We should have done
something earlier. It's, it's a joke that he's in school. Can you help us?" I'm
thinking that I can't even help myself, much less them or Dane.

I hear the screech of tires barely audible above Leslie's voice. I see Dane
crumple on the pavement as a blue BelAir pulls to the curb. The driver mud-
dles his way back to the place where tires and body met. I can't make my feet
work.

Next thing I know I'm leaning over Dane. He looks pale and small. "Jesus," the driver's saying as I inch my way beside him. "Do something," pounds
through my head. I hear one of the Jeffers kids babbling on the outskirts of
this scene. "Dane ran for the ball and this guy came too fast and Dane was in
the street and the car was too fast. Boy, I wouldn't wanna be this guy. Dane's
dad'll sue him."

"Dane and his dad might learn a lesson," I say to myself.

"What?" the driver is saying. "What did you say?"

"Nothin'. I'm thinking we need to do something."

The driver is as pale as Dane. "Damn kids. I didn't see the damn kid, he

reverse ni delig

ran out fast. I didn't see him, and I stopped the car and my brakes work good. There just wasn't a kid there until zoom, there he was. No time to stop. Kids, what is it with kids?"

This isn't a kid, I'm thinking. Dane lies very still. I wonder if Leslie is in the room talking about Dane as if I'm still there, if she's rounding up a group to go see the school board, if she's packing her things and heading home with the resolve to do something about Dane. I wonder why I think about such things at this moment.

Dane lifts his head slowly, then drops to the pavement again. Leaning down, I start talking to him. "Hey, Dane. Dane. You hear me?" He shakes his head as if to free himself of my voice. I reach out to touch him but hesitate when he starts to pull himself up. The driver reaches out to help. Dane recoils from his grasp. By now the crowd has grown in a circle around us. "Don't touch me," he whispers to the driver. "You've made enough contact with me for one day. A little embarrassing in front of my friends, don't you think?"

Dane rests on his knees for a long time, bends down to pick up the contents from his pocket and wallet that have spilled on the road. I circle and kneel down to help. I pick up his keys, a social security card, a military ID, and reach for a small foil-wrapped square just as his hand comes down hard on mine. "I wouldn't go touchin' that if I was you," he bows his head under my chin to make eye contact, "unless you're serious, Ma'am, about me teaching you something." He laughs the Dane laugh. The driver laughs, relieved, that the kid is still fit for joking even though he's not sure about what.

I feel the blood settle deep into my face and look into Dane's eyes. "Keep it up," I whisper. "Make sure nobody but nobody can get through your thick skin. Not even car tires. Maybe next time you won't be so lucky. Maybe you'll get what's coming to you." I stop myself, surprised at what I've said. "I didn't mean that, Dane." I extend my hand to help him up, but he stands on his own.

"Oh, you meant it. What's coming to me," a frown settles deep into Dane's face, "is what's coming to you and everybody else." I simply watch him as he brushes the dirt off his T-shirt and jeans. He arranges everything back in his wallet and pockets. The crowd around is a still life—a few whispers, shifting of feet. The driver asks, "Can I give you a lift? It's the least I can do. Do you want my phone number in case you're hurting in the morning? Your parents will want my insurance company's number. Where do we start?"

"We start with you just shuttin' your trap, old man. I don't want nothin' from you or your insurance, and I won't give my dear daddy the pleasure of knowing he might have the opportunity."

Dane looks at me hard, waiting and needing for me to say something, make some gesture. I don't move. "Here, Mister, here's the hurt," Dane says pounding on his breastbone. He turns to smile at me, "Thanks for the advice," and heads across the field toward his car.

Right now, I just want it to be morning again—starting the day over, right before the first bell.

As I remember it, Dane had the final word that day. I've tried to write this story several times during the thirty years since Dane and I shared a year together, each time attempting to lead up, as I thought fine narrative should, to moments of joy and lamentation, a moral to the story—potent and ripe with possibility—of lessons learned and those unspoken. What I found instead was that the story could not be tamed—one story led to others and each one singly was demonstrably incoherent and irrational. As my brother used to say, "You can't tame a polecat by caging it. All you do is fool yourself into thinking because it seems docile behind the wire mesh and will come to eat out of your hand that a polecat's become something other than itself." I think the same is true of memory and story. You can't cage memory neatly into words or form. I sit here for a long time thinking back. At one point, from far off, I hear the sound of Dane's laughter, feel his hand slamming mine down onto concrete when I reach for the small square packet—later I will know that this was a condom, which will help me finally understand what Dane meant by the statement that he could "teach me something." Were these the actual words he spoke? I can't know exactly. What is absent and what has been filled, the gaping hole of memory around which Dane's words take form constructs other stories, patterning different tellings in the same silent spaces. Meaning formed in words often falls away like shattering glass or the echo of a cry.

A long time passes before I write the next sentence: "The rose hues of sky forecast snow." I contemplate how the idea of snow tangles with my memories of Dane and the first year of teaching. Suddenly, a familiar voice makes my ears hum as I strain to hear.

"Ma'am."

"Yes, Dane. What is it?"

"If you want a little instruction in ways of the adult world, I could read what I'm working on. I feel lucky today." Dane fingers the cigarette pack in his shirt pocket.

I half look at him, stalling while I play out my options. "Are we going to embarrass anyone here?"

"I'll teach you all a thing or two—about writin', Ma'am. Don't get all worried. This is a story about snow. What could be more harmless than snow?"

"God in Heaven," I'm thinking. "Fool," I call myself as I hear the words slip out: "Have at it. I'll stop you if . . ."

"Yeah, yeah. I know." Dane sits on the stool behind the podium. "Now, class . . . this is a story about a ski trip." The sarcasm oozes from his voice as best I can tell. He reads: *Ann is a flat-faced skier I met at Jackson Hole. Around lunchtime she knocks on the window of my VW. I'm leading the strings into the dizzying parts of Dance Suite, where the trombones come in boo-bwah-bwah-bwum-bum. I point her to the passenger's side. I reach over and open the door. I'm into this very intricate place, both hands busy as hell, so Ann is an interruption.*

"I feel I'm inside a drum," Ann says. I frown. She is hard to hear through the music. I put on a little dog, now, swaying with my eyes closed, and make shallow figure eights with my head. I sneak a peek. She isn't watching. "Wait 'til you hear the horns."

"Where are your socks?" She points at my feet spread maybe twelve inches apart. Just at the bottom where the floorboard tilts up. Just then I get the horns in. I could listen forever, especially where Bartok goes wiry, all the lines running all over. By now Ann has her tongue in my ear.

"Perfect snow," she says. "Get your socks on." She runs her tongue over each clavicle. "Dane, the crew is waiting, let's go, puh-leaas?" I turn off the radio and slip into my socks and boots. I remove my skis from the Eagle-Safe Ski-Carrier I'd bolted onto the side of the VW. Then I follow Ann, not quite forgiving her for interrupting. I walk behind, cool and critical of the way her buns move perfectly, like the rhythmic little jumps of a tea kettle when the water's got way too hot."

I'd still like to claim the last sentence as my own, make it the starting line of another story, but mostly the line reminds me of the "rhythmic little jumps" of living in the same space with Dane for a school year. I don't know whether or not Dane wrote a longer piece around this story; I can't seem to recall how much of it he read to the class that day. I do remember my heart falling through the space of my mind, dread for what he might read mixing with the exhilaration of what he was reading. In a folder from that first year, all that I have of Dane's writing is this single, folded sheet, scrawled out in a hurried script. I'm certain it was a first draft.

This isn't the end of the story, however. That would be neat and tidy—Dane tamed after the car hit him or Dane won over by something inexplicable. As it was, Dane read to the class sometime in early December, long before the visit to my mother, soon after the YMCA, maybe even before Sarah read. I don't think it was before the bat bite. Maybe after my talk with Godfrey, but certainly before we read *Lord of the Flies*.

You see the problem? What I know of the story of my first year of teaching is partially buried in boxes of unsorted folders stacked in a closet that I left in our Idaho home when I moved what I thought were the essentials of teaching to New York. In trying to tame a story of Dane, I opened those boxes and spent the better part of two days rustling through assignments I'd made, faded purple runes of what I thought was teaching. Some still carry the yeasty smell of the ditto fluid, which to this day reminds me of the smell of the bread rising by my grandmother's pot-bellied stove, reminding me of other stories.

Student writing—names of faces I've long forgotten. Faces I can see through the haze of years. I find stories of their great-grandparents, chance encounters, and childhood friends. I say their names as a mantra to memory: Rachel. Sarah. Jefferson. Godfrey. Leah. Dane. Fragments settle together as I roam my mind, fleeting glimpses reassemble themselves yet again. I will have to let go what's left unspoken or what my mind denies, and embrace what I'm lucky enough to remember. Yes, I'm trying to tell you yet again that meaning formed in words often falls away like shattering glass or the echo of a cry.

14

Film Clips and
the Master's Tools

LILLIAN BRIDWELL-BOWLES

For the master's tools will never dismantle the master's house. They may enable us temporarily to beat him at his own game, but they will never enable us to bring about genuine change. And this fact is only threatening to those women who still define the master's house as their only source of support.

—AUDRE LORDE

When I left the South eighteen years ago, I thought I was an expert on multiculturalism. I had grown up as a white woman with the Civil Rights movement and had witnessed school desegregation firsthand, both as a student and a teacher. In the Midwest, I planned to teach others how to reform themselves, just as my family, my friends, and I had reformed ourselves. If we could do it, they could do it. I was downright arrogant about the "unexamined racism" in the Midwest. I thought then, and still occasionally think, that Southerners know more about social revolution than people in other parts of this country. I had what a brave Midwestern friend has described as "a condescending, liberal Southern attitude" toward Midwesterners. My memories of race and class in the South still play like Technicolor film clips in my brain.

FILM CLIP 1: The KKK at the Door

SETTING: *A rural part of Florida that is nothing like Disney World. For comparison, see the film version of* Cross Creek *about the life of Marjorie Kinnan Rawlings.*

142

A delegation of Ku Klux Klan members knocks on our front door and asks my father for permission to hold a rally on our property. These men are members of a family we refer to as "those Atchisons." My father curses and throws them out of the house just like my Sunday School Jesus chasing the moneychangers out of the Temple.

Even though my father rejects the possibility of KKK rallies, he sympathizes with their issues when he talks to his friends. His rejection is more a class issue than a race issue. This white father comes from people who protect black families from poor whites because it is in their economic interest to do so.

FILM CLIP 2: Epilepsy and Poor White Trash

SETTING: *The Atchisons' compound, a cluster of shacks down the road from our larger house.*

I go with my mother to take care of Willie Atchison, who suffers from epilepsy. My mother was a nurse during World War II, and they have come for her again because Willie is having a grand mal seizure. I stand out by the road, not allowed to go in, but I recognize Willie's father as one of the KKK men who came to our door.

I don't know what epilepsy is, but I associate it with shacks and poverty. I have never been allowed to play with Willie. I don't know if he goes to school; he has never gone to my school, even though he is white and could. I wonder what his father did that upset my father so much. I wonder if it has anything to do with Willie. I see *Gone with the Wind* a few years later and the Atchisons look just like the Slatterys. I don't know any black people, but I imagine they all live like the Atchisons.

FILM CLIP 3: Handshakes

SETTING: *Mount Olive, North Carolina, where my parents were raised; tobacco country, in my uncle's country store on the edge of my grandfather's land.*

I am playing with the brass keys on the cash register behind the counter. I reach up to touch the keys; I am six years old. I look over the counter to a group of white men talking to my father. He looks up, notices someone in the back of the store, and smiles as the man walks toward him. The man my

father has noticed is an African American man. As he approaches, he extends his hand in greeting. My father's hand stays at his side.
Freeze frame.
After a pause, they talk about the heat. I ask what is happening.

I learn later that this is my father's childhood playmate, his best boyhood friend. They grew up together on my grandfather's farm.

FILM CLIP 4: Diabetes and Pecan Pie

SETTING: *My uncle's farm (my father's "homeplace").*

A little boy pounds on the screen door in the middle of the night and screams for my uncle to come and take "Aunt Charlotte" to the hospital. My uncle leaves and is gone the rest of the night. He tells us at breakfast that Aunt Charlotte ran out of insulin.

Aunt Charlotte is an eighty-year-old brittle diabetic who has gone into a coma. When she is able, she still cleans my aunt's house and bakes pecan pies that are her specialty. There are twenty of her pies in the deep freezer.

As a child I know there are things wrong with these pictures. I wonder why some people see the pictures and don't see anything wrong. I wonder why I do. What is wrong with me? None of the adults talks to me about black people or patriarchy or dependency. Somehow I know not to ask too many questions.

FILM CLIP 5: Civil Rights Wars

SETTING: *The breakfast table in our home in Florida.*

My brother and I are arguing with our father. He says the entire fabric of Southern culture is being torn apart by the Civil Rights movement. We say he is a racist. He says we don't know what we're talking about because we haven't grown up with black people. We tell him again that he is a racist. He jumps up from the table and goes outside to get away from us. My mother, the peace-maker, tells us that we just don't understand him, that he was raised in a very different place. That he really isn't a racist.

FILM CLIP 6: White School

SETTING: *Later that morning, going to school.*

I pass by the black school on the way to my white school. I see a "Whites Only" sign above the water fountain in the park downtown. I go to my first-hour English class, and we read Wordsworth's "Lines Composed a Few Miles Above

Tinturn Abbey." I get a paper back with an A on it. I don't care about anything it says, except that I need to keep the A's coming to insure my spot as
valedictorian. I go to more classes where I study physics, trigonometry, and
white American history.

Not one word about riots or desegregation is uttered by my All-white teachers
in my All-white classrooms. Race is a taboo subject.

FILM CLIPS 7 AND 8: Sidney Poitier, Martin Luther King, and College

SETTING: *My dorm room at Florida State University.*

> *I open a letter from my mother in which she tells me, matter-of-factly, that she
> has invited a black coworker of my father to dinner at our home. I see a scene
> from* Guess Who's Coming to Dinner. *I sit in my college dorm stunned by
> what this casual bit of day-to-day news represents. I want to call my father
> and tell him how proud I am that he can do this, but I do not call attention to
> it in any way.*

Later that year in the same dorm room.

> *I hear the news report of Martin Luther King's assassination on the radio. The
> reporter announces an all-night vigil at the historically black university across
> town. I want to join others who have gone over to Florida A. and M. to express
> their grief. I am afraid. I talk to a few friends on the phone; they're thinking
> about going, too. I continue to sit on my bed. The reporters talk of fires and ri-
> ots. I am trying to read my anthology for a course in Southern literature. All
> the authors are white. Hundreds of tissue-paper pages of white Southern writ-
> ing between yellow covers. I think my professors must be afraid, too.*

FILM CLIP 9: Changing the World

SETTING: *Winter Haven, Florida; Winter Haven High School, one year
into desegregation.*

> *I am in front of the class, pretending to be an adult. I have only recently shed
> my love beads. I am teaching a unit entitled "Doing Your Own Thing." I have
> chosen to abandon England in Literature, especially Wordsworth, at least for
> now. I have all black students in the room with me for the first time. I feel very
> pale. They laugh at me, and tell me I have no soul, and give me a $33^{1}/_{3}$ Mo-
> town album so that I will have some.*

Throughout my term as a student teacher, I am afraid that I will do something wrong. I want desperately to reach out to them, but they are not happy
about being at the white school. They want their old school back.

EXTENDED SCENE 1: Leslie Lee, Linguistics, Literacy, and a Dog

SETTING: *A sparkling new, integrated school, about half white and half black in the Florida Panhandle.*
Nearly all of the students are poor. The government owns most of the land in the county. None of it is fit for farming; fishing off the Gulf coast is the only source of income for most families, and the median family income is $3,000. This is my first real job and I'm making $9,000 a year. White linguists from Minnesota have installed brand-new Plato terminals for a new kind of computer-assisted instruction. The programs are pattern practice drills to change the black students' dialects to a Midwestern standard. The white students, who have a similar dialect, are not required to go. The brand-new Plato Computer Classroom is a showplace, and school administrators come from all over the South to see it.

Leslie Lee sits down at the terminal, and the words on the screen announce, "Today you will learn the difference between 'ask' and 'akst.' Now let's practice . . ." He goes through about one hundred drills. He's having a good time with the new toy, and he scores 100 percent on the post-test. He walks out into the hall and laughs about the stupid computer.

Leslie Lee keeps his dialect. He has no plans to leave his home and family in Wakulla County. He also suffers from acute sickle-cell anemia. Sometimes he is gone from my eighth-grade English class for weeks at a time.

SETTING: *School office*

The guidance counselor comes in and says she's heard that Leslie Lee will be out of school for a while, and she wonders if I could take him some books to read. She tells me that his house is off the main highway that I take every day to get back to Tallahassee. She also tells me that it's one of three houses that belong to a family with one father and three mothers, each in a separate shack. She thinks Leslie Lee has more than a dozen brothers and sisters, but she's not sure. She knows he likes me, and she thinks a visit from me might help.

SETTING: *Off the road between Wakulla Springs and Tallahassee.*

I drive several miles down a winding sand and shell road into scrub oak woods. I reach a clearing where there are three unpainted shacks with tin roofs. Leslie Lee's is the one on the left. Unpainted boards leave cracks an inch wide. Broken-down cars are perched on blocks. Burning trash smolders in holes in the front yard. Mangy dogs bark at me as I get out of the car. A little sister comes running out to greet me, kicking the dogs away. I give her the book bag and leave quickly without seeing Leslie Lee. I sit in my car and shake.

I have never seen houses like this up close. I remember Willie Atchison's family's compound, which I only saw from a distance. I was never supposed to go there.

SETTING: *Homeroom*

> *Leslie Lee returns to school on crutches. "Thank you for the books," he says. "I read them all. I'm glad to be back in school. I hope I can finish the eighth grade." No sign of a nonstandard dialect as he talks to me. A couple of days later . . . I notice that Leslie Lee has his head down on his desk. I'm afraid he's sick again, so I go over to check on him. "I'm OK," he says, "but my dog died this morning." Tears begin to spill from his eyes as he tells me. We both cry, sobbing, in front of a whole class of eighth graders. "Let's go to the restroom and wash our faces," I tell him. I go to the teacher's lounge where it takes half a box of tissues to stop the flow. I just keep blowing my nose and throwing the tissues angrily into the trash. I hear a knock on the door, and it's Leslie Lee. "I didn't mean to make you cry," he says. We cry all over again, and off and on all day.*

I'm a sucker for dog stories. *Lassie Come Home* and *Old Yeller* are two of my favorite movies. I wonder which one of the pack was Leslie Lee's dog. I can't get those dogs out of my mind. At the end of the school year, I write a special letter to the guidance counselor arguing that Leslie Lee has done enough work at home to pass my class. He is promoted to the ninth grade. I leave that school at the end of the year and move to another school in Georgia. In the fall, I hear from him.

> Dear Mrs. Bridwell,
>
> Well, I made it to the ninth grade. Thanks for all you did for me. I'll never forget you. I like the ninth grade and I'm still reading books. Love, Leslie Lee

More weeping. More thoughts about those dogs and things I didn't do.

EXTENDED SCENE 2: Black-White/Black-White and Paper Clips by the Dozen

SETTING: *North Georgia. A large, popular high school with a long and serious history of winning football.*

I am assigned to direct the senior class play at my new school. I have no idea how to find a play so I ask the students to propose one.

"We want to do Cheaper by the Dozen," *Darryl says. "How boring," I say. Darryl comes right back, "But you don't know how we want to cast it. We want Jerome to be the father and Corabell to be the mother. We can have the kids line up—black-white, black-white!" "Groovy," I say. "You're on."*

Jerome is the black captain of the basketball team. Corabell is the white daughter of the local newspaper publisher. There's a double-page spread in the paper with the alternating black and white children lined up on the stage. The principal watches me like a hawk, shakes his head when he sees me in the hall, and refers to me always as "that female English teacher." This school has been integrated three years; people are still nervous. I'm not, because I am pregnant and sleepy. I take naps backstage on folding metal chairs while the students rehearse.

SETTING: *Play practice, stage in the cafeteria.*

Corabell comes in to play practice and tells everyone that her great aunt invited her to tea at her fancy antebellum house on Oak Street. The occasion, she reports, was to ask her not to kiss Jerome in the play. She says she's assured her aunt that it's not in the script. Jerome kisses her on the lips.

Jerome does not touch her during the performances. Black and white families pack the cafeteria three nights running.

SETTING: *Drama class, that same year.*

We have just won the state one-act play competition, and the principal tells me to tell the students to return their medals because an ineligible member competed.

"We have to return the medals because someone was ineligible," I say. "No!" they shout in disbelief. "Who was it? Why?" "I don't know. I only know one thing. I can't find my medal." I smile as I twist the chain where it hangs around my neck. I tuck it inside my shirt. The students smile, too.

They understand passive resistance. The ineligible student is a nineteen-year-old African American student who has had several babies and is not on the state's timetable for graduation. The football coach reported to the state officials that she was too old to act in the play.

SETTING: *School office, three years later.*

I'm grading a mountain of papers, and I go to the office for paper clips. The secretary doesn't believe I can be entrusted with a whole box of clips. "How many do you want? Three? Four?" A switch flips in my brain. I resign that day.

I have to have more authority over what I'm doing. I go back to graduate school to become a professor and fantasize that I might get more authority, maybe even more respect. I get my degree and leave the South.

I read *My Antonia* on the plane on the way to the interview at the University of Nebraska. I think Nebraska is the way Willa Cather has constructed it. I have never been to the Midwest before. Shortly after I arrive permanently, a colleague invites me to his folks' home.

FILM CLIP 10: Southern Girl Meets the Midwest

SETTING: *Alan's boyhood trails on a Nebraska farm. The only vegetation along the path is corn stubble and a lonely cottonwood tree in a gentle ravine.*

As we walk down the slope toward the cottonwood tree, three deer come out of nowhere and run across our path. I blurt out, "My God, where do they procreate?" My colleague laughs at me, and says, "Lilly, only you would wonder that, and only a 'Southern belle' would put it that way."

I miss sprawling oak trees draped with Spanish moss and swamps filled with lush subtropical ferns. I feel very exposed on this barren and dry terrain. The sky is everywhere.

In the first week in my new job as a professor, I go out to observe student teachers, and I see all-white classrooms for the first time since my childhood. Rows of late-model cars fill the student parking lot. The students all look like white models for *Seventeen* magazine. Again, I feel that this is a barren place. I feel alien and exposed.

I struggle to put "multicultural" readings into the curriculum in the department where I am teaching. I take my white students on an exotic bus tour, exposing them to all kinds of cultures different from their own. I am on a crusade. Like good tourists, they enjoy the trip, but they stay on the bus, not much affected. I do not invite them to take me on any more tours of their countryside. I don't have my bearings yet. I miss the South.

I am teaching a literature course for students who want to become teachers, and for the first time in this place, I have an African American student in class. I feel like calling the editor of the campus paper and reporting a major news event—something like, "First Black Student Enrolls at the University of Nebraska, More Than 20 Years After Alabama"—but I know this would be unwise. I know there have been African American students on Nebraska's football team for years, and a few others scattered around campus in small pockets, but they are still few in number and isolated from the white students on campus.

On the first day, I pass out the syllabus and a hefty bibliography of selected books for adolescents. The list is divided into categories, and at the top, in alphabetical order, is "African American Literature." I have expanded the notion of "adolescent literature," adding African American authors, even though their work is primarily for adults—Toni Morrison, Alice Walker, Zora Neale Hurston, Malcolm X, Langston Hughes, Richard Wright, Ralph Ellison, W. E. B. Du Bois, Booker T. Washington, and so on.

FILM CLIP 11: Saying "African American" Out Loud in Nebraska

SETTING: *My classroom*

> *As I begin to describe* Their Eyes Were Watching God, *I notice that Karla, the African American student, begins to bristle, twisting and turning in her seat as if she needs to excuse herself. She sends me really bad body language. As I speak I notice how thick my southern dialect is. I think she thinks I am a racist. I try to sound more like a Nebraskan, but it comes off phony. I go on talking about* Sula *and* The Bluest Eye *by Toni Morrison and whether or not they are suitable for teenagers. I ask them if they have read any of these African American writers. Nobody is saying a word in this lily-white-plus-one class. I am aware that they are nervous. I am not aware, at this moment, that Karla has reached the boiling point. But she has, and is about to blow. Another student turns to her and asks, "Is this novel really an accurate depiction of African American culture?" She stomps out saying something about mothers in relation to me, to everyone in the class, and to the entire University of Nebraska.*

Even issues of sexuality and Pecola's rape by her father in *The Bluest Eye* are eclipsed for these students by issues of race. Some of them have never met a black person, never read a novel by a person of color, and never had a black classmate. This class is too much for them. But I am too confused to deal with what has happened. I dismiss the class, flee to my office, hide, and try to figure out what I have done to make Karla so angry. After an hour, I call her up and ask her to meet with me. She declines. I beg. Finally, she agrees—the next day, my office, 3:00 P.M.

FILM CLIP 12: I Am a Racist

SETTING: *My office*

> *For fifteen minutes I hear the word* racist *used in every imaginable syntactic construction, usually with me as the subject. I defend myself: "No, I'm not a racist. Listen to my history. Get to know me. I am not just another white bigot."*

"But look at what you did," she shouts at me. "You have tokenized African American novels by putting them in a separate, special-but-not-equal category. They are in the 'other' department on your list. And then you set up that white student's question. Am I supposed to tell everybody what being an African American is like? Look, lady, I grew up in a suburb in Omaha. I don't talk like Toni Morrison's characters, and nobody I know talks like them. I don't know anything about southern blacks, and I don't want you or anybody else to stereotype me this way. If you judge me by the color of my skin, you are a racist." Karla leaves my office and does not to return to the class.

At first, I am disappointed in her and in myself because I can't convince her to come back and express her point of view. Then I get mad. Who does she think she is, rejecting black culture? I think she's an Oreo. I have no patience for Karla. She doesn't fit the script for my crusade.

Today, many years later, as I reflect on multicultural experiences in my classrooms, I don't walk on so many eggshells. I accept that I am a product of a racist culture. I know that there are bits and pieces of this racism embedded in me. But I also know that when one surfaces, I can learn something and try to do something about it. I am aware that I need help to see most issues from multiple perspectives, and I invite students to try to see themselves in new ways, too. I tell them that I am often blinded by my own history. I ask them if they are blinded by theirs.

I am particularly challenged by Audre Lorde's assertion. I grew up in the master's house, and I learned to use his tools very well. As I try to dismantle the house, I don't know what cultural walls I'll run into next. I only know that there is something deep within me that wants to demolish the racist parts of myself and the schools where I work.

Works Cited

Lorde, Audre. 1981. "The Master's Tools Will Never Dismantle the Master's House." *In This Bridge Called My Back: Writings by Radical Women of Color,* edited by Cherrie Moraga and Gloria Anzaldua, pp. 98–101. Watertown, MA: Persephone Press.

15

Satire, Sartre, Cookies, and the Classroom

JOEL J. GOLD

ven after thirty years of teaching I cannot explain why some classes are
special. The right combination of students and teacher, a spark to ignite—
whoosh! and off we go. Every professor, I suppose, has tucked away in
some corner of his or her mind an image of an idealized self as Mark Hopkins
on one end of the log and a receptive student on the other end. It hardly ever
works out like that.

Take my Honors Proseminar in Satire, for example. Juniors and seniors
who wish to graduate with honors in English must take one of these prosem-
inars, a plum for any faculty member to teach. Bright students from other
fields in the university are also welcome and often show up. I enrolled English majors and computer buffs, a couple of art history students, a poet, and a
few assorted walk-ons: eleven individuals who wanted to read Swift, Voltaire,
Orwell, and the rest.

Or so I thought. Some teachers undoubtedly attract students by reputation or force of personality; evidently, I acquire them by accident. About a
month into the semester I was discussing with one of my Satire students the
embarrassing number of spelling errors in his first paper.

"I'm really sorry," he said. "I'm dyslexic."

It was my turn to be sorry. I told him his ideas were first-rate and assured him that we could work out something. He was pleased at my willingness to accommodate him and remarked that actually dyslexia was not
always a bad thing. Puzzled, I asked him to explain.

"Well," he said, "when I read the timetable of classes, I thought you
were teaching an Honors Proseminar in Sartre. It sounded pretty interesting."

"But didn't you wonder at the first few periods on *Mac Flecknoe* and *Gulliver's Travels*?"

"Yes," he admitted. "I could see it would be a long time before we got to Sartre, but I really liked Dryden and Swift."

I took it as a compliment. What else could I do? I think Sartre would have approved.

What might have stumped even Jean-Paul, however, were the homemade cookies in a brown paper bag that appeared one afternoon. I had been grading papers for a couple of hours and had just stepped out for a break. On my desk sat an ordinary small lunch bag, on which someone had written in fat blue lines with a Magic Marker: "Dr. Gold—Happy Paper Grading" and signed it with a little blue happy face. Inside the bag were four, round, chocolate cookies, each about the size of a golf ball, sprinkled with what looked like powdered sugar. I examined the bag again, but except for the few words and the drawing, there was nothing else. The Satire class was the only one for which I was currently grading anything, so it was likely that the gift came from one of them. But which one? The happy face was encouraging but did not resemble any of my students.

I picked out a fat cookie and considered popping it in my mouth. Then I sniffed it. I fingered the powdered sugar but refrained from licking it. What, I thought, if there is an A student who is getting a C? Do any of us really know what students are thinking? Could I tell confectioner's sugar from cyanide? Soon enough? You get the idea.

Timidly, I decided to wait until I could ask my honors students about the anonymous donor. When they heard the question and understood my concerns, they all smiled benevolently at me, but nobody confessed to being the bashful baker.

Fortunately, I recalled that my new diet prohibited cookies. It would be prudent, not cowardly, to avoid them. So the brown bag sat untouched on my desk. I finished my grading, reached the end of the semester, and still had not tasted a crumb.

Toward the end of the term my students filled out the requisite teaching evaluation form—better known as "The Student's Revenge." To encourage free expression by the respondents, the instructor does not see these remarks until after the grades are in. When that moment finally came for me, I sat in my office, feet up, the brown bag settled amid the debris on my desk. I opened the first of the evaluations. There, buried in the middle of the sheet, was what I had been waiting for. "I baked the cookies," it read, and the student had signed her name. What a relief! I had recorded an A for her. I reached for a stale cookie while I opened the second evaluation.

I had the cookie nearly to my mouth when I read the paralyzing sentence in the second paper: "I sent you the cookies." This was impossible. I grabbed the sheaf of evaluations and raced through them. All but one or two assured me: "I gave you the cookies."

I sighed and emptied the bag into my wastebasket. I know when I've been had.

Of course, I had been tipped off to the special talents of this class earlier in the term when I had told them the story of the hand-lettered sign at the bottom of my door, which read "Paper Shredder," a joke about what would happen to late papers. One winter afternoon a few years earlier, I had waited in my darkened office and, when the last paper came tentatively through, I had tugged it from the student's grasp, muttering an audible "Chomp! Chomp! CHOMP!" as I tore up some scrap paper. And—foolishly—I told them of another practical joke I had played on the Comic Spirit class, in which I regretfully announced the "accidental" shredding of their papers. As proof, I had overturned a large grocery bag of confetti—the remains, alas, of their work. The Satire class paid close attention and chortled at all the right places before we went on to more scholarly matters.

The day I realized just how closely they had been attending to my stories was the day their papers were due by 5:00 P.M. I stayed away from my office until nearly 5:30. As I unlocked my door—the very same one with the PAPER SHREDDER sign—I saw on the floor a few hundred strips of shredded paper. I have to admit my initial confusion: Without quite understanding what had happened, I gathered up the scraps of paper and carried them to my desk. I found myself carefully fitting scraps together and deciphering a few words here and there. I appeared to be in possession of ten or eleven (it was a little hard to tell) critical essays on ". . . andide and Saint Joan," "The Innocen . . . Volpone and Can . . . ," and "Satiri . . . Travels." Page numbers helped me to piece parts of essays together. Then I realized that all of these scraps appeared to be on copier paper: They were not originals. On a hunch I went to see the departmental secretaries. Grinning widely, they handed me a large envelope filled with the original uncut essays.

Those wags in the proseminar had photocopied their papers, shredded the copies, slid them under my door, and left the originals for safekeeping with the appreciative secretaries to whom, obviously, they had explained the whole scam. They were learning the lessons of satire exceedingly well.

If the Cookie Caper and the Paper Shredder Scam showed what they could do when they put their minds to it, the Catch-22 Uproar revealed them at their spontaneous best. We had finished Animal Farm and were in the second period on Catch-22, a book they had loved. There came a moment when I slowed in my remarks about satire, corruption, Milo Minderbinder, and the missing morphine packets.

Three students were having a vigorous discussion. Right there in class. In the middle of my lecture! From what I could gather they *were* talking about *Catch-22*, but *still*. I paused and gave them my special penetrating stare. The pause was fatal: Four students on the other side of the room began to argue among themselves whether Heller was attacking the army or *all* organizations. I looked pointedly from one group of talkers to the other. Both groups ignored me. Someone in the heretofore silent middle offered an opinion to the person next to him. Two students in the front row turned around and disagreed.

The class was now joyously out of control. Around the room three separate but heated arguments flourished. I heard my Sartre student manage at last to bring existentialism into it.

After a few minutes the din grew less fearsome, and there were occasional patches of relative calm. I began to wave my arms about. "Hey," I shouted. "Hey, I'm the teacher. When do *I* get to talk?"

A few of them glanced up, perplexed. I think they were trying to recall who I was. Gradually, the buzz died down, the varying viewpoints had been aired, and they were now ready to see what I might like to contribute to the *Catch-22* discussion. Well, I did put in a few words (it's in my contract), and they listened politely, even taking a few notes to encourage me.

Later, back in my office, I reflected on those three or four minutes of uncontrolled fragmented arguments, eleven juniors and seniors so caught up in a work of literature that they didn't have time to wait for their professor. I guess a class comfortable enough to bake their instructor cookies and then keep him twisting nervously, too timid to take the first bite, a class that would shred their own papers and make their teacher the laughingstock of the secretarial staff, was primed to take the classroom experience to the next level. It certainly wasn't Mark Hopkins on one end of the log and a student on the other. They had all climbed up on that log, set it spinning wildly until I splashed into the water, and then they had a high old time.

It was the best class I never taught.

16

The Teflon Lesson
and Why It Didn't Stick

CECELIA TICHI

Much was written about the eight-year "Teflon" presidency of Ronald Reagan, but this essay concerns the Teflon college classroom lesson and why it did not stick. Let's recall, first, that without the DuPont Corporation's nonstick surface so useful for stovetop cooking, countless newspaper and magazine journalists would have been struck dumb between 1977 and 1984. It was Representative Patricia Schroeder, Democrat of Colorado, who first coined the term *Teflon presidency*, which became the pundits' term—their key word—for the phenomenon by which President Reagan evaded public responsibility for such items as the burgeoning of the national debt, the unconstitutional handling of foreign policy (e.g., the arms-for-hostages deal with Iran), the effort to fob off catsup as a *bona fide* vegetable in the national school lunch program intended to serve nutritious meals to poor children. Whatever affronts to citizenship and the Republic occurred on the watch of this commander in chief simply skidded off. No traction, no friction. (Yes, the journalists' term might just as well have been *Scotchguard*, but DuPont beat out the 3M Corporation as the lexical choice, and we know the rest.)

This is about a Teflon lesson in the college/university classroom, a lesson that did not stick even though the students grasped it, embraced it, gave themselves one of the most vibrant classroom sessions of the semester—indeed, of my teaching career—on its complexities. This is about the amnesia that sets in when cultural messages encountered just outside the classroom door pulp and shred new thoughts before they have half a chance to grip down. This is a story about the limits of learning when the lesson lies upstream of cultural currents so powerful that the boat is indeed, in F. Scott Fitzgerald's term, beat back.

It was early October 1995, a good point in the semester for English 160 (American Literature from the Beginning to 1900), a survey whose syllabus showed the instructor's perennial jostling between broad coverage and in-depth treatment. This term, English 160 would be a high-speed, time-lapse tour of Native American creation narratives, colonial diaries, letters, and po-ems (Anne Bradstreet, Edward Taylor) until the students disembarked at, say, Twain or Rebecca Harding Davis' *Life in the Iron Mills* in December.

As a veteran of this and courses like it, I could predict certain student responses—earnest pieties over the Native American material; eager engage-ment in Mary Rowlandson's narrative of captivity by the Wampanoag Indi-ans in 1676 (Was she *really* spiritual or were those biblical quotations only the lip service of a secularist?); more pieties over Franklin's *Autobiography* because its bourgeois ethic of success so closely mirrors my students' own as-pirations; then an empathetic righteous indignation for Frederick Douglass (as long as the racialized struggle seemed safely tucked away in another cen-tury); excitement over Whitman. And so on. But there would be some sur-prises, new viewpoints to emerge, texts refreshed and made new by the interchange within this particular class.

My goal is always student involvement, my in-class tactic the insistence that everybody respond to interpretive questions in a notebook for a mo-ment before we discuss the issues (e.g., Why do you think Margaret Fuller casts her essay "Woman in the Nineteenth Century" as a lawsuit? Why a legal case?). Everybody writes for a minute or two, then we talk. I can start any-where in the room, with the shyest or the most outspoken. (This pedagogical strategy *gratis* from John Warnock, now of the University of Arizona, who punctured my balloon when he pointed out that a roomful of raised hands is not synonymous with a roomful of fired-up minds.)

Our work relationship in English 160 seemed healthy too. The course, designed for sophomores majoring in English and for liberal arts students working off their core requirements, actually included several juniors and se-niors who had not scheduled it in chronological sequence. We met in the new neo-Egyptian psychology building, a clean, well-lighted place just a bit stuffy and antiseptic for my taste but acoustically decent. A few students had taken a course or two of mine previously, including Jake, who could be counted on to raise important issues in a style just short of provocative. To move discus-sion along, as I knew by now, we could count on Caroline, who identified herself as eager to learn more about Puritanism; or the genial Roger, who brought platonic issues to bear on the readings; or Pat, the premed sci-tech student interested in a humanities course but constantly worried about do-ing well enough to keep his grades high. And on seven or eight others who could be named in the group of thirty-five. The car crash that would nearly kill Heather's brother had not yet happened. The sudden death of someone very close to Matt (whether parent, lover, brother, sister, or friend, I never learned) was still weeks in the offing. For now, the group had "jelled," and the onslaught of midterm exams had not yet brought on the fatigue that would intensify toward Thanksgiving and turn into the semiannual marathon of all-nighter papers and finals just before the holidays. Apart from the affliction of allergy season in Nashville, the students and I were healthy, the weather was good, the leaves just turning.

According to my syllabus, it was time to read Ralph Waldo Emerson, a problematic moment in part because the whole of an Emersonian essay—in this instance, "Self-Reliance"—often strikes the students as dense, dry, abstruse. But they love his aphorisms. "Insist on yourself; never imitate"— sounds like a clarion call to the selfhood each is struggling to attain. My colleague, the Miltonist, dismisses Ralph Waldo as the ur-narcissist of a perpetually adolescent nation. I do not dismiss the notion. But certainly, to a roomful of young people trying to get out from under parents, guardians, authorities (including teachers) of every stripe, statements such as "trust thyself" rings like the Liberty Bell.

But the other side of Emerson's "Self-Reliance" needs to be called to their attention too. Women students often cite the sexist preponderance of male pronouns and the denigration of women in sideswipes at "feminine rage" and the like. But the dangerous Emerson seems to me a figure of relentless binary divisions between the heroic individual and others dismissed as conformists, skulkers, bastards, the timid, the whimperers. Society in his world is an undifferentiated "wave" or a "mob." Emerson's hero is the individual American jack-of-all-trades restlessly sampling occupational possibilities, though solely for his own benefit. He is the New England sturdy lad who "tries all the professions, who teams it, farms it, peddles, keeps a school, preaches, edits a newspaper, goes to Congress, buys a township, and so forth, in successive years, and always, like a cat, falls on his feet" (43). He is, in short, a political and occupational success, a new version of the Franklin figure (references here to September's course work just two weeks earlier).

But I insist that students pause to consider how the versatile, successful Emersonian American individual got that way. Who brought him up?

Nobody, as we learn from Emerson's verse epigraph to the essay. The self-made American is a parentless American "bantling" or infant cast onto rocks, suckled by a she-wolf (shades of the imperial Romulous and Remus!), and raised by none other than the hawk and fox. No parents, no mentors, no pediatric caregivers to minister to the abrasions or concussions from the collision with the rocks. No big brothers or sisters, no village to raise the child who becomes the self-reliant American starting life as a glorious orphan.

And a good thing too, given the sorry state of the ambient population in Emerson's world. The census of his others consists of dull, inertial blood relatives, of the contemptible mob, skulkers, conformists, incompetents, etc. The heroes are all the self-made isolates, all others wretched refuse.

The student-readers identify with this self-reliant figure—and who can blame them? Vitality lies on the side of the self-reliant American, while inertia and contempt mark everybody else like red dye from a bungled bank job. The reader lines up readily on the side of the self-reliant because there is no feasible alternative.

I care, however, that the students learn to recognize these rhetorical maneuvers. In fact, it took me years to grasp them myself, having been trained to ventriloquize as a female grad student eons ago before I had heard the term, false consciousness. Much more than a rectification of my generation's and gender's schooling is at issue. I am convinced that societal identity is at stake when a major American writer of Emerson's stature, influence, longevity conveys the idea that the individual is "the centre of things," that all others inhabit at best a periphery. I want my students to consider the possibility that not everybody is able to buy a township and to land on his tomcat feet in life, and to ask whether the others ought therefore to be dismissed as "a mob," a bunch of skulkers or servile "valet[s]."

How to invite such consideration—that is the challenge. In years past, I would press for close readings of terms and images, perhaps start a chart on the board. At about this point in the term, however, I had been rereading some Tocqueville, whose words virtually leaped off the page as a potential handout that could work far better than an instructor's outline. Alexis de Tocqueville's "Individualism in Democratic Countries," I realized, could stimulate an against-the-grain reading of Emerson. After all, *Democracy in America* was published just six years before "Self-Reliance." Let the two voices enter a debate whose terms the students could analyze and discuss.

The copy machine hummed, and I distributed the handouts, explaining that in the 1830s the French aristocrat traveled throughout the new states and territories from New York City to Boston, then westward to Green Bay, Wisconsin, north into Canada, and south as far as New Orleans, all the while noting social conditions and governmental structures of the new American democracy. I told the class that Tocqueville coined the term *individualism*, and I asked them to notice its definition within the essay.

So we went through "Individualism in Democratic Countries." Individualism, the students noticed, is not mere selfishness (*egoisme*), which, Tocqueville notes, is a vice "as old as the world" but is, in his view, "of democratic origin." At first, Tocqueville's usage seems laudatory, the students saw, since individualism is democratic and known to be "a calm and mature feeling." Soon, however, the Frenchman's tone changes. Individualism, we learn, "proceeds from erroneous judgment" and originates in "deficiencies of mind" and "perversity of heart." It "saps the virtues of public life." Individualists, moreover, satisfy their own wants and habitually consider themselves to be "standing alone" and falsely "imagine that their own destiny is in their hands." Ultimately, the individualist is thrown "forever upon himself alone and . . . threatens to confine himself entirely in the solitude of his own heart" (88–89).

It was the perfect handout for the workshop moment—short, incisive, apprehendable. We returned to Emerson. Now the Latin epigraph to "Self-Reliance"—*Ne te quaesiveris extra*, Do not seek outside yourself—sounded less lofty, the ringing statements of the essay less like transcendent truth than contestable positions. Those despised may seem, through Tocqueville's lens, less innately despicable (e.g., the skulking "charity boy, bastard, [and] interloper"). The binary Emersonian split between the laudatory "strong" and the pitiful "weak" seems less natural despite the plethora of organic nature figures in support of the former throughout "Self-Reliance." The "friend, wife, father, child" seem less easily relegated to Emerson's categorical "petulance" and "folly." The self-reliant "genius" authorizing and valorizing a shunning of parents, spouse, siblings seems less an entitlement than a claim (26–48).

"Your isolation . . . must be elevation" says Emerson (43), but the students of English 160 were now equipped with the Tocquevillian rejoinder that the individualist is not godlike but imprisoned in solitary confinement. The "self-trust" that in Emerson brings "new power" is countered by Tocqueville's warning that via individualism, the civic, public trust is sapped of its strength.

The class discussion was intense, the kind that wells up once, maybe twice a term if one is very fortunate. Of course, an instructor is well reminded that effective learning is not necessarily a correlate of vigorous in-class discussion, that an office conference, a walkway word, an onscreen exchange, or a quiet moment of student reflection on a text can have greater and more durable impact than a heated in-class hour. The classroom is not a pep rally. It may seem as though everyone in the room is involved, but the caution lies on the qualifier, *as though*.

Still, there is an incomparable electricity in that moment when the class takes off, when as instructor one becomes the facilitator because the discussion is peer-centered. Articulate, respectful of one another, attentive, citing textual evidence for one another, the class became one big study group, listening, debating, arguing, and extending argument. I went to the board and started two headings, "Self-Reliance" and "Individualism," and became the stenographer for the group. Exhilaration was in the air as oppositional terms were juxtaposed and differentiated, each with its own problematic, as, for instance, it was noted that Emerson regarded history as a shackle, Tocqueville as a binding of generations and of proper social hierarchy across generations.

Above all, the group grasped the fundamental antitheses between the terms *self-reliance* and *individualism*. The two terms critiqued each other in polar opposition, and the students of English 160 understood the radical division and the implications for social and individual identity. Many students spoke that day, calling out thoughts as I chalked them on the board. They cited one another. Roger capsuled Caroline's statement on Tocquevillian egoism so he could build upon it with a thought of his own, at which Caroline nodded in appreciative agreement at the collaboration. From the far side of the room, Heather took issue with Pat's suggestion that both Emerson and Tocqueville were champions of democracy, the first hopeful, the latter fearful. Students turned in their seats to see one another's faces, to address classmates directly—always with courtesy and respect. As needed, I directed traffic, but the thought and energy were all theirs. I believe they sensed the extraordinary occasion. In the moment, they were living their own education. And the class was justifiably pleased with itself. With one another's help, as a group, they had brought forth insights on conceptions of the individual self. In doing so, they became an intellectual community.

How shocking, then, to find that within a very few class meetings the lesson disappeared, slipped away, vanished. Within two weeks, it was as though the Emerson-Tocqueville session had never taken place. In discussion, in student essays, on quizzes, the terms began to cross into one another, to be used synonymously (e.g., "In Emerson's 'Self-Reliance,' we see the power of individualism to enable a person to rise to their greatest level of genius . . ."). In class discussion, the two terms became interchangeable despite my constant reminders of the mid-October hour when we grasped their semantic opposition. "Oh, right—" Catherine said, correcting herself in midcomment when I prompted recollection of the day the group learned the lesson so energetically. But her "oh, right" sounded almost annoyed, as if the insight were now inconvenient.

Catherine was typical. Roger, Pat, Matt, Heather—singly and all together—fell back to truisms on the Emersonian individual self. No matter how many times I reminded, prompted, and corrected them as the class made its way through Emily Dickinson, Whitman, Rebecca Harding Davis, the students persisted in using individualism as a synonym for Emersonian self-reliance. Tocqueville's term was folded into Emerson to enhance the viewpoint of "Self-Reliance." The social critique vanished. The devastating image of the individualist "confine[d] entirely within the solitude of his own heart" had been forgotten. The Teflon lesson was complete.

How did this roomful of bright young people get amnesia? How did individualism so easily collapse into self-reliance? After all, these were smart, accomplished students, responsible and diligent. They sought good grades as a measure of self-regard, and they were career-minded too. They were quick learners. They would not accept an identity as shirkers, as lazy, as irresponsible. So how did the lesson get forgotten so fast?

Colleagues in psychology would doubtless tell me that my reinforcement schedule needed heft, that if Tocquevillian individualism was to be a crucial concept in the course, it needed to be hammered in constantly through quizzes, exams, other assignments. Possibly the psychologists would have a point, though I suspect their method would only briefly delay the Teflon moment.

Why? Because Tocqueville's message fell casualty to the limits of the classroom *vis-à-vis* the larger culture. This does not mean the student culture of the Greek system, sports, parties, the weekends that often start on Thursday night. I mean American culture, with its drumbeat of Emersonian messages celebrating the autonomous solo self in ads, TV shows, pop fiction. A quick flip-through is revealing. The United States Army, an organization based on interdependence, camaraderie, *esprit de corps,* recruits young people with the slogan "Be all that you can be." The Hitachi Corporation promotes sales of its notebook computer with this come-on: "From now on wherever YOU are, is exactly where you should be." Taylor Made Golf Clubs uses this copytext in its ad: "The Perfect Game isn't out there, waiting for you to find it. It's inside you, waiting for you to tap into it." A software company concedes that to make a killing in sales "it pays to work together" but says its product is "great for lone wolves too."

Of course, the lone wolves are onscreen from John Wayne to James Bond (surely an honorary American) to Arnold Schwarzenegger. On a new TV talk show, Rosie O'Donnell does a comedy skit on children in playgrounds forced to share their toys in a cultural double standard. Adults, the comedian reminds us, are hardly ever called upon to share.

Manufacturers, of course, want it that way. Every suburban household should have its own lawn care equipment, snow thrower, chain saw, exercise machines, what have you. Members of such households who fall victim to the 1980s and 1990s mania for massive corporate layoffs (the euphemism for firing) are encouraged to consider themselves freed from slavish conformity into a new state of personal career independence. As Louise Uchitelle observed in *The New York Times,* "During the Depression, when so many people felt vulnerable to poverty, America developed a 'one for all' economic system" as "the federal Government established safety net programs such as Social Security" and "corporations took on new responsibilities for the well-being of their workers." Now, the article continues, "this communal system is giving way to a do-it-yourself approach. . . [a] shift in the American ethic toward greater self-reliance, even for those who don't make ends meet" (Uchitelle 1997, A1, A11). Now, laid-off employees are told they can become self-reliant individualists who take charge of their careers in ways that were impossible when they drew dull paychecks from AT&T or Mobil or Warnoco. The layoffs have really set them free to discover their Emersonian genius.

In academic life, of course, we insist on students doing their *own* work. Cheating is disheartening, infuriating. Yet those of us serving on honor councils from time to time encounter the ethos of Ralph Waldo Emerson when international students are hauled up for plagiarism and are baffled by the charge against them because their culture has no concept of private intellectual property or the individual possession of thought.

Politicians on the national scene love to invoke the Puritan Governor John Winthrop's figure of the "city on a hill" to describe the exemplary America. But they omit his injunction that we are "knit together" in a social commonwealth. In English 160, the students are hardly to be blamed for failing to sustain a critique that goes to the center of the culture they inhabit. The so-called real world very seldom allows them to consider the radical challenge posed by Tocqueville in the 1830s. Emerson's version is the winner's version. The students of English 160 never had much of a chance.

Works Cited

Emerson, Ralph Waldo. [1841]. 1979. *The Collected Works of Ralph Waldo Emerson*. Volume 2. Introduction by Joseph Slater. Cambridge: Harvard University Press.

Tocqueville, Alexis de. [1835]. 1990. *Democracy in America*. Volume. 2. New York: Vintage.

Uchitelle, Louis. 1997. "A Shift to Self-Reliance." *The New York Times*. National Edition. January 13: A1 and A11.

17

Testing the Limits of Tolerance in the Democratic Classroom

JOHN CLIFFORD

I

For teachers of my generation this tale—since it is a story about classrooms and authority—begins long ago and far away in the late 1960s when everything changed. I drift back to Greenwich Village on a warm evening in mid-September 1969 to a seminar room overlooking Washington Square Park, a bucolic refuge vitally alive with an edgy bohemian flavor: a microcosm of the ubiquitous zeitgeist of rebellion. Earlier, I had walked through the park to class, relishing the pungency of marijuana and incense as they combined with the eclectic aromas wafting from the vendors' carts filled with pretzels, popcorn, hot dogs, and cheap sauerkraut—all this mixed in with the acrid exhaust from hundreds of taxis.

Inside the room I sat around a table with my fellow students, half there, half still in the park. Like me, they were harried, tired. I looked wistfully out the window at the energized tapestry of the park. This was a familiar feeling, my emotional and intellectual allegiance torn between the iconoclasm of the sixties and the tradition of the academy.

I was waiting for Louise Rosenblatt's seminar on Literature and the Crisis in Values to begin, hoping it would reinvigorate my commitment to teaching and my belief in the transformational power of literature after four stale years of graduate training in New Criticism. When I had started the canonical literature program at New York University, I had no idea how interconnected reading was with teaching, how a formalist explication created a pedagogy where the teacher was more like a priest or rabbi initiating novices into the subtleties of sacred texts. This had been driven home when I had

164

tried and failed to make Spenser and Milton come alive for my all-male, working-class students in a high school in Brooklyn. In that context, learning meant filling their notebooks with lots of information.

My chair at the time, a gruff, muscular man, told me to give them "a Cook's Tour" of English Literature. He encouraged me to convey as much knowledge about literature to my passive students as they would endure. This was a pedagogy that had little to do with critical thinking and nothing to do with helping my students look at fictional characters as representations of themselves and their struggles in a tumultuous world. "Hey, Mr. Clifford," they often complained, "how come we have to read stuff like *The Faerie Queene?* Why can't we study Bob Dylan or Ken Kesey?" I fumbled for an answer. "It's going to be on the SATs," I would say, convincing no one.

I didn't need more literary information in graduate school; I needed a new vision, a new pedagogy. Like my high school students, I was also caught up in the cataclysmic changes of the sixties. We thought that things would never be the same, that we were in the vortex of a profound cultural shift. We felt it in our bones, saw it in our zany bell-bottoms, in the energized music of The Who and Jefferson Airplane, in our protests against Vietnam and racism, in our confrontational attitudes toward sexual codes, authority figures, institutions, and traditions. I was also learning an important lesson about my teaching: to sustain my commitment, I had to believe that what I was doing mattered, for my students, for society. Does a comprehensive knowledge of literature change people's lives, make them more tolerant, ethical? After teaching Milton and Spencer to stupefied students hungry for voices that spoke to them about their lives, I knew I wanted literature to be an impetus for students, to help them understand the zeitgeist and to become intellectually aggressive, to question everything, to feel betrayed that the democratic rhetoric of our culture had fallen short. I hoped that literature might provide a way to transform ethical complacency.

I admit that was a lot to be thinking, gazing out at Washington Square Park, waiting for Louise Rosenblatt, but these feelings were roiling as I tried to make sense of the disparity between my elite training in literature and the raw needs of my working-class students. She finally arrived, looking a lot like my grandmother: short, gray, assertive, confidently in charge. As we introduced ourselves, she asked what I did. "I teach high school English in Brooklyn," I said. "Oh," she replied, "not high school students?" A cogent response that worked its way deep into my consciousness, helping to clarify my conflicting feelings about what I needed to do in the classroom.

Rosenblatt's seminar was a perfect fit. Her course was a revelation—completely different from the "touchy-feely" stereotype reader-response teaching had in traditional literature programs. Louise's spirited defense of the democratic rights of readers had the immediate ring of truth. Her insistence that literature needs to be intimately connected to one's inner life suddenly seemed not just refreshing but a compelling antidote to the barren transmission of information.

I remember a discussion late in the semester about Ralph Ellison's "Battle Royal," the opening chapter of *Invisible Man*. My traditional chair at school had urged me to use the last ten minutes of class to sum up. But Rosenblatt's class was quite different. There was no closure at the end of our vigorous debate. We were arguing about whether the grandfather's injunction that blacks need to be a secret, subversive enemy in the master's house was cowardly, pragmatic, or expedient. There was no consensus, only multiple possibilities. But maybe that's too easy an insight: One especially heated part of the debate surfaces. There was an older Franciscan brother in the seminar. We had clashed several times. His comments were judicious; mine seemed impassioned. "I think the grandfather is an ethical man," he calmly averred, "a kind of Gandian precursor of Martin Luther King." "I don't think so," I challenged. "He's more like the Uncle Toms that are too afraid to confront injustice." I was right; I knew it.

Rosenblatt, sensing my self-righteousness, intervened: "John, is there some way you can be right without Brother Timothy being wrong?" In a doctoral seminar in reader-response theory, I had to agree, of course. But I've been perplexed about that discussion over the years. Caught up in the activism of the sixties, I was convinced that the grandfather's passivity was ethically flawed. Perhaps though, I missed the larger picture about the necessity for competing voices in a democratic classroom. Perhaps I was too strongly written by a masculine discourse in which winning is always the goal. But Rosenblatt was urging us to adopt another discourse, one in which everyone had a contributing voice. "The point" she maintained, "is not being right; the point is the democratic negotiation, the communal understanding of how meaning gets made by each individual." But perhaps that's not always the case. Both Brother Timothy's and my positions were credible; both were within "acceptable discursive parameters." But, what if one of the participant's values falls outside the norm?

II

That seminar happened twenty-five years ago. I left high school teaching as the war ended and taught writing for four years at Queens College, CUNY. I have since been teaching at the University of North Carolina, Wilmington and also teaching a summer course in Responding to Literature at the University of Pennsylvania, which brings me, as way leads on to way, to another narrative.

A seminar room overlooking a busy street in West Philadelphia, hermetically sealed against the noise and heat of morning rush hour. Waiting for me were fourteen students, sitting around a large table, all women in their twenties and thirties, racially diverse and evenly divided between master and doctoral students. I had been teaching this course in Responding to Literature for several summers. This group seemed typical: highly motivated, disciplined, intelligent, and progressive. And quite willing and able to be open and personal. In a course informed by personal engagement, these were ideal students. The master students were usually school teachers; the doctoral students hoped to work in colleges as administrators, teachers, supervisors. I knew one student, Stephanie. She was in another course of mine the summer before. With an honors degree from Stanford, she was articulate, intellectually aggressive, and urbane. She was the kind of student who immediately understood how to be the good student. She was serious, engaged.

At the beginning of the first class, I passed out William Stafford's "Traveling through the Dark," a brief narrative poem about a driver who comes upon a slain deer on a dark, narrow, mountainous road. Even after he discovers that a fawn is still alive inside the mother, in order to avoid a disaster on that dangerous road, Stafford writes, "I thought hard for us all—my only swerving—,/then pushed her over the edge into the river." The poem contains obvious ethical dilemmas that encourage personal involvement, but the text also has provocative gaps—spaces that engaged readers can't help but fill in with their own experiences, their own views on questions of life, death, responsibility. The discussion was going well, I thought: lots of seemingly committed responses, lots of sophisticated ideas about making moral decisions. I tried to involve everyone in the discussion the first day; this breaks the ice, sets a pattern. However, one student heldback: Constance, an elementary school teacher, dressed quite conservatively with brown hair to her waist. I assumed she was shy, unsure of herself amidst her more experienced and informed classmates. But for some reason, I didn't draw her out. I let her be.

Since part of what I am trying to do is to be a model for response teaching, I usually attempt to encourage quiet students to join the discussion. In a significant way the credibility of the course rests on how I behave. To me, there is a deep irony (if not hypocrisy) to response theorists lecturing, to proponents of collaboration holding forth in front of the room, to postmodernists confidently solving what is problematic. Unless all the students sitting around the table are involved in the process of meaning making, what good does it do to tout the virtues of a participatory pedagogy? So I press on, trying to encourage the quiet, the recalcitrant, the passive.

Since we met for three hours every day for two weeks, a sense of community developed quickly; graduate students like feeling a part of an energized community and know how to support its goals. Stephanie was clearly the intellectual leader. The others respected her and, sensing her commitment, seemed eager to get involved.

I was moving along, championing the democratic value of tolerance for difference, of the necessity to negotiate conflicts. I hoped for consensus but tried to be flexible enough to see that agreement was not always possible or necessary or even helpful. About halfway through the course, however, there was a dramatic turn for the worse, a seemingly innocent event that even today I am still trying to fathom, one that changed the dynamics of the course and tested the limits of tolerance in a democratic classroom.

Constance was still the only student not in the fold. We had been discussing James Wright's "Lying in a Hammock" (1980). I like the poem because the last line, "I have wasted my life," is a complete surprise, forcing readers back to the text, refiguring the images so they fit with the evolving hypotheses that are necessary in the making of meaning. As often happens, students had created two distinct narratives. Stephanie asserted, "The narrator is sorry he has not spent his life in harmony with nature." Another student, Kezia, maintained, "The narrator wishes he had spent his days away from the limitations of farm life."

"Interesting," I said, "how we read our own values into poems. And fitting, too. We want our students to create their own meaning, not simply to mimic the interpretations of their teachers. We resent being told what to think; we should not dominate the vision of our students with our authority. Democracy needs a critical consciousness."

But suddenly Constance spoke: "I think you are doing a disservice to students, making them believe there is no truth, no right or wrong. It's an abdication of your ethical responsibility. You might be confused about what wasting your life means, but reasonable people know that standards exist that need to be followed."

In my seminars, I have always taken the relativity of truth so much for granted that Constance's comment stunned me. Almost all the discussion that day had been focused on the students' diverse reasons for the narrator's feeling that he had wasted his life. Constance's comment was cold water on my enthusiasm. I was comfortable negotiating diverse, even bizarre interpretations, but I couldn't remember a graduate student resisting openness, tolerance, and ambiguity.

I paused for a moment and simply said, "I think it's good for young students even in the sixth or seventh grade to understand that truth depends on context, on how you look at something." A weak response perhaps, but I was impatient. Like a stage performer, I could sense that no one wanted to debate Constance's point. But the seed of dissent had been planted in our group, indeed a sour taste of my authority, even of my bullying, lingered in the air, at least in my mind.

The next day was worse. The topic was Robert Lowell's "To Speak of Woe That Is in Marriage" and a chapter from Louise Rosenblatt's *Literature as Exploration*. Like many of the poems I use, Lowell's sonnet is ambiguous, full of provocative gaps. The female narrator is bemoaning a painful marriage, but her credibility is in question. Some students blame the husband, others the wife, some marriage itself. I use the poem to illustrate Rosenblatt's seminal idea that readers create meaning out of their own cultural assumptions and expectations, that texts provide the score, that readers play the music. Constance was waiting, pumped up, ready to amplify her earlier stance against the evils of relativity. This time her comments were not only about the value of affirming truth. She asked quite boldly, "Why do you choose a poem that denigrates marriage, that focuses on sexual perversion, that encourages cynicism and despair? I think this discussion has been conducted in an ethical vacuum." Impassioned and insistent, Constance dominated the discussion. I was frustrated at not being able to decide on an effective strategy.

When Stephanie came to my office before class the next morning, I was surprised how seriously she was responding to Constance. "No one is interested in those discussions with Constance. She's taking up time better spent on the connection between theory and practice." Although I agreed, I said, "But doesn't she have a right to defend her values, her experience? That's what I am professing; that's the attitude I am trying to persuade the class to adopt." Indeed my crisis was that I believed just that: students do have a right to create meaning, have a right not to have meaning imposed on them by those in power. Since Rosenblatt's class in the sixties, that idea has been central to my teaching. But Stephanie also seemed right. The women in this class were progressive, open-minded, and I assumed, tolerant. Constance was a Christian fundamentalist whose husband was a Baptist minister. He probably supported her confrontational posture in class, and they both decided that she should take a stand, defending the tenets of their beliefs against their sworn enemies: situation ethics, secular humanism, and postmodern skepticism.

But did I really believe in Constance's right to argue her position? Or was there an implicit agenda hidden in my approach? There had been when Brother Timothy and I had argued years ago. Constance was affirming her deeply held beliefs; so was I. But unless I did something, I was in danger of losing the class to boredom, anger, or frustration. Stephanie was blunt about her point of view: "The tuition at Penn is too expensive to waste time on a point of view everyone thinks is antithetical to the life of the mind." It was clear that Stephanie was the spokesperson for the class. After a difficult night, I decided I would not call on Constance and not follow up on her responses.

The next day we read "Rape," Adrienne Rich's razor-sharp denunciation of male complicity in the oppression and silencing of women. Constance spoke first: "It is women like this and hysterical antiestablishment sentiments like these that make feminists look foolish, antimale and not worth taking seriously." I quickly called on Stephanie for a response. She said, "I especially like the scary way she connects the rapist to the cop. That was really powerful." Stephanie simply ignored Constance, refocusing the discussion on her own perceptions and on Rich's accusatory last line, "will you lie your way home."

The other students quickly joined the conspiracy. Although Constance made a few more comments, each was ignored. We simply went about our discussion as if she were invisible. Except, of course, that she wasn't, and her dwindling comments still reverberated through the room, creating tension, unease, guilt. Something was wrong, but no one had the will to fix it. In spite of this, the semester moved along reasonably, I thought. In our typical workshop fashion, we read poems and stories, discussed the implications for teaching, and were in general agreement about the democratic and pedagogical benefits of response teaching. At the end of the table, however, sullen yet completely confident and vindicated, Constance sat, secure in her fundamentalist certainty that she had not capitulated to the postmodernists. She came with the truth and left with it. And thus the course ended.

III

A year later, I was back at Penn, once more immersed in my summer course. Stephanie called to ask my advice about taking a position at a local college. As we sat in a cafe on Locust Walk, under a thick canopy of oak trees, the uneasy memories of last year's course seemed distant and dreamlike. But only for awhile. I asked Stephanie if she ever ran into Constance again. "Oh, her!" she said with a casual dismissiveness, "Boy! Did she ruin that course." I found her comment too sharp to process, too painful to pursue with her. "Good luck with the interview," I told her, distractedly wandering down Locust Walk, gradually letting the force of her comment sink in, weave its way into my troubled memories of the course. "'Ruin!' she said, 'Ruin!'" I still couldn't get my emotions, my sense of academic responsibility, my commitment to democratic teaching to rest harmoniously with my sense of failure, of an opportunity missed, of misused authority. I meandered for a long time along the paths that amble through campus, examining my equivocal response to Stephanie's perception. I conceded that I had learned something about the limitations of my response theories, about the powerful hold ideology has on our behavior, about the simultaneous success and failure of teaching. Without planning to, I started to think of the next day's class and our discussion of "Traveling through the Dark," of the narrator's poignant decision to abandon the deer on a dark road, of his imperfect weighing of ethical priorities, of his probable second-guessing the next morning.

IV

Months later I sat in a large convention hall waiting for Stanley Fish. His topic, "Boutique Multiculturalism," sounded intriguing but ambiguous— typical Fish. My thoughts that evening were far from my classroom fiasco with Constance, actually closer to the next day's visit to the Baltimore Aquarium. But Fish's talk was more than his typical bravura performance, at least for me. What he said helped me sort out the interconnected web I was caught in with Constance, Stephanie, and Louise Rosenblatt.

Fish mesmerized us with a narrative of tolerance and its limits: The novelist Paul Theroux encounters a Pakistani taxi driver with an advanced degree in science. Their ride evolves into a tour as they cordially exchange views about the differences between their respective cultures. The urbane conversation moves easily from classroom behavior to attitudes about sports, food, driving. The affable rapport that Theroux feels with this man from a distant culture pleases him until the conversation moves to literature and the fiction of Salmon Rushdie. The driver's amiable countenance changes; he begins chanting bitterly, "Rushdie must die! Rushdie must die!"

Theroux is shocked. As he later writes, he tells the driver that these are "ignorant and barbarous sentiments" (Fish 1997, 383). Theroux's arguments about free speech are to no avail. For the driver, the greater virtue is the *fatwa* that protects the sacred, not the artistic freedom that would profane. He cannot dissuade the driver from his commitment to religious authority and the rooted solidity of received truth. Fish's story is powerful, its implications provocative. Perhaps our tolerance for other cultures can only extend so far, perhaps only to an appreciation of the superficial cultural differences of food and style. But when serious differences emerge like those between religious dogma and democratic inquiry, where is the common ground for negotiating? Can we respect the taxi driver's right to believe Rushdie must die? We could, of course, but only by privileging one cultural ethic over another. Even in a postmodern environment, we cannot hold that Rushdie must live and Rushdie must die.

Could I allow Constance's belief in an absolute truth to influence a classroom discussion grounded in a democratic ethic that encourages students to interrogate authority, to create meaning out of the dialectic of self and community? Can tolerance of the Other be extended to Constance's abhorrence of "secular humanists" and their relativist attitudes? Can I be proud that I initially provided a safe place for Constance, one that allowed her to assert a fundamentalist ethic largely marginalized at secular universities? In this environment, Constance at first seemed to flourish in our animated, committed discourse. But her voice was finally silenced because our dominant discourse community did not value her perspective, did not wish to engage in a seemingly irrelevant and annoying dialogue. I reluctantly agreed with them because I could not otherwise reconcile the demands of Constance and Stephanie. This choice still seems, for all my good intentions and reasonable justification, a failure, a missed opportunity for democratic promise. Although I surely want to, I cannot yet write this narrative with myself as the hero. Constance somehow should not have felt alienated in my classroom; the rest of us should not have felt superior. Constance tested the boundaries of my tolerance. Somehow, these inevitable limits should be written into all our narratives about school, about authority.

Works Cited

Fish, Stanley. 1997. "Boutique Multiculturalism . . ." *Critical Inquiry 23* (Winter): 378–95. A revised version of his 1995 SAMLA talk.

Lowell, Robert. 1975. "To Speak of Woe That Is in Marriage." *Selected Poems.* New York: Farrar, Straus & Giroux.

Rich, Adrienne. 1984. "Rape." *The Fact of a Doorframe.* New York: W. W. Norton.

Stafford, William. 1960. "Traveling through the Dark." *Stories That Could Be True: New and Collected Poems.* New York: Harper.

Wright, James. 1980. "Lying in a Hammock at William Duffy's Farm in Pine Island, Minnesota." *Collected Poems.* Middletown: Wesleyan University Press.

18

Facing the Other
The Emergence of Ethics and Selfhood in a Cross-Cultural Writing Classroom

SONDRA PERL

January 6, 1996. The phone rings. It's Susan Weil, a faculty member at City College, CUNY, inviting me to teach two graduate courses in a program she helps to direct. The students, it turns out, are two American and nine Austrian teachers of English enrolled in an M.A. program in Language and Literacy. What is unusual is that while the teachers receive their M.A.s from City, they never actually attend classes there. Instead the program arranges for CUNY faculty to teach the courses in Austria in two- to three-week blocks. Susan is wondering whether I would be interested in working with the eleven teachers in the Innsbruck group.

"Interested?" I respond. "For years, I have dreamed of working with teachers in an international setting. If the dates work and my family agrees to do without me, I would love to."

So begins my odyssey—a journey that brings me face-to-face with the issue of my own identity. For what I do not say to Susan is this: Although I yearn to travel and work with teachers in other countries, my imagined trips always take me to France or Spain, India or Japan. Germany is the last place on earth I want to go. Austria is a close second.

June 28, 1996: Sitting on the plane, I imagine two and a half weeks without kids and dogs, family and friends, phone calls and car pools. What a luxury, I tell myself, to be fully self-sufficient, not needing to respond to the needs of other human beings, needing only to devote myself to the courses and what is required of me professionally.

Every few minutes, on a large screen at the front of the cabin, a map charting our progress appears—the countries and major cities are labelled

173

first in German, then in English. I hear the voice of my mother: "If we had been born there instead of here, we would not have survived." Childhood memories of the Holocaust come unbidden: emaciated prisoners in striped pajamas, their agonies clearly visible in their hollow eyes, their haggard faces; film clips of Hitler, right arm raised in the *Sieg Heil*; the worn pages of a novel I cherished, Meyer Levin's *Eva*, the story of a young Jewish girl who tried to survive by "passing." At thirteen, I was gripped by her courage and imagined myself in her place, reading this book over and over again, using it repeatedly for book reports. A question I asked myself then: "If I had been born there, would I have survived?" A question that has haunted me ever since.

For weeks I have joked, "If only this program took place in Paris I'd really be excited." For although I have agreed to go, beneath my humor lies a deep-seated prejudice, one I can only admit to loved ones: I have inherited my mother's hatred of Germans and her conviction that no matter what they say or do, no matter how stunning their accomplishments in art, music, and philosophy, within every German citizen there lies a Nazi in disguise.

Why have I accepted this invitation, I wonder, not for the first time. I know it is related to being so homebound for the past twelve years, busy raising my children—a twelve-year-old daughter and nine-year-old twin sons—and my immediate thrill not only with the prospect of travelling but also with the idea of bringing what I know about the teaching of writing and literature to other teachers. The fact that the country is Austria and the teachers mostly Austrian I have tried to ignore.

While on the plane I jot a note to myself: "For several days now, maybe weeks, I've been dealing with my questions about Germans—Austrians—Nazis—my deep prejudices. Now that I am on the way, it seems clear that I must differentiate between national stereotypes and individual people—it is not possible that everyone is a Nazi."

June 29, 1996: I arrive in Innsbruck and am greeted by Tanja Westfall, one of the two American teachers in the course. Tanja serves as the course coordinator and has also offered to be my guide, inviting me to stay with her in the tiny village of Hatting, a short train ride from the city and the University of Innsbruck where the courses are to be held. As soon as I deplane, I am struck by the extraordinary beauty that surrounds me: the snowcapped peaks of the mountains, the lush and nuanced greens of the fields, the flowers that bloom in the window boxes that dot the wooden balconies of the houses. So struck am I that for moments at a time I am able to forget that this exquisite land harbors unspeakable horrors.

We arrive at Tanja's flat, and while she is making lunch I unpack and settle in. As I look out the window, I see an old man in the garden opposite. He is using a scythe to cut the grass, rhythmically swaying back and forth, back and forth. It is a scene from another world, but my reverie is broken by intruding thoughts. "What did he do during the war? What would he say if he knew a Jew was sleeping next door to him?"

July 1: The first day of class. Tanja and I arrive early to set up the room. The tables and chairs are in rows. A teacher's lectern is at the front. I ask her to help me rearrange the furniture. We move the tables into a large square and place twelve chairs around the perimeter. I know the message I want to convey here. This will be a collaborative endeavor; we will be speaking to and with one another. I will be included in the conversation but will not dominate or control. From the privileged position of professor, I will look to model a more egalitarian possibility.

The teachers arrive. Handshakes. Introductions. People seem kind, warm, waiting to see what I have brought to them. The teachers have received my precourse assignments and have some questions about how we will proceed. We have two courses to complete, "Composition Theory and Practice" and "The Teaching of Adolescent Literature from a Reader-Response Perspective." I plan to switch back and forth between them, sometimes focusing on issues of composing, other times working on the teaching of literature. We have eight class sessions spread over two weeks with large blocks of time at our disposal (some six-hour blocks, a few eight-hour days, and even two ten-hour days that will extend into the evening); I put a schedule on the board and explain that we will meet in both large and small groups and have extended periods of time for writing, reading, and group work. At the end of each evening, we will reconvene as a large group in order to write "Reflections." Above all, I am interested in making sure the teachers reflect on what they are doing and learning, to consider the relevance of our work for their own classrooms.

We begin the first night with an activity in which we write and examine our own composing processes. I write too. Then I model ways of responding to each person's draft. We listen to the stories people tell about their memories of writing. We laugh with recognition. We sympathize with pain recollected. Writing is hard work. Many vividly recount the harsh criticism they received at the hands of their professors. So many memories are tinged with fear. At the end of the first night, after everyone has read and commented, Max leads the group in rapping their knuckles on the tabletops. My startled expression occasions an explanation. "Great night. Thanks." Later that evening, Tanja tells me this is high praise.

July 2: The second night. We begin with an inquiry into their experiences as readers and then a discussion of their responses to two texts I had assigned prior to the beginning of the course: Chapter 1 of Vito Perrone's *A Letter to Teachers* (1991) and the full text of Louise Rosenblatt's *Literature as Exploration* ([1938] 1995). I have always liked using Perrone in a class of teachers. In a frank and open tone, he invites us to consider important questions, asking, for example, "What do we most want our students to come to understand as a result of their schooling?" (4). And he articulates a clear and hopeful vision of what is possible in classrooms: "If we saw the development of active inquirers as a major goal, much that now exists—workbooks and textbooks, predetermined curriculum, reductionism, teaching to tests— would, I believe, begin to fade. Teachers would be free to address the world, to make living in the world a larger part of the curriculum" (9). It is statements like these that I expect to discuss with the Austrian teachers.

But the teachers are struck by something else Perrone has written, something so obvious to me that I have never before stopped to think about it: "Education at its best is first and foremost a moral and intellectual endeavor ..." (1). Later on, he asserts, "Adults are having increasing difficulty explaining their commitments to their children. But children and young people need to know that their parents and teachers have important values" (7).

Tentatively, at first, the teachers begin to ask, "What does this mean?" "Do you honestly think education is connected to morality?" Initially they want to argue that no such statement should be made. What they say to me and what I hear repeatedly as they speak with one another in small groups are versions of the following: "We have been trained to keep ourselves and our personal values outside of the curriculum." "We all follow the same procedures." "Teachers here are taught not to speak about what they believe." "We can't deal with morality in the classroom."

When we come to Rosenblatt, the conversations are even more troubled. I chose Rosenblatt for many of the same reasons I chose Perrone. She writes clearly and speaks directly to teachers. I also find her book balanced in its understanding of textuality. Rosenblatt not only affirms the existence of texts and readers but also succeeds in clarifying the nature of the transaction that occurs between them. But when the Austrian teachers begin to respond, I once again discover that what has always been obvious to me is quite unsettling to them.

In her opening chapter, Rosenblatt writes, "The teaching of literature inevitably involves the conscious or unconscious reinforcement of ethical attitudes. It is practically impossible to treat ... any literary work of art in a vital manner without confronting some problem of ethics and without speaking out of the context of some social philosophy. A framework of values is essential to any discussion of human life" (16). She continues, "A teacher will do neither literature nor students a service if he tries to evade ethical issues" (17). Later on, she argues that a teacher should not "try to pose as a completely objective person. The assumption of a mask of unemotional objectivity or impartial omniscience is one reason why teachers and college professors sometimes seem not quite human to their students. A much more wholesome educational situation is created when the teacher is a really live person who has examined his own attitudes and assumptions and who, when appropriate, states them frankly and honestly" (124).

Several teachers ask, "How can one be a whole human being in the classroom?" But most reassert their claim to what they call "moral neutrality." These conversations are tentative, polite. Only a few teachers are willing to talk; most are waiting to see, I suspect, how I will respond. Am I about to impose a new agenda, one that conflicts with their training and inclinations? Can they risk resisting me and the messages in the texts I have assigned? And for me the pedagogical question becomes, can I keep this inquiry open? Is there room for negotiation here? Can I model an alternative to the authoritarian teaching they have been subjected to with its expectations for conformity? And how can I enact the moral and ethical stances called for by Rosenblatt and Perrone? For unbeknownst to them, I am also engaged in another, silent conversation:

First voice: You are working with the children or grandchildren of Nazis. What if they knew you were Jewish? Would they be so receptive to your teaching then?

Second voice: This is not an issue. Almost everyone in the room looks younger than you are and you were born after the war. These teachers in front of you are not responsible for what happened.

First voice: Well, their parents were alive then. Your father served in the U. S. Army. Their parents could easily be the same age as yours. What did their parents or even their grandparents do?

Second voice: You are not here to accuse them. You are here to teach them.

But I realize this is precisely the issue. What am I teaching in these courses? What am I looking to impart to these teachers? How important are the ethical questions that concern me? Do they have a place here, especially in a course in which we are reading about the importance of a teacher's values in framing the curriculum, of the social philosophy necessary to create a coherent classroom?

While I am holding these private conversations with myself and while the teachers are working on their responses to readings, we are also working on assignments related to the composition course. Here, I want them to compose a piece of writing that matters to them, a piece for which they choose both the form and the content. I plan to write too and to share my drafts and revisions with the class and within a small group.

July 4: Outside at Tanja's. I am sitting at a wooden table under a fruit tree. The sun feels warm on my back; flies buzz around my head. The day before, during class, I led the teachers in some writing activities designed to help them discover or clarify issues or topics of interest to them. At home, they are supposed to be working on their drafts. I have come outside to work on mine. Annoyed at the flies, I swat them away with one hand as I finger my pen in the other. I look into the distance and once again am haunted by thoughts of the Holocaust, of what happened literally on the ground on which I am now walking, living, breathing. And so, tired of censoring myself, unable to imagine anything else anyway, I permit these thoughts to come, and I write:

> What am I doing here
> in the homeland of Hitler's birth?
> Why have I come
> across an ocean
> to a land and a language
> I've never wanted to know?

> Never would I come here
> to the land where Nazis reigned,
> to the place where your people
> turned my people
> into objects of derision and hate.

> Like the numbers
> etched into their forearms
> images are seared in my brain
> of bodies, piled high
> in ditches, of hair
> and teeth, piled high
> in corners.

> I see the laboratories where
> the wombs of young women

are filled with concrete,
the bodies of babies
flung aside
And the Mengele selection,
the preference for twins
Oh my twins

This thought brings me to a full stop. "This is ridiculous," I say to my-self. "You cannot write about this. How could you ever read this to that room full of teachers?" I open my journal and try to describe the struggle I am in: "It is impossible for me to be here, in Austria, and not ask what happened. Jews were the playtoys of the Germans—teased, raped, tortured, destroyed. The bitterness runs deep—a well so deep it drowns. But have I suddenly be-come the accuser? I am not Zola. *J'accuse* is not my intention."

This line prompts me to continue writing, to clarify my position: "I am, at least for now, the inquirer. The same questions keep returning to me. I want to know, what happened here? This land of such overwhelming beauty, of such towering granite faces, peaks that dwarf any sense I have of human power, this land gave birth to Adolf Hitler. How does one understand that? What does it mean to have inherited the responsibility for this twentieth-century self-styled God goose-stepping his way to power?"

I lift up my pen and stop, not knowing how to let myself go any further.

July 5: The fourth evening of the course. A few teachers express dismay. They are finding it excruciatingly difficult to write. No matter how many prompts I offer or how many different prewriting techniques I show them, when they have to sit down and face a blank page or a computer screen, they freeze. I have seen this before. American teachers who have written only academic pa-pers often resist their first invitations to write more creatively, but never be-fore have I seen such deep distress in a group.

Renate begins, "I just can't do this. Why should I write when I can more easily talk?"

Max concurs, "There is no point in writing if the teacher does not give you a topic. I do not mean to be rude, but this activity seems like a waste of time."

It is clear that they see no purpose in what I am asking them to do. Nor, I suspect, do they believe that anything they have to say is worth writing.

I comment, "This is interesting. Why do you think this is so hard for you? What is going on as you try to write?"

Renate once again responds, "Our professors never asked us to be inven-tive. Our writing has consisted primarily in reporting back to our teachers what they have told us."

I recognize the standard school game: figuring out what the teacher wants and providing it. Obviously these teachers have been good at this. They've become teachers themselves and have never been asked to think or act differently. No wonder my invitation seems so threatening. I am asking them to write in a voice they choose, not one designed merely to please me or provide me with the correct answer. I am asking them to be more of a human being in the classroom than anyone has asked before—to bring at least something of themselves here.

I sense the importance of this moment. I am aware that how I respond is crucial. Eleven teachers are watching me.

"It sounds as if many of you are blocked." I can see the relief on their faces. "In fact, it sounds to me as if it's even worse than being blocked. It sounds to me as if you are describing a kind of paralysis."

Again, I see by their faces that I have adequately named their dilemma. While I am speaking, I realize that I am also speaking about myself, that they are mirroring my own paralysis. My mind is racing. Should I tell them what is going on with me? How much should I say? I'm not sure I should say anything. Would it be useful or just complicate matters? Uncertain, I bide my time.

"Look," I respond, "let's pay attention to what is making this seem so hard for you. There are lots of answers I could give you. In fact, in the articles you'll be reading tonight by Nancy Sommers and Donald Murray, you will find many answers to the question, 'Why write?' But I think for now it's important just to notice that for some of you this whole invitation to write is paralyzing. Let's see what happens as you go to your writing groups. Talk about what is paralyzing. See what others have written and keep this as an important question for you. If this is something you are experiencing, your students will likely face a similar dilemma."

For the moment, my comments seem sufficient to handle their anxiety and we proceed with the plan for the evening, which includes time for small groups to read and respond to drafts.

I have placed myself in a group with three women: Gerlinde, Margret, and Rosie, all Austrians.

We are seated together at a small rectangular table. Two have written stunning pieces: In a quiet voice, at several moments tearful, Rosie reads to us a narrative about her mother's struggle with cancer and her final days of life; Margret uses a child's point of view to describe an abusive father and a child's sense of the abyss. "How can you cross the chasm if the bridge is not there?" the child wonders at the end of this piece. Gerlinde describes her inability to write anything, explaining that she is exhausted from work during the school year and not yet ready to compose.

When my turn comes, I explain that I have been keeping a journal about my experiences in Austria but I doubt whether I can mention to them what I am writing about. They look perplexed. I recall Rosie's tears as she read about her dying mother, and I picture the chasm Margret has just described. "It's a lot like Margret's chasm," I say. "I don't know if there is a bridge here." Again they watch me quietly, waiting for me to go on. I look back at them and in a halting voice, I say, "The more I walk on this land, the more my mind fills with images of the Holocaust. But how can I read this to you? I, well, I don't know how to talk about this or how to ask you about it."

Margret's eyes widen. She looks straight at me and says, "How can you not talk about this? We never discuss our past, but we must! Of course, you should continue to write and you must let us hear it."

I am astonished. Margret wants to talk? She is encouraging me to make this more public? Is there more here than my personal issue? Can my dilemma offer something to the group, something that has the resonance of ethical issues, something that shows them not only my fears as a writer but also who I am as a human being? When I ask them if they think I ought to raise my concerns with the group, they wholeheartedly agree: "Yes. Of course you should." I tell them I'll think about it.

At the end of the evening when the entire group comes together to reflect on the night's work, I have made up my mind to speak. Although I know I am taking a risk, the encouragement of my group makes me think the risk is worth taking. How better to enact for these teachers what it means to be a human being in the classroom than to be the person I am with my fear of raising one of the most compelling moral dilemmas of the twentieth century—one in which, in very different ways, we are all implicated?

My heart pounds as I begin. "Before we write reflections, I want to say something about the paralysis that Renate and Max talked about tonight. I not only understand what you are talking about, I, too, have been experiencing it. I have found it almost impossible to write. In fact, for the past four days, every time I try to write, I silence myself. I refuse to go on. Because what is emerging is just too upsetting, and I don't think I'll be able to read any of it to any of you."

Not a sound in the room.

I go on. "I came here to teach. But I now realize I also came here with a lot of questions. I raised these questions with my group tonight, and they have encouraged me to raise them with you. My questions have to do with what happened here sixty years ago. I don't expect you to explain the war to me. But I am curious about all of you. How do you cope with the knowledge of what happened here? How do you understand it? What sense do you make of it now?

"For the past few days, I have been plagued by these questions. But I felt I could not ask them, that this is not my job or what I am being paid to do here. But I also realize that I am not morally neutral, and if I pretend neutrality or innocence, then what I am trying to show you is a lie. I will be pretending to be someone I am not. The course will be an empty gesture. And what we are reading, theories I value and believe in, will also turn into lies."

I take a breath and look at them sitting around the table. Silence. "I don't want you to answer me now. Just let my questions sink in and see if you have something to say in return. If you do, I'd be interested to listen. But I mention this now because I want you to see that I, too, have been blocked and have been silencing myself. I don't think that is an effective way to teach writing or to show you what I believe to be powerful or important about teaching. So why don't we all write some reflections, now, on whatever comes to mind about tonight's work."

People pick up their pens. The concentrated quiet in the room tells me that everyone is writing and the writing matters. I have no idea if they are angry, offended, or shocked, or if I have made a huge mistake. I pick up my pen and write, "I have raised with them the questions that have been plaguing me. What will happen? Will we find a way to continue this inquiry? Should we?"

When I ask for volunteers to read, some teachers excitedly describe what is happening in their own writing groups. Others reflect on how valuable it is to hear and respond to what their peers are writing. Still others express interest in changing topics. Margret waits to read last. "How can we not address Sondra's questions?" she reads. "How can we avoid talking about the fascism in our land, our country, our blood? How can we not teach our children who they are and be willing to take the beating of the world? We are the generation that must respond. Our parents can't and won't. We must own our dark side."

Margret looks up. Our eyes meet. This night as we leave, there is no knuckle rapping. Only a great silence.

July 6: The fifth session. We have an eight-hour class planned with a range of activities: reading groups, writing groups, more time for writing, discussions of responses to articles, a dinner break, selections of Young Adult novels to be read in small groups. I know we can resume with business as usual or we can pause and acknowledge what I opened up the night before. I feel it is important to note what has occurred, to mark it in some way. I am aware that once a large space is opened, the tendency in most groups is to close it down and retreat to safer ground. Since our schedule now calls for a break of four days, I want to make sure no one is left hanging or feeling terribly unsettled by the personal and historic turn we have just taken. I want both to reassure the class that we can proceed with our work and still affirm that we have touched upon something important.

I begin by naming what has occurred: the paralysis issue raised by Renate; the question of "Why bother writing?" mentioned by Max; the importance of not foreclosing on these issues but rather inquiring into them and attempting to see what answers can come from our own experiences as writers; the power that writing groups seem to be generating for individuals to pursue what matters to them; how through the language we use and bring to our groups, we express who we are; how, through these written expressions, we come to know one another more fully; the courage it takes to reveal what is most deep and present in us; and my desire not to impose an agenda on the group but rather to give everyone the widest possible room to be a participant in a classroom where the teacher is also someone who can voice her concerns and questions. Finally, I conclude, "We have an unusual opportunity here. We can, as many groups would, pretend that nothing momentous happened, or we can approach these questions with care and respect and see what occurs. We have a chance, I think, to speak across cultures."

It is not lost on me that I am no longer the same person who began this course, that by opening this issue I have opened myself to them. Still, I wonder, how will they respond? And, still I debate, what will I write?

The hours in class pass quickly. In reading groups, we are concluding our discussion of Toni Morrison's *Sula* (1973, 1982), which gives me the opportunity to raise the problem of racism in America. The teachers are finding it useful to record their reactions to Morrison in response journals and then to discuss them in small groups. When writing groups meet, the teachers seem even more engaged. One writing group does not return for a scheduled activity. They report later, shocked at their own behavior, that they just couldn't stop. What they were doing together was just too compelling to cut short. I am secretly delighted by their disobedience.

Gerlinde, Margret, and Rosie ask me to read what I have written. I consent, but I lower my eyes as I recite the lines about Nazis, about "your people" and "my people." I know I am starkly naming our difference; giving voice to this leaves me feeling scared, naked, unmasked. I am aware that until now, I have not actually said I am Jewish. After this reading, however, I assume that through whatever classroom grapevine exists, my identity will become common knowledge.

That night after class, I join six of the teachers for drinks in a local bar: Max, Freya, Alex, Tanja, Johanna, and Gerlinde. My notes say it was "Fun. Easy." Then I recount a story. Johanna, a young woman in her late twenties and a mother of two, is asking me about life in New York. She wants to know if it is safe. "Can you, for instance, leave your baby in a car while you run into a shop?" This is a common practice in Innsbruck. I describe my fear of having my kids out of eyesight for even a minute whether we're in a supermarket or at a playground. Then she asks, "Is it safe to visit Chinatown and Harlem and the Jewish quarter?" Her question strikes me as enormously funny, and I burst out laughing, responding with a line I've heard my non-Jewish friends use: "In New York, there is no Jewish section. In New York, everything is Jewish."

In retrospect, I can't imagine that Johanna or anyone else actually understood what I was referring to, but somehow everyone joins in laughing and something, stemming from Johanna's naïveté or my own sense of humor, brings us a greater sense of ease in each other's presence.

July 11: The seventh day. I record in my journal: "There seems to be much less fear of writing in the room. We all seem more willing to encounter the uncomfortable experience of 'not knowing' what we will say or write. Also people are beginning to form their own answers to the question, 'Why write?'"

I am referring here to Renate's wonderful burst of energy. Having read Maxine Hairston's article "The Winds of Change" (1982) over our small break, Renate enters the room claiming to have had a "paradigm shift." "I see now," she exclaims, "what this is about. Writing is a process. It's exciting. I'm so excited." And on the last night of the course, she has us all laughing until tears come as she reads aloud her piece on the pleasures of organic gardening, punctuated by a gardener's pain at the sight of proliferating slugs.

But only a few teachers attempt to answer my questions. Most choose not to talk about the Holocaust or their views of what happened. The two who do are members of my small group. Rosie is deeply engrossed in her piece about her mother. It is taking beautiful shape and she seems to want to say something but doesn't. Gerlinde, who still lacks the energy to write, tells me that my questions leave her feeling helpless, that she is not sure what to say. Then she tells me, "We lived in the country. My mother had nine children. She refused Hitler's medal of honor. My parents thought the Nazis were terrible; to them it was a time to survive, to get through."

It is Margret who responds most fully. With Margret I seem to have asked a question she has been waiting to answer for years. One afternoon, speaking slowly, she reveals that her in-laws, well-respected natives of Innsbruck, with whom she and her husband and daughter currently live, were enthusiastic supporters of the Nazis. Her father-in-law was an official in the Nazi party; her mother-in-law was the leader of a Hitler youth group of Tyrolean girls, proud that her framed picture hung on the wall of Hitler's study.

Margret finds this knowledge unbearable, has never found a way to make peace with it. Finds it even more problematic that she has no way to talk about this with her daughter. No way to have a conversation about the events in which her husband's family were so complicit. She and her husband, it turns out, met at an antinuclear rally; they share certain basic values. But where a critique of National Socialism is concerned, there is silence in her home.

Rosie and Gerlinde sit with us as Margret and I look at one another. There is no interpretation anyone needs to offer. Each of us is, in some way, thinking about our mothers and our daughters and what it means to be born into a particular culture, a particular time and place, what it is we each have to pass on; what it is we might pass on to one another.

I am reminded of my own complex relationship to Judaism, marked at first by the exuberance of my extended family's Passover Seders, when eighty or more of us would gather in the basement of a shul in Irvington, New Jersey, and those of us who were kids would run around and ignore the more observant grandparents, who bent over prayer books and took all of this so seriously; then how this same Judaism was deeply colored by the hate my mother communicated to me concerning anything German, my fascination with photographs that depicted the horrors of the Holocaust, and my child's knowledge that had my parents been born in Europe rather than America, they too would likely have perished at the hands of the Nazis; and finally how my Jewish fate seemed to be sealed when my father's financial success moved us out of my grandparents' world of immigrant Jews and into a world of privilege and power, where, like Eva, I too learned to pass, to blend in, to remake myself in the image of my Christian schoolmates.

On this next to last day of the course, Margret and I discover that our daughters are the same age, born in the same year, on the same day. When we mention this to the class, Alex jokes, "You mean that both of you were in labor at the same time?" We all laugh at this thought. But alone, Margret and I speculate about the possibility of our daughters writing to one another. We both know we are looking to say how much we want to stay in touch, how much the other's presence has begun to mean to us.

That afternoon, I find myself writing with greater ease, less compulsion: "Gerlinde's comment that this whole issue 'leaves her speechless' stays with me. It is, of course, overwhelming, beyond words. And yet now I see that one must speak. One must look again at the sense we can make of this, the images we carry within us and how we hold them, the stories we have been told and can now tell. . . . What was transformative for me was speaking out, giving voice to my concerns, not pretending to be someone who didn't care or didn't have questions or was morally neutral. On Austrian soil, I am not innocent. I see now that I could not have come here and remained silent, could not have made myself blend in as if nothing happened here. . . . All of this is rich and revealing to me. Powerful, evocative, freeing."

The teachers, too, are more at ease, busy, reading, writing, working on book presentations, meeting the demands of the course. Margret produces poem after poem, what she calls her Holocaust series, and shares with the group an insight she has had about writing in a second language. "I could not have written these poems in my mother tongue," she explains. "I tried but I always felt a sickness creeping up my legs. This [experience] has changed my relationship to English. I believe I have fully grown into it."

July 13: The last night of the course. Among many concluding activities (book presentations, final responses to readings, a potluck dinner in the classroom, discussions of classroom practices and future plans), I have scheduled time for each person to read a particular piece of writing to the group and then one last opportunity to write reflections, to sum up, to comment upon, and to mark what it is we are taking away with us.

The read-around is a time for each of us to listen to and appreciate one another's work and to acknowledge, as well, what it took for us to arrive at this point. There is no necessary order to the readings. One person volunteers to read. We listen, clap, and move on. Often a sad piece is followed by a humorous one. Connections seem to emerge. And when someone from one's own small group reads, the shared sense of pleasure and pride is palpable.

This evening, we hear, among others, Freya's piece about a woman who wakes up to find herself in a hospital partially paralyzed after a car accident; Alex's science-fiction rendering of a woman intent on destroying the lives of the men she loves; Barbara's careful description of a trip through France; Tanja's story of adoption. Margret reads a poem she calls "Innocence":

> We didn't mean to
> brand your arms
> We didn't mean to
> rip off your clothes
> We didn't mean to
> make you crawl on your knees
> We didn't mean to
> select you on the ramp
> We didn't mean to
> send you to the gas
> We didn't mean to
> hurt anyone on our march to Norway

We didn't mean to
load a cross on our offspring's shoulders
We didn't mean to
cut off the human bond
We *don't* mean to
say "Forgive us.
We were wrong the same!"

I have come to expect something dramatic from Margret. An unacknowledged leader of the group, her words often speak to and for the others. So it is Gerlinde who in some ways surprises me the most on our last night together. Never having focused on a topic, frequently preoccupied with ongoing commitments she had made to her school, Gerlinde has maintained until the end of the course the position of the nonwriter. Yet this night, she reads a piece that shows how carefully she has been listening. It is a letter to Louise Rosenblatt, a rewrite of an earlier assignment I have given them:

Dear Mrs. Rosenblatt,
You originally wrote your book, *Literature as Exploration* in 1938, one of the darkest years of Austrian history. While you were writing, enlightened by cultural pluralism, terrible things happened here from the "occupation" to *Kristallnacht*. And so many Austrians, Jewish Austrians, who wrote the best literature were in danger, not allowed to publish, and had to leave the country. May I express my deepest regret for all of the atrocities.
Yours sincerely,
Gerlinde Egger

Teaching is always so surprising to me. I knew that Rosenblatt first published her book in 1938. But I was so busy focusing on the relevance of her message for these teachers today, I hadn't thought to look back to her earliest publication date or to consider what the year 1938 would mean to them. It took Gerlinde's observation and her imaginative reaching out across time and space, in writing, to remind me again how soil, the terrain we stand on, the land we inhabit, alters the way we read and write and changes the meaning we make.

These courses altered my sense of my issue too. In the final days, while we were each attempting to complete the pieces we had begun, I found myself composing in a different tone, with different kinds of questions:

What pain has lain
dormant inside me?
This is not my
history. I was not born

here. But the souls
of six million
still haunt, still call.

What is this hatred, born here
nurtured here, turned hysterical?
So overwhelming, so encompassing,
it annihilates the other?

Can I find this hatred
in myself? Or is the higher ground
of victim preferable?

For protection, I have
hated you. All of you. There was
no distinction to make.
Germans? They're all Nazis,
I said. Austrians? The same.
Was there a difference?
Who cared?

But now, I have come
among you. You have given
me room to speak. Now, I
see you with your passion
and your pain. Your human side
opens to me and so
the opening starts,
the caring begins,
to ask, to be heard, to know.

I choose not to read this to the group. It is too unformed, too raw. I'm not
ready to read it aloud to them or to anyone. I choose instead to read a piece I
have written on e-mail to my daughter who, my husband has written, is hor-
ribly homesick during her first experience at sleep-away camp. In this piece, I
try to convey to her how each of us comes up against our own fears, our own
demons, whenever we venture into the unknown. The irony here is not lost
on me.

In final reflections that night, we find it easy to acknowledge one another, the importance of the questions we have asked, the good humor
that has accompanied us, the power of the pedagogy we have engaged in.
Many teachers express a desire to reform what they are doing in their

classrooms, to devise with their students a more learner-centered curriculum. No one is more adamant than Margret, who reads to us a reflection on teaching:

> I want to support my students in resisting all those leaders who seek to turn their minds into copies of their own, unquestioningly taking what they are offered. A mind that asks questions, reflects, and dares to speak out for all the values once acknowledged to be worthy . . . will be the goal I set for the students in my classroom. Is this utopian? . . . I don't know but considering our tradition, I have come to ask the following question: Are there any mistakes a teacher could make that are worse than contributing . . . to a belief that makes young people march joyfully into an atrocious war?"

We find it hard to end. We know, in some sense, there is no end. But this time, when everyone raps knuckles, I do the same.

July 16: On the plane home. I think about the courses, the students, the little bit of German I now understand and can begin to speak, the exhilarating and exhausting hikes up to the snow peaks that Margret, her husband, and Tanja took me on during our days off, my aching muscles, my family awaiting me in New York. I recall the scene in the airport that morning: As Tanja and I arrive, we are greeted by Margret, Gerlinde, and Max, who have formed themselves into an impromptu good-bye party. We exchange hugs. Margret hands me a package with a letter inside. In the form of a thank-you, she writes:

> I was so eager to bring to words what had been brooding in my heart for such a long time. . . . This experience of reading each other's words and of responding to each other had its climax in a feeling of revelation. If you, Sondra, hadn't been so courageous to ask your careful questions, I would never have been able to answer them. When I eventually realized you were Jewish, it hit me right in my heart and my brain: you are kin to all those people who suffered inconceivably by atrocities committed by my people. History became real and present. I could hardly bear it. I had nothing to offer. An apology would just have been a token weighing so little that the scales of justice would not have moved an inch. Yet with you I have learned that some people are willing to look closer even if it seems impossible to bear doing so. Thus others get the chance to learn.

I relax into my seat, watch the progress of the plane on the screen in front of me, and marvel, not for the first time, at the power of teaching.

Works Cited

Hairston, Maxine. 1994. "The Winds of Change: Thomas Kuhn and the Revolution in the Teaching of Writing." *Landmark Essays on Writing Process,* edited by Sondra Perl, pp. 113–126. Hillsdale, NJ: Lawrence Erlbaum Associates.

Morrison, Toni. 1973, 1982. *Sula.* New York: Penguin.

Perrone, Vito. 1991. *A Letter to Teachers: A Reflection on Schooling and the Art of Teaching.* San Francisco: Jossey-Bass.

Rosenblatt, Louise. [1938] 1995. *Literature as Exploration.* New York: Modern Language Association.

19

What We Don't Like, Don't Admit, Don't Understand Can't Hurt Us. Or Can It?

On Writing, Teaching, Living

WENDY BISHOP

In the movie *Michael*, the Andie Macdowell character—a dog trainer who wants to be a country-western singer but who is pretending to be an angel expert—looks at John Travolta, who plays the Archangel Michael and who has a dazzling smile and bad hygiene, and challenges him. She demands to know: If he's an angel and all the women are falling in love with him, why isn't she? He answers with what will surely be a much-quoted line, because even my nine-year-old son quoted it yesterday, giggling: "I put a block on you."

I've blocked on writing this essay for more than a year, which gives the word *block* much more than comic import for me. Most writers delay—it's not bad, really, it's necessary even, sometimes—but those who know me as a writer know it spells big trouble. I don't usually admit impediment in writing or in life. I'm always figuring out a new way to run. And I don't usually talk about teaching difficulties: the subject I want to address head-on in this essay. Yet even now I'm blocking, taking the long way around, going cross-country with every sentence, but I forgive myself, for now since I am finally in motion, I can't be stopped. I want to talk about those events, students, subjects, a happily practicing teacher has to block out, and why, and what it means to do so in one's teaching life and to one's teaching soul. By doing this, I also, of course, want to examine what it might mean to teachers to relax some of those blocks, to at least look back and learn from the necessary emotional maintenance we all undertake in the classroom. What angels know is that humans were made for happiness, but what they also know is it's very hard to achieve happiness—in a lived life or in a teaching life. And aren't these two really, after all, the same thing?

192 · NARRATION AS KNOWLEDGE

For nearly two decades, I've been a committed writing teacher who goes overboard in my advocacy for students. I have tried *never* not to like students, and largely succeeded. In fact, I've been presumptuously judgmental about other teachers who put students down in large or small ways. I've been self-deceptive about that judgment, carefully making a case against calling students "kids," say, in a research study and then slipping into that not unexpected type-of-talk naturally as I began to age well beyond my first-year students.

Certainly I believe that I/we should respect students enormously though I have learned as Peter Elbow suggests there is probably a normal need to let off steam and in privacy "make-fun" of the priceless excuse or the incredible English opening sentence. By ignoring such a need, I denied the times when I conflated students/kids in word or thought or when in aid of professional conviviality I too tried to tell a "funny" teaching story (I realize now that I was saved and sanctimonious mainly because I'm not a good storyteller in the traditional, "here's a joke" sense). These habits of mind and of accident kept me in a state of functional denial. Generally, I deny bad teaching memories. I did this rather relentlessly during the five years I trained new teachers of writing—I mean, they didn't need to hear "bad" stories, did they? Of course, you realize easily, as I realized after some time, that I may have done them a disservice, for new teachers immediately plunge into teaching-learning problems in their own classes and too rosy a picture does them no good (just as too cynical a picture is problematic also).

Anyway, in the last four years or so, I began to suspect my teaching narratives—a bit. I began to worry that I've tended to hide the tracks of difficulty and disaster. Those frail and distant and lost images of students who frustrated me (whom I frustrated in return) flit like Pandora's "ills" and "evils" in my interior teaching files—a secret locked file cabinet. My personal and effective party line was, and mostly still is, that I shouldn't, don't, and can't dislike a student. That students who don't like me—visibly, audibly, or invisibly on university evaluation forms—are not my enemy; if they do dislike me, I can turn that to account, trying harder to be a better, bolder, more understanding teacher. Don't resistant students make me look good to the degree that I can survive them with understanding, empathy, or a refusing-to-be-baited shrug toward a grading form? And isn't it true that without some denial we wouldn't return, paper after paper, student after student, term after term to our sometimes soberingly difficult writing classrooms?

I'm a liberal. I intentionally strive to be ethical. I have had to tell myself certain stories. And because of my inclinations, I need now to explore new teaching narratives.

Over the last ten years, working with graduate students, I denied even more thoroughly. I relate to these individuals as colleagues. I would claim—and it is/was true—that I preferred graduate students to most colleague-professors even as my salary and career gains were moving me away from those friends at a seemingly unbridgeable rate. Older graduate students like the ones I often work with are generally engaged in learning, and those not engaged rapidly disappear into busy alternate lives.

But one day, a teacher whom I liked dropped out of a teacher-education program, showing me how losing a student I was mentoring can hurt. (Probably) because she reminded me of me in an earlier career incarnation, I was trying so hard to make her in my image. I thought she was a good teacher, yet she found teaching writing made her so nervous she would throw up before her first-year class. We're friends today, sort of. Or would be if I ever saw her. She tried to keep up the friendship more vigorously and I let it drift, busy with "active" students. But I like her and feel guilty and detect some undertone of guilt in that drift. She left the "fold" and I may be punishing her by not keeping up. Or maybe I just worry too much?

Next came a graduate student whom I mentored and liked though I could hear some of the department static on my antenna and knew that for others she was sometimes too intense (a common issue, I've noticed with goal-directed older women students—I should know this, I was a very prickly one in the summer of 1985). She was difficult to like: independent, older than me, motivated in the way of reentry women students that I admired. And I admired her. When she resisted conventional writing styles and forms, I encouraged her to write her skillful alternately styled essays (drawing on her background as a creative writer and her growing commitment as a teacher-researcher). Some time later, I found her resistance was not purely aesthetic, for I was astonished to find that this fluent writer's attempts at plain style, test-taking academic discourse for her qualifying exams were dismal. I was dismayed. She had been so fluent in her ability to write creative nonfiction and personally voiced teaching essays, I had wrongly assumed she would be fluent when needing to show knowledge. I was pretty sure she knew what she should know, but I wasn't completely sure given the confusing prose in these exams. Problematic. Her problem or mine? Hers of course— she was old enough to know that wanting institutions to be different doesn't make them so and that there are still rules and rituals to be followed. And mine of course—I was experienced enough to know that I was avoiding confrontation with her as a person when I let her always choose her writing forms. I was avoiding examining my own belief/practices that said by "supporting" a student in the writing she preferred to do I was doing all the teaching toward the degree that needed to be done.

The exams weren't strong but I/her committee made what I/we thought were appropriate allowances. I tried obliquely but couldn't tell her point-blank that she had barely passed and that I expected something . . . more. Or did I tell her point-blank and did she look at me blankly, not understanding what I was saying? Even now I don't know. But I wanted from her that intangible perfect performance that would make me proud and show off the person I thought she was. By the time she proposed a dissertation, I was again distressed. It wasn't a "research" dissertation proposal as I thought I'd made clear it needed to be, as I thought I'd taught her to do in an (albeit informally taught) research methods course. And I couldn't make this go right—by responding, avoiding, or advising. She had an agenda—to complete her later-in-life degree quickly, and I was discovering that I had an agenda too. So, though a champion of good teaching (I was on my life's journey, of course, aiming to right some bad graduate teaching I had experienced in my own past), I was suddenly the "other." The teacher with a "problem" student. The harder I tried to solve the student, the more frustrated we both became. I finally gave up, suggested she switch to another dissertation chair and declare another area of English studies. Eventually, she completed her degree and asked me for a teaching recommendation, and it is the first one, ever, that I didn't finish. She's a fine teacher. I feel petty. Or is she a normal anomaly?

Recently, I found a note from her to me. As I search for it again this morning, I realize I threw it out ten days ago even as I knew I should have saved it (as I had saved it for two years) to quote in an essay. But I didn't. Seeing it again hurt—my memory says she wrote something like, "Wendy, I've now completed setting up a new committee and I wanted to let you know. I've appreciated the time you spent working with me and I want you to know that I've benefited from our interactions, especially those early on in our acquaintance." This isn't quite her voice (remember, I can't tell jokes well) but it is her import—she formally expressed appreciation—she mentioned benefit. I know she was a better writer than I am for her here; she didn't choose the stiff words *interaction* or *acquaintance*—those words come from my sadness. But she did say something like "early on"—that was the phrase that hurt, that led me to the wastebasket as if the simple note were burning my fingers. Teaching relationships don't last. I was good for her and she for me—early on—but not later on. From her, I learn that I need to learn to identify these moments of change and learn how to let students go and to let my ego go with them (or better yet, before them).

What's at stake? I've seen glimmers of answers in the essays Lad Tobin writes—looking at how classrooms feel and what really goes on in them and how writing instruction inevitably leads us into important self-examinations as teachers. As people. I want to say, Let's talk about this stuff more. It's not mere lore or conference bar gossip. A lot of this has to do with surviving our own mentoring and learning how to mentor others, because ours—teaching writing—is a person-to-person profession with all the issues that arise when persons interact. The things I've found myself most avoiding in these inter-actions are facing the outcomes of educational liberalism and the teaching hopes that liberalism engenders; in addressing our emotions, the way love, anger, passion, anxiety are present in the classroom contract; and, yes, in looking at teaching as "life itself."

My writing block seems more understandable now, I expect, and it wasn't placed upon me by an angel but by my own desire for teaching survival: these are tough issues to explore, especially as we begin to teach and need to have specific and practical help. They are more important as we age, weary, or wear as teachers and have ever more need of spiritual help.

Students and teaching writing have moved and touched and hurt and pleased and pained and surprised and astonished and impressed and moved and touched me.

Some days, I'm tempted to write to all the students at the poles of my memory: those who made my teaching life blessed and those who have caused me the most concern. I was tempted to write this essay as letters to each of them and then to construct their imaginary answers back. Maybe I should make this essay an (im)pure fiction, a story about someone who sends such letters and gets answers? What will those answers be? I don't know. I know, to get to these issues—authority, emotion, and existence—I would steal any story technique and grammar B stylistic technique (like those I've used recently to trick myself into being more honest in my nonfic-tion) because I need to explore the aching tooth, the underbelly of guilt, that my memories/interactions with these students raise. But then I block, my emotions swinging from paranoia to self-indulgence (jeez, maybe this thing—teaching—just doesn't work out sometimes, relax, forgive yourself) to fascination with what I won't let myself talk about and admit.

Why did these teachers/colleagues/students, whom I know to be honor-able, human, striving teachers/colleagues/students, push my buttons, make me feel used somehow, make me feel resentful, make me feel unsuccessful? Why do some make me feel euphoric and distressingly godlike, more impor-tant than I know I merit? I think exploring these territories will make me reevaluate my "labeled" successful teaching in useful ways. And I'm willing to do this fairly unpleasant thing for the sake of that knowledge, guessing other teachers might find the journey worth starting on with me, though each will end it in her or his own way.

So, I was going to continue with an academic effort—dividing the rest of my space into useful thirds that would go this way:

The Liberal Self-Delusion—Authority Is as Authority Does
Emotional (Self)-Delusions: How Real People (Especially Women-Type People) Survive in Teaching/Learning Places
Life Itself: Where We All Meet

But such separations proved of little worth for developing narrative knowledge. Instead, I took the black dog Lucy for a run—we're all running here on this resolution-filled morning in my suburban neighborhood, the first of January. Black dogs are a great salve for quandaries in love and teaching and life. A good, endorphin-inducing, writing-block-solving, temporary solution. My friend Libby Rankin can vouch for this and also provide the lyrics she's written to "Beautiful Dreamer" that begin "Beautiful black dog." Obviously, we exchange dog pictures and writing advice.

I found my narrative thread (or leash or lead) on that run. This is all about love—the necessity of and the possibility of. Of sentences and people. Some of those sentences are my own, some are my students'. Generally, actually absolutely, my love life has been less successful than my teaching life, but these two lives have also intertwined. Intentionally, I use the word *love* imprecisely. We are also talking about authority—and there are many -ists who can talk about authority with more élan than I can, though for my money the French feminist ones and Trinh Minh-ha and my friend Kate Haake do it best. I could go to philosophers. But I don't really get them. Or, like so much in my life, I get them enough to know that I don't quite get them, even though I suspect they do engage in something get-at-able. Ditto with the very scholarly.

Simply, many years ago I fell in love with a professor. He was eighteen years older than me, and in this year's Christmas letter, just arrived, he still feels cranky about being older. At the time, it was a wonderful opportunity for an unsure woman graduate student to be accelerated into something that felt like adulthood and respect. He valued my mind—really—and my very nice young body. I valued his warmth, knew he replaced in some ways my just-dead father. We shared words. We still do. And poetry. He read aloud to me and I learned how to cook while being read to (and miss it). I kept him guessing and listened well though he lectured sometimes and I grew restive sometimes—wanting to be, not to be told.

Right now, this month, I'll be forty-four—that is, five years older than he was when I met him so many years ago, when his thirty-nine seemed so old, when, as a young student, I needed mentoring. Through him, I met famous writers and learned to distrust famous writers (both useful lessons) who—mainly male—wanted to mentor me in ways less benevolent than my now good friend. I learned that I could get sucked up and lose my identity in that of someone more established, that I didn't want or dare to be the girlfriend but also that the role *was* seductive. We went to Europe. We wrote good poems and stories—his more immediately successful than mine but still informing me. I found that many of his colleagues were also sleeping with students, learned sad stories of English department affairs, indulgences, and inequities. In some ways I learned too much, moved from naïve to jaded and left the academy for a restless while, though I know now these stories are true of any workplace, for any workplace is a human living place. Because of this way of coming into the academy as a woman, I determinedly put up roadblocks and mental blinders to the power seductions and potential sensuality of mentorings. I would be different. I would be feminist, collegial, peer—grad student to my grad students. I would disperse authority, love everyone equally and unromantically.

I did OK at this. But I suppressed stories and voices, fissures and sensualities. Once as a young teacher I was visited by a supervisor who reminded me that the young man in the back row was in love with me. I ignored her statement until it resurfaced in a short story—proving I heard her very well indeed. Once, in my late thirties, a young writer came to my office again and again. My marriage was on rocky ground, I was floundering. I wrote a poem to him. And ignored my feelings, subverted them. So they ran away with me shortly later in an e-mail word love affair, just as such things were being invented. Understandable, but hurtful to the soul, for colleague-to-colleague is not necessarily smarter or safer. Power—of words, people, presence—is always at issue. An issue.

My students fall in love with me in many ways. One says:

My essays were good kids out on their own, your class the proud parent, always there to provide stability and guidance.

Another says:

You said it: my problem with writing seems to be that I don't know what I want to be as a writer. You might just be right about this because I've got some real questions about who I am as a human being. I've been going through big changes of life lately and I think they might be reflected in my writing: I'm not sure what my voice is because I'm not sure who I am.

I never meant to be a parent to my students—quite the reverse as you see from my initial teaching decision never to call students "kids." And I never meant to tell someone what his problem was and have him believe it. And I never meant to half fall in love with a student or fully fall in love with a professor. No, I fooled myself into thinking things were as I declared them to be. And even then I could be disappointed. When an independent student told me that he learned more from his peers than from me—was I proud midwife (as I professed) or wounded mentor (as I have to admit I felt)? Or a little of both:

> No kiss-ass letters wanted. None given. I learned most not from you, but from those around me. I learned humility, respect for diversity, and the art of communication. But that's what you intended, isn't it. Not to teach us, but for us to teach one another?

"Good," my benevolent teacher self says. "But I created that class atmosphere," the craven person who teaches says. Do I need to confess that the first two more flattering students received A grades? The last received a C grade. Is it more or less confessional to explain that the C-earning student continues to return to talk to me about writing, sees me as his mentor, when I saw myself as mentor to the other two students? Do we name ourselves as teachers or are we named? Like love, these outcomes are bewildering, bothering, worth pondering.

I'm writing about love here on the first day of January because I want to clear the decks. Last night, I broke up with a lover. Someone I've known eight years, loved six months, who in bookendlike reversal (though three years older than me) is novice to my expert. Two decades after I started teaching, I'm the successful professor and he's the late-in-life, newly minted Ph.D. without, as yet, a tenure-line job and with student loans enough for a lifetime. We can't bridge the authority/power differential of this undoable relationship. I can no more be right for him than my professor way-back-when was right for me or than my e-mail-life-love and I could hold on to one another: each of these discoveries has been a lesson and a painful one. I know professors and students who have made it together—often male professor/female student pairings. I know the seduction of youth or of (a)vocation-related familiarity. Like most of us, I distrusted and craved both. Unable to deal with such tensions, I denied them. I denied authority. I regularly begin classes with a Moby Dick riff of "Call me Wendy." I'll do this next week—assert my accessibility even as I protect my privacy with every distanced step I take to keep my personal life separate from my teaching life. In fact, these days I have authority by the full-professor fistfuls and must learn to deal with this. And still be liberal. And still be ethical. And still be a committed social-expressivist (process) teacher. And still believe that writing personal narratives in first-year classes is necessary and hasn't needlessly, wantonly, led me to this sorry confessional/professional pass.

I've always been sure I knew how to live my teaching life. I seemed to observe its boundaries and behaviors better than I did those of my private life. Now I'm not so sure in either direction. I go to the classroom for connection, I can even say, for love. I understand why bell hooks, even though she seems outrageous (and wants to) when she does, calls our attention to the sexual and sensual potentialities of mentoring. I'm advocating nothing, just admitting everything. I know I mentor women mostly, and more comfortably, for to mentor more men, more often might take me into danger zones (just as I've learned to love women more from mentoring them and to respect the several lesbian couples I've become friends with this way). And that's just it. Teaching is the life I live in. It's life itself. Filled with authority teeter-totters. Me and him/her. Me and my department chair. My students and me. Me and my teaching friends. Shadows, lovers, learners, listeners, solid good plain friends, potentials, all. A world of potential.

I need to ask myself different questions as I age as a teacher—what is making me anxious, uneasy, happy, easy about this or that teaching relationship? Some of my graduate students have become my best friends. How did we make this passage, and why? What need did we fill, each for the other? Some have left mad at me, very. Because I wasn't "their" mentor or couldn't like or teach them. Don't worry, I try to tell myself, let that one— that experience with that person—go. Though sometimes—often—I can't. I just saw one of these students. She had written me a burning final class evaluation, one I still have but won't dig out for you. In fact, I don't dare throw it away for that would seem, somehow, unethical, not playing fair. Anyway, her dislike and resistance eclipsed the enthusiasm of nine other students that term. At a recent South Atlantic MLA conference, she was talking to her partner and a friend of mine introduced us. "We already know each other" she said. "Yes," I said. And lots of distance passed in the look between us.

Teaching does have a beginning, middle, and end. Sort of. Maybe. Sometimes. Lots of them. Teaching produces a compelling narrative, as long as it goes on. Again and again and again. A fool for love. A fool for teaching. I'd rather in some ways still be blocked, be under the bedsheet of desire, be telling the black dog I'm too sated and tired for a walk today; but I also know I can come back to this territory of teaching and know that I'm in another phase of my life there. I don't care much anymore for the shoulds and should-nots, the taking sides of my early scholarly life. Sometimes it seems my best teaching friends are burning out at an alarming rate—complaining about 4Cs this, literature folks that. But I want to be an optimist. Sometimes I can't be. More times I can be. I know what I am and am not—I'm a writer who loves to and needs to teach writing; who loves to and needs to write; who loves, and will again, and needs to.

I'll end with another movie. It's the Christmas season and I'm house-bound in Florida with a nine-year-old son and a nearly thirteen-year-old daughter—dear children both. My recently lost loved one and a girlfriend (once a graduate student; "my" Ph.D. candidate) and I went to see *The English Patient* ten short days ago. No wonder my text today is love, blocking and unblocking, what can and can't hurt us. This friend and I had recently exchanged e-mails before she came south to visit only to find that she had picked the same quote from the novel that I had picked when I read the book a year earlier, choosing the lines for a poem epigraph. We both scooped these words out of a book of hundreds of rich pages. Then, at the theatre, we listened to the same lines quoted near the end of the movie. Flanking either side of my soon-not-to-be lover, she and I inhaled sharp breaths of recognition. I call this life-triangulation. Michael Ondaatje writes:

> We die containing a richness of lovers and tribes, tastes we have swallowed, bodies we have plunged into and swum up as if rivers of wisdom, characters we have climbed into as if trees, fears we have hidden in as if caves. . . . We are communal histories, communal books. We are not owned or monogamous in our taste or experience. (261)

It has started to hurt me, this not admitting, exploring, tasting, touching, or understanding the real moments of the writing classroom. Which includes, of course, the everyday student-rich, back and forth, predictable extraordinary productive plainness of pages and drafts and work groups and book bags dripping on a rainy day as well as the enlivened unwrapping of narratives and histories and tastes and experiences that are shared there—relationships between people, words, places, work, and wonder. I'm not fully unblocked. I'm not sure I've said all I could or should say. But I'm ready to plunge in again—to listen, watch, experience, trust, worry, learn. To love.

Happy new year. May a teaching archangel watch over you as you make your way through it and maybe even make you laugh. I think, sometimes we're meant to be blocked. And other times we need to work harder to love the angel.

Works Cited

Ondaatje, Michael. 1992. *The English Patient*. New York: Random.

Contributors

Chris M. Anson is Morse-Alumni Distinguished Teaching Professor of English at the University of Minnesota. His books include *Scenarios for Teaching Writing; Journals in the Classroom; Writing and Response;* and *The Longman Handbook for Writers and Readers.*

Wendy Bishop teaches writing at Florida State University. Her books include edited and coauthored volumes—*The Subject Is Writing; Genre and Writing; Metro; Elements of Alternate Style*—as well as *Something Old, Something New; Released into Language; Working Words; Thirteen Ways of Looking for a Poem;* and *Teaching Lives.*

Lynn Z. Bloom is Professor of English and Aetna Chair of Writing at the University of Connecticut. Her recent publications include "Freshman Composition as a Middle-Class Enterprise" in *College English;* the coedited *Composition in the 21st Century: Crisis and Change;* and *The Essay Connection.*

Neal Bowers is Professor of English and Distinguished Professor of Liberal Arts and Sciences at Iowa State University, where he teaches modern and contemporary poetry and poetry writing. His books include three collections of poems, most recently *Night Vision;* studies of the poetry of Theodore Roethke and James Dickey; and a nonfiction volume titled *Words for the Taking: The Hunt for a Plagiarist.*

Lillian Bridwell-Bowles is Professor of English and Women's Studies at the University of Minnesota where she directs the Center for Interdisciplinary Studies of Writing. She is the author of numerous articles, monographs, and books, including *Identity Matters: Rhetorics of Difference.*

John Clifford teaches writing, literature, and theory at the University of North Carolina at Wilmington. His books include *Modern American Prose* and *Writing Theory and Critical Theory.* He is currently working on a textbook with John Schilb, *Arguing About Literature.*

203

Patricia Shelley Fox is an Assistant Professor of English and Director of the Coastal Georgia Writing Project at Armstrong Atlantic State University in Savannah, Georgia. She has published most recently in *Assessing Writing* and the *Connecticut Journal of English*.

Toby Fulwiler teaches writing and directs the writing-across-the-curriculum program at the University of Vermont. His books include *The Journal Book; College Writing; The Blair Handbook;* and *When Writing Teachers Teach Literature*.

Joel J. Gold teaches humor, writing, and eighteenth-century literature at the University of Kansas. He writes regularly for *The Chronicle of Higher Education;* his books include *The Wayward Professor* and an edition of Samuel Johnson's *A Voyage to Abyssinia* for the Yale Edition of *The Works of Samuel Johnson*.

Sharon J. Hamilton is Associate Dean for External Affairs and Director of Campus Writing at Indiana University-Purdue University at Indianapolis (IUPUI). Her books include *My Name's Not Susie: A Life Transformed by Literacy* and *Collaborative Learning: Underlying Assumptions and Effective Techniques* (coedited with Kris Bosworth).

Michael Martone teaches writing at the University of Alabama. His books include *Seeing Eye; Pensees: The Thoughts of Dan Quayle; Fort Wayne Is Seventh on Hitler's List;* and *Safety Patrol*.

Joy Passanante teaches literature, creative writing, and business writing at the University of Idaho. She is also a freelance writer and editor. Her essays, stories, and poems have appeared in journals such as *College English*, *Short Story*, and *Long Pond Review*.

Sondra Perl is Professor of English at Lehman College and the Graduate School and University Center of the City University of New York, where she has been teaching for more than twenty-five years. She was the recipient of the Carnegie Foundation's 1996-97 New York State Professor of the Year Award, and her books include *Landmark Essays on Writing Process*.

Kim Stafford directs the Northwest Writing Institute at Lewis & Clark College, where he serves as Artist-in-Residence in the Graduate School. He is the author of *Having Everything Right: Essays of Place*.

Cecelia Tichi is Professor of English at Vanderbilt University, where she has won the Ellen Gregg Ingalls Award for Excellence in Undergraduate Teaching. Her books include *Shifting Gears: Technology, Literature;*

Culture in Modernist America; Electronic Hearth: Creating an American Television Culture; and *High Lonesome: The American Culture of Country Music.*

Lad Tobin teaches English, trains TAs, and directs the writing program at Boston College. He is the author of *Writing Relationships* and the coeditor with Tom Newkirk of *Taking Stock.*

Joseph F. Trimmer teaches writing and cultural studies at Ball State University. His books include *Fictions; Understanding Others: Cultural and Cross-Cultural Studies and the Teaching of Literature;* and *Writing with a Purpose.*

Victor Villanueva Jr. teaches writing, writing theory, and rhetoric at Washington State University. His books include *Bootstraps: From an American Academic of Color.*

Ruth Vinz taught high school for twenty-three years before joining the faculty in English education at Teachers College, Columbia University. She is author of *Composing a Teaching Life* and coauthor of *Learning the Landscapes; Recasting the Text;* and *Inside Out.*